Fault Lines

In some years elections bring about enduring changes to the American political scene. In 2006, a pivotal election year, the Republicans suffered a resounding defeat, losing the House and Senate for the first time since the 1994 "Republican Revolution." But what caused this pivotal shift? The essays in *Fault Lines* provide both a wealth of insight regarding what happened in the 2006 congressional elections and a framework to aid in understanding the possible significance of the 2006 outcome for subsequent developments in American politics.

Contributors to *Fault Lines*, who all draw on the data from the 2006 Congressional Elections Study, include many of the nation's most prominent and accomplished observers of Congress and congressional elections. This book promises to be an influential contribution to our understanding of Congress, congressional elections, the Bush administration, media and politics, political communication, and partisan polarization.

Part of the *Controversies in Electoral Democracy and Representation* series, edited by Matthew J. Streb.

Jeffery J. Mondak is the James M. Benson Chair of Political Science at the University of Illinois at Urbana-Champaign.

Dona-Gene Mitchell is an assistant professor in the Political Science Department at the University of Nebraska-Lincoln.

Controversies in Electoral Democracy and Representation
Matthew J. Streb, Series Editor

The Routledge series *Controversies in Electoral Democracy and Representation* presents cutting edge scholarship and innovative thinking on a broad range of issues relating to democratic practice and theory. An electoral democracy, to be effective, must show a strong relationship between representation and a fair open election process. Designed to foster debate and challenge assumptions about how elections and democratic representation *should* work, titles in the series will present a strong but fair argument on topics related to elections, voting behavior, party and media involvement, representation, and democratic theory.

Titles in the series:

Rethinking American Electoral Democracy
Matthew J. Streb

Redistricting and Representation
Why Competitive Elections Are Bad for America
Thomas L. Brunell

Fault Lines
Why the Republicans Lost Congress
Edited by Jeffery J. Mondak and Dona-Gene Mitchell

Fault Lines

Why the Republicans Lost Congress

Edited by
Jeffery J. Mondak
University of Illinois at Urbana-Champaign

Dona-Gene Mitchell
University of Nebraska-Lincoln

NEW YORK AND LONDON

First published 2009
by Routledge
270 Madison Ave, New York, NY 10016

Simultaneously published in the UK
by Routledge
2 Park Square, Milton Park, Abingdon, Oxon OX14 4RN

Routledge is an imprint of the Taylor & Francis Group, an informa business

Typeset in Galliard and Gill Sans by
Florence Production Ltd, Stoodleigh, Devon
Printed and bound in the United States of America on acid-free paper by
Edwards Brothers, Inc

Library of Congress Cataloging in Publication Data
Fault lines: why the Republicans lost Congress/edited by
   Jeffery J. Mondak, Dona-Gene Mitchell.
      p.cm. – (Controversies in electoral democracy and representation)
   Includes bibliographical references and index.
   1. United States. Congress–Elections, 2006. 2. Republican Party
   (U.S.: 1854–)–History–21st century. 3. Elections–United States.
   4. Bush, George W. (George Walker), 1946– . 5. United States–
   Politics and government–2001– . I. Mondak, Jeffery J., 1962– .
   II. Mitchell, Dona-Gene.
   JK19682006.F38 2008
   324.973'0931–dc22   2008012557

ISBN10: 0–415–99361–X (hbk)
ISBN10: 0–415–99362–8 (pbk)
ISBN10: 0–203–89090–6 (ebk)

ISBN13: 978–0–415–99361–6 (hbk)
ISBN13: 978–0–415–99362–3 (pbk)
ISBN13: 978–0–203–89090–5 (ebk)

Contents

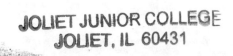

Illustrations

Figures

Tables

Foreword

by Lee H. Hamilton

The 109th Congress, in 2005–06, was, in the view of many, one of the low points for Congress. There were all kinds of concerns: ethics and lobbying scandals, intense partisanship, lack of oversight of the executive branch, and a distressing willingness to skirt the normal deliberative process, which is supposed to afford an opportunity for competing points of view to be aired and debated.

I write a bi-weekly column on Congress, in which I try to explain the institution to ordinary Americans and encourage them to get more civically involved. Quite often in 2006 I took a dim view of Congress, writing columns with titles such as "Why Does the Congress Want to Give up Power?", "Wouldn't it be Nice if the Congress Showed Up for Work?," and "Spotlight on a Congress in Institutional Crisis." It was a very tough time for those of us who care deeply about the institution of the Congress.

In my columns, I identified a lot of different ways that Congress could improve itself. I said it should become a more independent branch of government, co-equal to the presidency. It should be much more robust in its oversight. Partisanship ought to be softened. Deliberation should be improved. Procedures should be fair and open. Members should hew to higher ethical standards. Congress should focus more on the future, maybe even the long-term future.

In the fall of 2006, around the time of the election, we conducted a survey on Congress, put together by Professor Ted Carmines of the Center on Congress at Indiana University, with help from some of the people whose work is published in this volume. We wanted to find out how the American public felt about the performance of Congress. Were they bothered by the problems I listed above? Did they think that the institution of Congress was under a lot of stress?

While those polled were somewhat satisfied with the way Congress made its activities open to the public, their overall assessment of Congress was fairly negative. They were highly critical of what they saw as excessive partisanship in Congress. They were very concerned about the power of special interests. And they felt Congress was failing to hold its members to high ethical standards.

The Center on Congress followed up on that poll of the public with another survey in December 2006, in which we asked leading political scientists who closely follow the legislative branch to evaluate the performance of Congress.

We found that the professors were pretty tough graders. Congress earned a few Bs, with members getting credit for being accessible to their constituents, and for keeping their workings and activities open to the public.

But there were a number of Cs, and a long list of Ds. The poorest grades came on some of the most important standards for judging Congress, as members were faulted for excessive partisanship, weak oversight, ethics lapses—many of the same shortcomings we had found when we surveyed the broader public.

With the 2006 election came a change of partisan control of Congress, and promises from the new Democratic majorities in the House and Senate that they would change the way Congress worked. The leadership's initial speeches about reform and openness, and working together all sounded quite promising.

At the end of 2007, midway through the 110th Congress, we again surveyed leading political scientists about the institution's performance. Overall, they graded Congress a notch higher than in 2006—not a dramatic improvement, but an indication that Congress does have the capacity to change.

The experts saw notable improvement during the year by Congress in "carrying out effective oversight of the president and executive branch" and "protecting its powers from presidential encroachment." Competition with a president of the opposite party led Congress to play a more important role in policymaking.

Congress also got better ratings on three questions related to operational performance: whether it "engages in productive discussion and allows all points of view to be heard"; "allows Members in the minority to play a role"; and "follows good process and conducts its business in a deliberate way."

The experts also gave Congress better marks in 2007 on the questions of "Does Congress keep the role of special interests within proper bounds?" and "Does Congress hold members to high standards of ethical conduct?"

But several weaknesses identified by the experts in 2006 remained problems in 2007. For instance, Congress still did a very poor job of "keeping excessive partisanship in check," the experts said. On 13 of the 19 questions posed in the survey, the experts gave Congress a grade of C.

I am encouraged that Congress has taken some steps toward improvement, even if many are modest. Congress is more sensitive now to its power being encroached upon by the executive branch. There is more disclosure of lobbying activities. There are signs of improvement in cooperation across party lines in some committees.

But there is obvious room for improvement in many ways. For example, closed rules are still far too prevalent, and the minority is still too constrained from playing a meaningful role, particularly in the House.

We should all be watching Congress closely, and pushing for additional progress. One way we can do this is through systematic research of the sort presented in this volume, research that helps us all to understand what citizens had on their minds as they voted in the 2006 elections. I believe that Congress, for all its faults, is a responsive body. If members hear consistently and forcefully from their constituents that Congress has gotten off track and is just not operating as it should, I think Congress will respond, and begin to change.

Congress ought to be a beacon of open, deliberative, and thoroughgoing debate, an institution that truly represents the diversity and fair-minded decency of ordinary Americans. Let us encourage our representatives to make Congress an institution we can all point to with pride.

Acknowledgments

The chapters in *Fault Lines* draw on papers first presented at the Illinois Conference on Congressional Elections, a conference held at the University of Illinois on October 18 and 19, 2007. The conference was sponsored by the Cline Center for Democracy. *Fault Lines* would not have been possible without the tremendous support, assistance, and encouragement provided by Peter Nardulli, the Director of the Cline Center, and by Cline Center administrative aide Sheila Roberts. We are also grateful for the support of this project offered by Richard and Carole Cline, and by the Charles J. and Ethel S. Merriam Fund.

Many individuals participated in the Illinois Conference on Congressional Elections, providing valuable input that informed much of the research reported in *Fault Lines*. For their insights and contributions, we thank Brian Gaines, Jim Kuklinski, Beth Popp, and Tracy Sulkin of the University of Illinois, political consultant Christopher Blunt, James McCann of Purdue University, and Scott McClurg of Southern Illinois University, along with the many students and faculty who attended sessions of the conference.

All of the chapters in *Fault Lines* report data from the 2006 Congressional Elections Survey (CES), a survey sponsored by the Center on Congress at Indiana University. We are extraordinarily grateful for the efforts of the Center's director, Rep. Lee Hamilton. In addition to writing the foreword for *Fault Lines*, Rep. Hamilton was also a featured presenter at the October conference, and, most importantly, he has been an enthusiastic supporter of scholarly research on Congress and congressional elections. Invaluable assistance on this project was also provided by Vicky Myers and Ken Nelson, both at the Center on Congress. We also wish to acknowledge the efforts of Herb Weisberg of Ohio State University, who helped to design the CES, of John Kennedy and his staff at the Center for Survey Research at Indiana University, and of the nearly 1,600 Americans who graciously took the time to respond to our survey.

Funding for the 2006 CES was provided by the Center on Congress, the Center on American Politics, and the Office of the Vice Provost for Research at Indiana University, the Cline Center for Democracy at the University of

Illinois Urbana-Champaign, and by the following individuals: Edward Carmines, John Hibbing, Robert Huckfeldt, Gary Jacobson, Jeffery Mondak, Walter Stone, and Herb Weisberg.

Matthew Streb of Northern Illinois University edits the series *Controversies in Electoral Democracy and Representation* for Routledge. He and Michael Kerns of Routledge saw the timeliness of the research in *Fault Lines*, and they worked very hard to shepherd the book through the publication process. We are grateful for their efforts, along with those of Felisa Salvago-Keyes of Routledge and the anonymous reviewers who provided insightful—and remarkably prompt—feedback on the volume's chapters.

Jeffery J. Mondak
Dona-Gene Mitchell

Contributors

Matthew Buttice is a doctoral student in the Department of Political Science at the University of California, Davis.

Edward G. Carmines is Warner O. Chapman Professor and Rudy Professor in the Department of Political Science at Indiana University.

Jessica C. Gerrity is an assistant professor in the Department of Political Science at Washington College.

Nathan J. Hadley is a doctoral student in the Department of Political Science at the University of California, Davis.

Lee H. Hamilton is the Director of the Center on Congress at Indiana University and President and Director of the Woodrow Wilson International Center for Scholars, in Washington, D.C. Prior to becoming Director of the Center on Congress and the Wilson Center, Lee Hamilton served from 1965 to 1999 as a U.S. Representative from Indiana.

David J. Hendry is a doctoral student in the Department of Political Science at the University of Illinois, Urbana-Champaign.

John R. Hibbing is Foundation Regents University Professor in the Department of Political Science at the University of Nebraska-Lincoln.

Robert Huckfeldt is Distinguished Professor and Chair of the Department of Political Science at the University of California, Davis.

Robert A. Jackson is an associate professor in the Department of Political Science at Florida State University.

Gary C. Jacobson is a professor in the Department of Political Science at the University of California, San Diego.

Cherie D. Maestas is an associate professor in the Department of Political Science at Florida State University.

L. Sandy Maisel is William R. Kenan Jr. Professor in the Department of Government at Colby College.

Dona-Gene Mitchell is an assistant professor in the Department of Political Science at the University of Nebraska-Lincoln.

Jeffery J. Mondak is James M. Benson Chair in Public Issues and Civic Leadership in the Department of Political Science at the University of Illinois, Urbana-Champaign.

Rolfe D. Peterson is a doctoral student in the Department of Political Science at the University of California, Davis.

John Barry Ryan is a doctoral student in the Department of Political Science at the University of California, Davis.

Walter J. Stone is a professor in the Department of Political Science at the University of California, Davis.

Elizabeth Theiss-Morse is a professor in the Department of Political Science at the University of Nebraska-Lincoln.

Michael W. Wagner is an assistant professor in the Department of Political Science at the University of Nebraska-Lincoln.

Eric Whitaker is a doctoral student in the Department of Political Science at the University of Nebraska-Lincoln.

Chapter 1

The Context for Defeat

Dona-Gene Mitchell and Jeffery J. Mondak

In most years, midterm congressional elections produce little in the way of noteworthy developments. Sparks may fly in a few individual races, but far more often than not the basic political landscape remains the same. Although only a handful of midterm elections in U.S. history brought fundamental political change, two of the last four are among them. In 1994, the Republican Party won control of both the U.S. House and the U.S. Senate for the first time in over 40 years. Republicans maintained a majority in the House throughout the next 12 years, and also controlled the Senate for all but a brief time in this period. In 2006, however, Democrats recaptured both the House and the Senate. For only the second time in over half a century, the majority party in Congress suffered a harsh rebuke.

Elections are coarse mechanisms. Countless factors can influence why a voter opted for one candidate over another, but the vote itself tells us little or nothing about those factors. Likewise, at the national level the reality that one party fared well in a given election year while the other fared poorly provides no ironclad insight as to the forces underlying these outcomes. Election results tell us what happened, but not why. One approach to this situation is to let the mystery be. We can file away the fact that, for whatever reason, Democrats regained control of Congress in 2006. Then, rather than dwelling on why this result occurred, we can look ahead to how American politics may change in the years to come. But if we are incurious, we almost surely will remain unenlightened. If a message was embedded in the 2006 elections, then it is essential that that message be deciphered so that we can assess the nature of representation and political accountability. For instance, knowledge regarding why voters turned out the Republican majority in 2006 may provide a basis for understanding what Democrats need to do to retain their new majority status, and what Republicans need to do to prevent the Democratic majority from becoming entrenched. Simply put, we need to know what voters had in mind so that we can determine whether Congress has answered that call.

The title of this book, *Fault Lines*, has two interrelated meanings, and the studies in this book pursue two interrelated ends. The first concerns the possible causes of the Republican defeat. Simply put, who or what was at fault? Much of the research in *Fault Lines* seeks to test a series of accounts regarding how and why the Republicans came to lose Congress in 2006. The second meaning concerns social and political fissures. Do the 2006 elections signal the presence of serious cleavages within the Republican coalition, and perhaps even within American society as a whole? Research in *Fault Lines* also tackles these questions, with an eye toward gleaning insight from the 2006 elections regarding broad matters such as the role of media in contemporary American campaigns, the characteristics of political conversation in a divided polity, and the nature of Americans' attitudes toward politics and government.

If the 2006 elections demand explanation, how should we proceed? One strategy entails identification of a particular interpretation that we think or wish to be true, followed by speculation in support of our thesis. Examples of this approach abounded in the popular press in the days and weeks following the 2006 elections. As if reading lines from a script, observers attributed fault for the Republican defeat here and there. Viewed in isolation, each of the various perspectives offered by pundits perhaps enjoyed an air of plausibility, yet, seen collectively, many of the accounts are difficult to reconcile with one another.

Three interrelated questions frame popular explanations of the Republican defeat. First, was 2006 about policy? Various schools of thought emerged on this question. Many conservative leaders insisted that the election represented not a public repudiation of conservative principles, but rather voter backlash against Republicans in Congress who had abandoned those principles.[1] If any one policy issue dominated the elections, many observers argued that that issue was the Iraq War. For instance, upon finding in exit poll data a correspondence between attitudes on Iraq and the vote choice, some analysts inferred that Iraq was the decisive issue: "Views on the Iraq war did the most to determine how people voted. Eight in 10 of those who opposed the war voted for Democrats; eight in 10 of those who supported the war voted for Republicans."[2] Commentator George Will advanced a similar position, arguing that "More than any congressional elections in history, last week's turned on a single burning national issue. Control of Congress has changed because of deep discontent about Iraq."[3] Although Iraq was the most visible policy concern, numerous other issues possibly influenced the vote in 2006, including the government's handling of Hurricane Katrina, along with immigration, social security, healthcare, energy prices, and others.[4]

Second, for those voters who turned away from Republican candidates in 2006, did the vote choice represent a referendum on the increasingly unpopular presidency of George W. Bush, a rebuff of Republican leadership in Congress, both, or neither? Attitudes toward the Iraq War and President Bush are intertwined, and many analysts saw these attitudes as decisive. For instance, pollster John Zogby posited that "this was, at the grass roots, a referendum against the war and the president."[5] Other observers, though, disagreed. The Republican leadership in Congress had been criticized on multiple fronts leading up to the 2006 elections, including for failing to pass legislation on key issues, for failing to restrain government spending, and for perceived inadequacies in its response to the numerous scandals that hit members of Congress, mostly Republicans, in 2005 and 2006. From this perspective, Republicans in Congress should shoulder some or all of the blame for their own fates rather than shifting responsibility to the White House. David Keene, president of the American Conservative Union, said "Republicans will blame everyone but themselves, but this will have been a referendum not on the ideas that brought them to power, but on the sorry way in which they've gone about either ignoring or implementing those ideas, as well as on their competence, integrity and morals."[6] Likewise, one editorial argued that "Members of Congress may flatter themselves by saying, in effect, 'It's not us—it's the guy in the White House.' But if those now in Congress think this election was only about Bush, and not also about them, they're dead wrong."[7]

For its part, the Bush administration sought to deny, or at least deflect, culpability. Bush adviser Karl Rove, who continued to forecast that Republicans would retain control of Congress right up to Election Day, later claimed that there was nothing either unusual or problematic for Republicans in the outcome: "The 2006 election was a normal off-year election . . . (I)t was a close loss . . . We lost fifteen contests by a combined total of 85,000 votes. We lost control of the Senate by 3,562 votes in Montana. Close election—the normal and ordinary thing you'd expect in a second midterm."[8]

The final question is whether voting in 2006 suggested a desire on the part of Americans for a specific new course. Did voters vote for policies advanced by Democrats, or did voters merely seek to convey dissatisfaction with the status quo? Many observers inferred the latter. For example, Matt Bennett of the progressive think tank Third Way said that the direction signaled by the 2006 elections is an "open question," and that, for Democrats in Congress, "the mandate is, 'Do something different, for God's sake.' "[9] Peter Beinart stated the matter even more forcefully: "Democrats shouldn't fool themselves. The American people haven't given them a mandate to govern; they have given them a mandate to stop Bush from governing."[10] If Karl Rove is correct that 2006 was a normal midterm and if Bennett and Beinart are right that the policy signal was ambiguous, then the seemingly dramatic change that occurred in 2006 may trace to rather ordinary, innocuous sources.

The various accounts of the 2006 elections described here are best seen as hypotheses rather than as explanations. These and other perspectives require rigorous examination. Toward this end, political scientists fielded several major surveys in 2006. With careful examination of data from these surveys, it will be possible to deepen our understanding of the causes and implications of voting behavior in the 2006 elections. The research reported in *Fault Lines* draws data primarily from the 2006 Congressional Elections Study. In the way of overview, the remainder of this chapter first describes that study, then uses data from that study to revisit key features of the political environment in 2006, and finally summarizes the outcomes of the 2006 U.S. House and Senate elections.

The 2006 Congressional Elections Study

To provide insight on voting behavior in the 2006 elections, a public opinion survey, the 2006 Congressional Elections Study (CES), was designed and administered. This survey is the central data source for the research reported in *Fault Lines*. Thus, a brief discussion of the study's attributes and procedures is warranted.

Three of the researchers[11] involved in the 2006 project fielded a survey on Congress and midterm congressional elections in 2002. Building on that effort, a more expansive investigation was carried out in 2006. As in 2002, survey interviews were conducted by telephone by the Center for Survey Research at Indiana University.

Respondents on the 2006 survey were drawn from a subset of U.S. congressional districts. First, 100 districts from the 48 contiguous states were randomly selected for inclusion in the project. Second, 72 districts were identified in which either the incumbent was not running for re-election in 2006 or pre-election forecasts had indicated that the race was likely to be competitive. Of these 72 districts, 17 were already included in the initial sample of 100, meaning respondents were drawn from a sample of 155 congressional districts. The decision to include an over sample of open and competitive districts was made to maximize the capacity to identify campaign effects. Had we drawn a simple random sample, a much larger portion of respondents would have lived in uncompetitive districts.

Four different interviews were conducted as part of the CES. First, 1,023 pre-election interviews were completed, including 515 with respondents from the 72 open seat and competitive congressional districts, and 508 with respondents drawn from the survey's remaining 83 districts.[12] These interviews were conducted between September 28, 2006, and the November 7 election. The median pre-election interview occurred on October 22, just over two weeks prior to Election Day. The survey included a large number of questions, and interviews lasted an average of 33 minutes. Second, a modified version of the full pre-election survey was completed by an additional 174 respondents later in November, after the elections. Third, among the 1,023 respondents interviewed prior to the election, 766, or 75 percent, also completed a post-election survey. These interviews took place between November 9 and December 30, with the vast majority (87 percent) occurring within two weeks of Election Day. The follow-up survey was briefer than the pre-election instrument, with interviews lasting an average of 22 minutes. Fourth, an additional 401 respondents not included as part of the pre-election sample were interviewed using a modified version of the post-election instrument;[13] these interviews were conducted in early 2007, between February 28 and April 24. Data from these various portions of the survey can be combined in multiple ways depending on the researcher's needs.

Data from the CES are put to creative use in the various studies reported in the chapters that follow, and these studies discuss many of the items asked as part of the survey. The survey was designed to pose questions on a wide array of subjects of possible relevance to the 2006 vote. Among these are standard measures of partisanship, ideology, and participation; various questions tapping respondents' positions on issues that were important in 2006; questions that provide data on respondents' levels of political knowledge, interest, and attentiveness to the news; and a variety of specific batteries on matters such as political discussion, religious attachments, and whether respondents had been targets of partisan mobilization efforts.

As an initial step toward making sense of the 2006 congressional elections, this chapter describes the elections in broad strokes. Relying primarily on data from the CES, our next task is to discuss the political context. We do so in order to call attention to a few of the major forces that may have influenced the political climate in 2006, forces that possibly affected how campaigns were waged and how voters decided which candidates to support. Following this review, we provide a summary of results from the 2006 U.S. House and Senate elections. The simple story, of course, is that the Republicans lost control of both houses. To begin to understand why this occurred, it is useful to review the numbers so that we can see how many seats changed hands in the House and Senate, and how many incumbents were defeated.

The Political Context

In many ways, congressional elections constitute local affairs. Which candidate wins a given election depends on factors such as the partisan composition of the state or district, whether the party out of office recruited a strong candidate, the relative success of the leading contenders in raising funds and in mobilizing voters, and whether the candidates avoided serious missteps on the campaign trail. But it does not follow that we can make sense of election results purely on a case-by-case basis. The national political context also matters. Each election cycle, forces beyond the borders of the state or district combine to make the going at least a bit easier for candidates of one party, and correspondingly more difficult for candidates of the opposing party. In some years, these forces are especially prominent, providing one party with a strong advantage. This advantage influences many of the purportedly "local" aspects of congressional elections, including candidate recruitment, campaign fundraising, and mobilization of the electorate.

As discussed in this chapter's first few pages, the political context in 2006 included several noteworthy components. For the most part, these factors worked to the benefit of Democratic candidates. First, President George W. Bush, who was in his sixth year in office, was not popular. Bush's poor standing enabled many Democratic candidates to campaign as much against the president as against their actual congressional opponents. Second, 12 years into the Republican Revolution, the Republican leadership in Congress was faltering. Republicans could point to few legislative accomplishments in recent years, and so much of the news about Congress concerned scandals that Democrats spoke of Republicans maintaining a "culture of corruption." Third, Americans were increasingly disgruntled with the perceived lack of progress in the Iraq War, a war well into its fourth year by Election Day. The popular accounts of the 2006 elections described above reveal disagreement on the precise combination of factors that led Democrats to regain control of the House and Senate. Disentangling these explanations is a central task of the research reported in *Fault Lines*. At this point, all that can safely be concluded is that, collectively, the factors described here formed a landscape relatively hospitable to Democrats, and relatively hostile to Republicans. The political context did not assure that any Democrat would win or any Republican would lose, but the context did place many Republican candidates on the defensive. Data from the CES reveal the specific nature of the obstacles Republicans faced.

George W. Bush

The political fortunes of the president affect the electoral prospects of the president's fellow partisans in Congress. For many years, research in political science described this link in terms of a somewhat coarse process of "surge and decline" in which presidents would provide a boost to the party in presidential election years, a boost that would then be absent in subsequent midterm elections (e.g., Campbell 1966).[14] In the mid 1970s, however, influential research established a more enduring connection, one discernible through study of the impact of presidential approval ratings and short-term party evaluations on midterm elections (e.g., Tufte 1975; Kernell 1977; Abramowitz, Cover and Norpoth 1986). At times when a president is politically strong, this link works to the benefit of the president's party. Conversely, in years such as 2006, the president's unpopularity may dampen the prospects for the party's congressional candidates.

With but a few exceptions in U.S. history, the president's party has lost ground in Congress as a consequence of midterm elections. However, two of the exceptions to this pattern occurred in the two prior midterm years, 2002 and 1998. The 2002 elections took place in the window between the September 11, 2001 terrorist attacks and the March 20, 2003 launch of the Iraq War. President George W. Bush enjoyed high approval ratings in this period, and the Republicans gained seats in both the House and the Senate. In the Senate, the two-seat gain was sufficient to restore Republicans to the majority.[15] In 1998, the middle of Bill Clinton's second term as president, Democrats gained a handful of seats in the U.S. House while the composition of the Senate remained unchanged. The 1998 outcome marked the only time in the modern era in which the president's party strengthened its position in Congress as a result of the president's second midterm election.

George W. Bush enjoyed high approval ratings in 2002, as Bill Clinton did in 1998. But President Bush was not popular in 2006. Comparison of pre-election data from our 2002 and 2006 surveys demonstrates this point. On both surveys, respondents were asked to indicate how favorable or unfavorable they felt toward the president, and also to answer a standard item on presidential approval. Data on favorability are depicted in Figure 1.1. The difference between the two years is striking. In 2002, just over 50 percent of respondents were favorable toward George Bush, and another 16 percent selected the center category on the five-point scale; less than one third of respondents indicated that they were unfavorable toward the president.[16] The situation changed dramatically by 2006. President Bush's favorability numbers fell off by nearly half from the 2002 mark, to under 28 percent, whereas 53.9 percent of respondents expressed unfavorable views of the president. Further, dissatisfaction with the president was not of a mild form; 41.2 percent of respondents opted for the "most unfavorable" category on our five-point measure.

If anything, public sentiment toward President Bush in 2006 appears even more critical when we consider data on presidential approval. In 2002, data

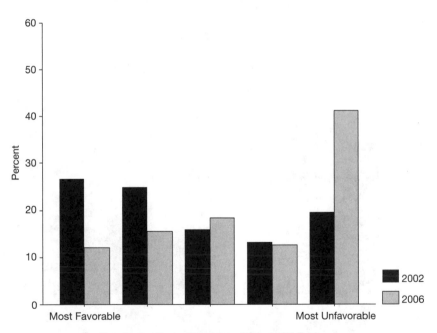

Figure 1.1 Favorability toward George W. Bush, 2002 and 2006.
Note: N = 1,137 (2002) and N = 1,011 (2006)

in Figure 1.2 reveal that 68.9 percent of respondents approved of the job George W. Bush was doing as president. By 2006, the president's approval had fallen to 41.2 percent, and a stunning 45.3 percent of respondents indicated that they strongly disapproved of Bush's performance. Moreover, this depiction is hardly unique to the CES. On 43 national surveys conducted between Labor Day and Election Day in 2006,[17] the highest raw approval mark President Bush attained was 44 percent on a mid-September *USA Today/ Gallup* poll, and Bush's average mark was 38.2 percent. As recoded here, with respondents who answered "don't know" and "no opinion" omitted, the president's approval on these 43 polls averaged 40.4 percent, just under the level observed on the CES.

Presidential approval is measured nationally, whereas congressional elections are contested locally. In many states and congressional districts, voters' sentiments regarding George W. Bush obviously were more positive than the national averages reported here. Nonetheless, Bush's decline in approval between 2002 and 2006 complicated the task of many Republican congressional candidates. For Republicans with safe seats, the president's standing was of minor consequence. For Republicans running in more marginal states and

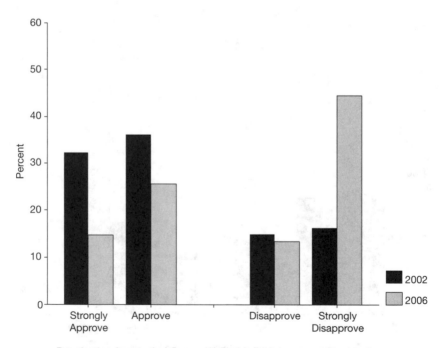

Pre-election Approval of George W. Bush's Performance as President

Figure 1.2 Presidential Approval, 2002 and 2006.
Note: N = 1,137 (2002) and N = 1,007 (2006)

districts, though, public displeasure with the president heightened the candidates' electoral peril. At least when defined in terms of presidential approval, the political context in 2006 was unfavorable for Republican congressional candidates.

Congress

Congressional incumbents routinely strive to develop personal attachments to their constituents (e.g., Fenno 1978; Cain, Ferejohn and Fiorina 1987). If the bond between legislator and voter transcends national politics, then the incumbent will endure even when national forces operate to the incumbent's disadvantage. But just as the president's standing shapes the political climate, so too does public sentiment toward Congress. Particularly for incumbents of the majority party, electoral prospects hinge in part on whether the current Congress has fared well or fared poorly in the public's eyes. In 2006, Congress was not held in high esteem, and, in particular, public concern had mounted regarding the tenure of the Republican majority.

Public skepticism regarding the performance of Congress is hardly unique to 2006. Indeed, much of the enduring dissatisfaction with Congress may arise from the public's uneasiness with the basic properties and processes of a democratic legislature (Hibbing and Theiss-Morse 1995, 2002). But this situation docs not necessarily impede incumbents seeking re-election, as some research suggests that citizens distinguish between Congress as a whole and their own representatives when forming performance evaluations (e.g., Fenno 1975; Parker and Davidson 1979; cf. Born 1990; Lipinski, Bianco, and Work 2003; McDermott and Jones 2003). Whether critical views of Congress do, in fact, ensnare individual representatives is partly a function of party and partly a function of the nature of the times. Representatives from the majority party will bear the brunt of public antipathy toward Congress (McDermott and Jones 2003), particularly in years in which anti-incumbent sentiments run high. For several reasons, 2006 was such a year.

But for the brief period when the Jeffords switch gave Democrats control of the Senate in 2001 and 2002, the Republicans had controlled both houses of Congress for 12 years by the time of the 2006 elections. Unfortunately for Republican incumbents, what had once been a revolution had, by 2006, become an unpopular status quo. Data in Figure 1.3 demonstrate that public approval of Congress was relatively high prior to the 2002 elections, with over 62 percent of respondents voicing approval just before the first post-September 11 elections.[18] By 2006, though, approval of Congress had fallen to 37 percent.

If this dissatisfaction adversely affected incumbents' electoral prospects, two factors suggest that Republicans were likely to be in especially great peril. First, as the majority party in Congress, and with a fellow partisan in the White House, Republicans were in no position to shift blame to the Democrats. Simply put,

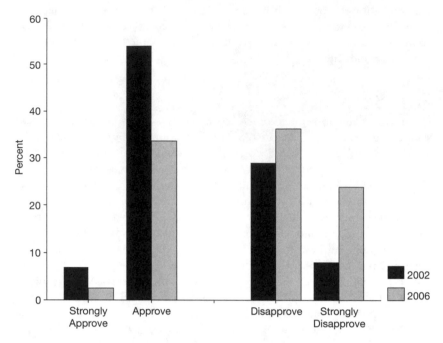

Pre-election Approval of Congress

Figure 1.3 Congressional Approval, 2002 and 2006.
Note: N = 1,120 (2002) and N = 986 (2006)

Americans disapproved of Congress in 2006—a Republican-controlled Congress. Second, even if some of the public dissatisfaction in 2006 was of a generic anti-incumbent variety, the fact that more incumbents were Republicans than Democrats meant that more Republicans were at risk. After all, a "throw the bums out" mentality works to the disadvantage of the majority party.

Data from the CES support the claim that public dissatisfaction with Congress was targeted more toward Republicans than toward Democrats, although the difference in views of the two parties is of modest magnitude. Respondents were asked to evaluate "congressional Republicans" and "congressional Democrats" using a five-point favorability scale. Republicans in Congress received unfavorable ratings from 49.9 percent of respondents, and neutral or favorable ratings from the remaining 51.1 percent. Democrats fared slightly better, with 41.4 percent of respondents rating the Democrats unfavorably.[19]

What was the basis of this dissatisfaction? In part, disapproval arose from the perception that Congress was doing a poor job on the issues. Respondents on the CES were asked to assign Congress grades on various dimensions, one being "for tackling the key issues facing the country." Data in Figure 1.4 reveal that a mere 17 percent of respondents awarded Congress a grade of A or B on this dimension, whereas 53.2 percent of respondents gave Congress a grade of D or F. But Congress was perceived even more negatively on a different matter: how the institution responded to misconduct by some of its members. Numerous members of Congress were embroiled in scandal in 2005 and 2006. Most of the scandal-plagued incumbents were Republicans,[20] and several were driven to resign from Congress or abandon their re-election bids. Two House members who resigned during the 109th Congress, Randall Cunningham (R-CA) and Bob Ney (R-OH), were sent to prison; Ney did not officially resign until November 3, only days before the election. The parade of charges understandably was disastrous for the implicated incumbents, but the reputation of Congress as a whole was also tarnished. When asked "what grade would you give Congress for holding its members to high standards of ethical conduct?" the data in Figure 1.5 demonstrate that nearly 28 percent of respondents assigned Congress a grade of D, and a staggering 42.5 percent gave Congress an F. In exit poll data, corruption was the issue ranked as "very important" by the largest portion of voters, 41 percent.[21] Voters saw corruption as relevant in 2006, and they saw Congress as performing poorly in addressing it.

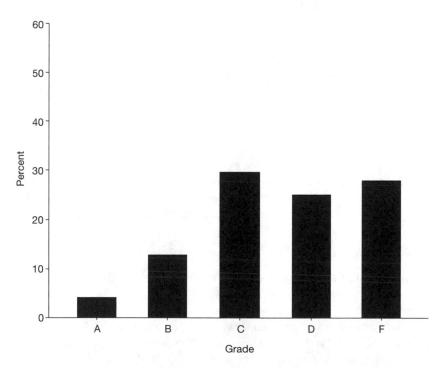

Figure 1.4 Evaluations of Congressional Success in Tackling Key Issues, 2006.

Note: N = 1,003

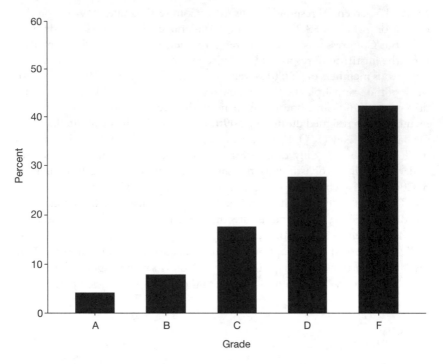

Figure 1.5 Evaluations of Congressional Success in Holding Members to High
Standards of Ethical Conduct, 2006.

Note: N = 1,008

When seeking re-election, members of Congress often attempt to run away from the institution. In some years, however, the Capitol's shadow is difficult to escape, particularly for incumbents from the majority party. In 2006, the political context was one in which Republican incumbents were hampered by their links to both an unpopular president and an unpopular legislature.

The Iraq War

George W. Bush's approval ratings languished throughout 2006, and Americans were similarly critical of Congress. Viewed in isolation, these low marks seemingly would suggest that Americans were experiencing fatigue in the sixth year of the Bush presidency, and perhaps also that idiosyncratic matters such as the various congressional scandals had brought a cumulative adverse effect on mass opinion. These interpretations may have some merit, but they do not tell the full story. No description of the political context in 2006 would be complete without mention of the Iraq War.

The U.S. invasion of Iraq was launched on March 19, 2003. Only six weeks later, on May 1, President Bush, standing in the shadow of an enormous banner reading "Mission Accomplished," declared that major combat operations in Iraq had ended. But three years later, as the 2006 elections neared, the war lingered on. By Labor Day, over 2,600 U.S. troops had been killed since the start of the war in Iraq, and another 20,000 had been injured. Americans were growing increasingly dissatisfied with the Bush administration's handling of the war effort, particularly since it was unclear how and when the administration planned on ending U.S. military action in Iraq.

Pre-election data from the CES reveal that respondents were strongly critical of the Iraq War. These data, depicted in Figure 1.6, show that only 26 percent of respondents expressed favorable views of the war at that time, whereas nearly 58 percent were unfavorable. Further, displeasure with the war was hardly mild; over 46 percent of respondents indicated that they were highly unfavorable toward the war.

In 2002, President Bush and Congress enjoyed high approval ratings in part because of the nation's forceful response to the September 11 terrorist attacks, a response that included toppling of the Taliban in Afghanistan.

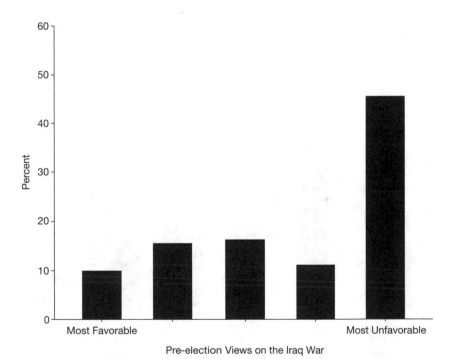

Figure 1.6 Opinion Regarding the War in Iraq, 2006.
Note: N = 1,011

In Figure 1.7, for instance, we see that on our 2002 survey over 71 percent of respondents voiced approval of George W. Bush's handling of the war on terrorism. By 2006, however, the Iraq War, the failure of America to capture Osama bin Laden, and some Americans' concerns over perceived infringements on civil liberties had combined to erode this approval; just under half of pre-election respondents expressed approval of George W. Bush's handling of terrorism in 2006. The foundation of the President's support had weakened. For Republican congressional candidates, it followed that their task grew much more complicated. Associating themselves with the President and with the War on Terror no longer constituted risk-free means to garner electoral support. To the contrary, for many Republicans, their links to President Bush and the Iraq War had become political liabilities.

This brief discussion of the political context in 2006 necessarily is far from exhaustive. Nonetheless, the points highlighted here paint an inhospitable, and perhaps even bleak, picture for Republican candidates. Association with an unpopular president, an unpopular Congress and an unpopular war put Republicans on the defensive. Meanwhile, Democrats were energized. The data examined here do not tell us the extent to which the political climate ultimately

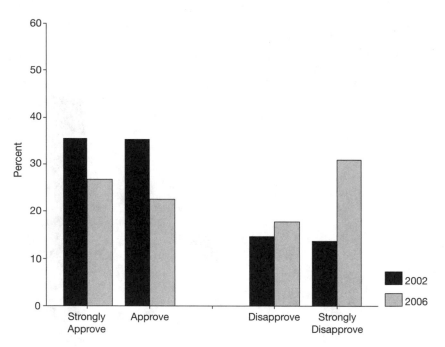

Pre-election Approval of George W. Bush's Performance on Terrorism

Figure 1.7 Approval of George W. Bush's Handling of Terrorism, 2002 and 2006.
Note: N = 1,136 (2002) and N = 1,005 (2006)

mattered in the 2006 elections. Context alone does not determine elections, but nor should context be ignored. Throughout 2006, all signs suggested it was likely to be a bad election year for Republicans, although few forecasts predicted how strong the Election Day repudiation would be.

Election Day

Heading into the 2006 elections, Republican majorities in both the House and the Senate were thin. In the House, Republicans held 232 seats to 203 for the Democrats,[22] meaning that Democrats required a net gain of only 15 seats to capture a minimal 218–217 majority. The pre-election partisan divide in the Senate was 55–45, and thus the Democrats needed a six-seat swing to win control.[23] As the election neared, it seemed likely that Democrats would end with a narrow majority in the House, although their prospects for capturing control of the Senate appeared much less certain. On Election Day, however, voters backed Democrats in stronger numbers than projected by most forecasters, with several close races ending in favor of the Democratic candidates. The final results are summarized in Table 1.1. Democrats won the House comfortably, picking up 30 seats to more than reverse the partisan divide there, from 232–203 Republican before the election to 233–202 Democratic after. In the Senate, Democrats secured exactly the number of victories needed to wrest control from the Republicans, achieving a net increase of six seats.

There are three keys if a political party is to record gains in congressional elections. First, the party must hold its current seats. Even in years that are strong for a party, a few of its seats are likely to be vulnerable. If the party does not retain all or most of these seats, it becomes much more difficult to accrue a net gain. Second, the party must defeat vulnerable incumbents from the opposing party. In 2006, the combination of national forces described above put many Republicans back on their heels. A further complication for several

Table 1.1 Seats Changes in the U.S. House and Senate as a Result of the 2006 Elections

	2004	2006	Net Change
A. U.S. House			
Seats held by Democrats[a] following the election	203	233	+30
Seats held by Republicans following the election	232	202	−30
B. U.S. Senate			
Seats held by Democrats[b] following the election	45	51	+6
Seats held by Republicans following the election	55	49	−6

Notes:
a Includes Bernard Sanders (I-VT) as a Democrat following the 2004 elections.
b Includes Jim Jeffords (I-VT) as a Democrat following the 2004 elections, and Bernard Sanders (I-VT) and Joe Lieberman (I-CT) as Democrats following the 2006 elections.

Republican incumbents was that they had been embroiled in scandal. To win back Congress, Democrats needed to capitalize where Republican incumbents were at risk. Third, to make gains in Congress, a party typically must win open seats. In 2006, 21 of the 33 open seats in the House were formerly held by Republicans, creating targets of opportunity for Democratic candidates. These opportunities were especially strong in districts in which Republican incumbents had resigned under the cloud of scandal. In the Senate, there were only five open seats, and only one was formerly held by a Republican. Consequently, Democratic opportunities to gain ground via open seats in the Senate were slim.

Using these keys as a guide, the components of the Democratic victory in 2006 are summarized in Table 1.2. Looking at the first two rows in each section, the first point to note is that Democratic candidates in both the House and the Senate pitched a perfect game in terms of retaining those seats held by Democrats prior to the election. In the House, Democrats controlled 203 seats going in to the election, and every single one of these was retained. Democrats also swept in the Senate, with all 15 Democratic incumbents winning re-election, and all three open seats previously held by the party remaining under Democratic control.

By holding their current seats, Democrats put themselves in a position to recapture Congress, but the crucial factor in their win was the defeat of Republican incumbents. In the House, Democrats gained 22 seats by toppling incumbents, more than enough to secure a majority. Democrats made further

Table 1.2 Sources of Seats Gains for Democrats in 2006

	Seats in Contention	Seats Won by Democrats
A. U.S. House		
Seats with Democratic incumbents running for re-election	191	191
Open seats with Democratic incumbents	12	12
Seats with Republican incumbents running for re-election	211	22
Open seats with Republican incumbents	21	8
B. U.S. Senate		
Seats with Democratic incumbents running for re-election	15	15
Open seats with Democratic incumbents	3	3
Seats with Republican incumbents running for re-election	14	6
Open seats with Republican incumbents	1	0

Note: Totals include independents who align with the Democratic caucus (see Table 1.1).

strides by winning eight Republican-held open seats in the House, but this was not the decisive blow. Although open seats played noteworthy roles in other recent elections (e.g., Gaddie and Bullock 2000), in 2006 Democrats took back the House by defeating Republican incumbents.[24] In the Senate, open seats had no impact at all in 2006. There, Democrats scored their victory by besting six of 14 Republican incumbents.

It warrants emphasis that Democrats were able to recapture Congress in 2006 in no small part because the pre-election partisan balances in the House and Senate were so even. By all accounts, 2006 was a bad year for Republicans, yet nearly 90 percent of Republican incumbents running for re-election to the House were victorious, and the six-seat swing in the Senate was smaller than the shifts seen in 1980, 1986, and 1994. One implication of this is that analysts are wise to be cautious when interpreting results of the 2006 elections. A change in party control of both houses of Congress is a dramatic outcome, yet the causes of this outcome conceivably could be relatively mundane. A second implication, looking ahead, is that hard-fought battles for control of Congress should be expected in the next few election cycles. It would be of little surprise were thin majorities to persist for some time in the House and Senate, and even were party control to shift again in the near future. At the time of writing, 2008 is shaping up to be a good election year for congressional Democrats. But even if this proves to be the case, it seems doubtful that Democrats will be able to build large enough majorities in 2008 to put the House and Senate safely in their grasp in 2010 and beyond. Their win in 2006 may be the first step toward resurgence for Democrats in Congress, but it also may be the beginning of an era of political back-and-forth.

Making Sense of 2006

The purpose of this chapter has been to provide an overview of the 2006 elections, not to reach any definitive conclusions regarding either why Republicans lost their congressional majorities or what these elections imply for the future. In 2006, several aspects of the political context were favorable to Democratic candidates, and enough Democrats apparently capitalized on these circumstances to revoke the Republican revolution. But these simple observations suggest far more questions than they answer. Did Republicans fare poorly in 2006 because voters consciously rejected Republican leadership, including the policies of the Bush administration and the war in Iraq? Alternately, did Republicans lose because Democrats fielded high-quality, well-funded candidates who constructed a Democratic win district by district and state by state? Or might it be that the Republican majorities in the House and the Senate could have endured but for the ethical lapses that became central points of discussion in many campaigns? Conceiving of the elections more broadly, did voters' decisions in 2006 mesh with our understanding of the fundamental bases of electoral behavior, or were there exceptional or atypical factors at work in these elections? By reclaiming control of the House and Senate, did the Democrats position themselves in 2006 to bring about meaningful new directions in public policy? Lastly, did the 2006 outcomes contribute to the political climate surrounding the 2008 presidential and congressional elections?

Progress toward answering these questions requires careful, systematic analysis. Collectively, the research reported in the chapters that follow provides a substantial amount of new insight regarding the causes and implications of the shift in control of Congress that followed the 2006 midterm elections. The next two chapters examine the role of information in 2006. In Chapter Two, Edward Carmines, Jessica Gerrity, and Michael Wagner report on patterns in media coverage during the 2006 campaigns, and link these patterns to voters' perceptions. Matthew Buttice, Robert Huckfeldt, and John Barry Ryan switch the focus to information disseminated through political conversation in Chapter Three, with research on the possibility that Americans' partisan perceptions are shaped by patterns in social communication. Following these examinations of the information context, the next two chapters focus on the significance of candidates. In Chapter Four, Walter Stone and his colleagues contrast patterns in candidate emergence in the 2002 and 2006 midterm elections, demonstrating that the decision to run in 2006 hinged on national partisan factors, whereas district-specific considerations had been more dominant in 2002. David Hendry and his collaborators then explore the specific matter of scandal in Chapter Five. Their analyses reveal how, and to what extent, scandal contributed to the Republicans' loss of Congress. Following that assessment, Dona-Gene Mitchell and Gary Jacobson investigate issue voting in 2006. In Chapter Six, Mitchell probes the myth and reality of issue voting in American elections. In Chapter Seven, Jacobson paints a rich portrait regarding the particular significance of the Iraq War for voters' judgments. Lastly, to come full circle, John Hibbing and his coauthors report on Americans' broader attitudes toward politics and government in Chapter Eight, revisiting many of the themes addressed in Rep. Lee Hamilton's insightful Foreword.

Notes

1 E.g., Ralph Z. Hallow, "Republican Blame Game Begins: Conservatives Say Party Abandoned Principles, Failed to Unite," *Washington Times*, 8 November 2006.
2 Susan Page, "GOP Coalition Fractured by Opposition to War: Republicans' Loss of Support among Prime Groups of Swing Voters is Democrats' Gain," *USA Today*, 8 November 2006.
3 George F. Will, Retreat from Exuberance, *Newsweek*, 20 November 2006.
4 For a discussion of the role of these issues, see David S. Broder, "Facing Up to Reality," *The Washington Post*, 9 November 2006.
5 Quoted in Hallow, "Republican Blame Game Begins."
6 Quoted in Hallow, "Republican Blame Game Begins."
7 "GOP's First Step: Admit the Problem." *Investor's Business Daily*, 9 November 2006.

8   "Interview with Karl Rove," *Fox News Sunday*, 20 August 2007.
9   Quoted in Page, "GOP Coalition Fractured by Opposition to War."
10 Peter Beinart, "Block Party," *New Republic*, 20 November 2006.
11 Edward Carmines, Robert Huckfeldt, and Jeffery Mondak. For an example of research utilizing data from the 2002 study, see Huckfeldt *et al.* 2007.
12 These numbers give a sense of the value of the over sample of competitive districts. Had the 1,023 respondents been drawn from a simple random sample, approximately 170 would have resided in competitive districts. By tripling that number, the over sample facilitates improved study of campaign effects.
13 The alternate post-election survey included nearly all of the same questions asked on the panel post-election instrument, along with key items on demographic and political attributes from the pre-election survey.
14 Campbell (1985, 1987, 1993) presents a revised depiction of the theory of surge and decline, one that includes presidential popularity as a factor in midterm congressional elections. See also Cover (1985).
15 The Republicans gained control of the U.S. Senate following the 1994 elections, and maintained their majority for the next six years. Following the 2000 election, the Senate was split 50–50, initially giving the Republicans a working majority via Vice President Dick Cheney's tie-breaking vote. A few months later, however, in May of 2001, Senator Jim Jeffords of Vermont switched from a Republican affiliation to independent, and caucused with the Democrats. This switch provided the Democrats with a thin majority in the Senate, one that they retained until the 2002 elections.
16 Data from the few respondents who indicated uncertainty are omitted from these calculations, and are excluded from this chapter's figures.
17 This discussion includes data from all surveys fielded or commissioned in this period by ABC, the AP, CBS, CNN, FOX, Gallup, NBC, the *New York Times*, *Newsweek*, Pew, *Time*, *USA Today*, the *Wall Street Journal*, and the *Washington Post*.
18 Whether Republicans in Congress benefited from this approval more than did Democrats is unclear, as Democrats maintained a working majority in the Senate in 2002.
19 The closest parallel questions in 2002 differed somewhat in focus, with respondents asked to evaluate "the Republican leaders in Congress" and "the Democratic leaders in Congress." On those measures, Republicans fared negligibly worse than Democrats, with 33.5 percent of respondents rating Republican leaders unfavorably versus 31.9 percent for Democratic leaders. On the 2006 post-election survey, favorability dropped relative to the pre-election measure for both Democrats and Republicans, but the Democrats' 10 percentage point advantage was maintained.
20 The most noteworthy exception was Rep. William Jefferson (D-LA), who was implicated in a corruption investigation in 2005. Jefferson was re-elected in 2006, but he was indicted on 16 federal criminal charges in June, 2007. A second exception was Rep. Patrick Kennedy (D-MA), who, following a late-night car crash on Capitol Hill in May, 2006, pleaded guilty on June 13 to driving under the influence of prescription drugs.
21 Page, "GOP Coalition Fractured by Opposition to War."
22 In these descriptions, we count independents with the Democrats or Republicans as appropriate. Thus, the count of 203 seats held by the Democrats includes Bernard Sanders (I-VT), who caucused with the Democrats throughout his tenure in the House.
23 With a five-seat gain, the Senate would have been split 50–50, in which case Republicans would have retained control via Vice President Dick Cheney's tie-breaking vote.

24 Although the Democrats' margin of victory in the House was secured by toppling Republican incumbents, the data in Table 1.2 do reveal that the Democrats were disproportionately successful in open seats. Specifically, Democrats won 38 percent of open seats previously held by Republicans, while defeating just over 10 percent of Republican incumbents.

References

Abramowitz, Alan I., Albert D. Cover, and Helmut Norpoth. 1986. "The President's Party in Midterm Elections: Going from Bad to Worse." *American Journal of Political Science* 30: 562–76.

Born, Richard. 1990. "The Shared Fortunes of Congress and Congressmen: Members May Run from Congress, but They Can't Hide." *Journal of Politics* 52: 1223–41.

Cain, Bruce, John Ferejohn, and Morris Fiorina. 1987. *The Personal Vote: Constituency Service and Electoral Independence.* Cambridge, Mass.: Harvard University Press.

Campbell, Angus. 1966. "Surge and Decline: A Study of Electoral Change." In Angus Campbell, Philip E. Converse, Warren E. Miller, and Donald E. Stokes, eds., *Elections and the Political Order.* New York: Wiley.

Campbell, James E. 1985. "Explaining Presidential Losses in Midterm Congressional Elections." *Journal of Politics* 47: 1140–57.

Campbell, James E. 1987. "The Revised Theory of Surge and Decline." *American Journal of Political Science* 31: 965–79.

Campbell, James E. 1993. *The Presidential Pulse of Congressional Elections.* Lexington, KY: University of Kentucky Press.

Cover, Albert D. 1985. "Surge and Decline in Congressional Elections." *Western Political Quarterly* 38: 606–19.

Fenno, Richard F., Jr. 1975. "If, As Ralph Nader Says, Congress is 'The Broken Branch,' How Come We Love Our Congressmen So Much?" In Norman J. Ornstein, ed., *Congress in Change: Evolution and Reform.* New York: Praeger.

Fenno, Richard F., Jr. 1978. *Home Style: House Members in Their Districts.* Boston: Little, Brown.

Gaddie, Ronald K. and Charles S. Bullock III. 2000. *Elections to Open Seats in the U.S. House: Where the Action Is.* Lanham, MD: Rowman and Littlefield.

Hibbing, John R. and Elizabeth Theiss-Morse. 1995. *Congress as Public Enemy: Public Attitudes toward American Political Institutions.* New York: Cambridge University Press.

Hibbing, John R. and Elizabeth Theiss-Morse. 2002. *Stealth Democracy: Americans' Beliefs about How Government Should Work.* New York: Cambridge University Press.

Huckfeldt, Robert, Edward G. Carmines, Jeffery J. Mondak, and Eric Zeemering. 2007. "Information, Activation, and Electoral Competition in the 2002 Congressional Elections." *Journal of Politics* 69: 798–812.

Kernell, Samuel. 1977. "Presidential Popularity and Negative Voting: An Alternative Explanation of the Midterm Congressional Decline of the President's Party." *American Political Science Review* 71: 44–66.

Lipinski, Daniel, William T. Bianco, and Ryan Work. 2003. "What Happens When House Members 'Run with Congress'?: The Electoral Consequences of Institutional Loyalty." *Legislative Studies Quarterly* 28: 413–29.

McDermott, Monika L. and David R. Jones. 2003. "Do Public Evaluations of Congress Matter?" *American Politics Research* 31: 155–77.

Parker, Glenn R. and Roger H. Davidson. 1979. "Why Do Americans Love Their Congressmen so Much More than Their Congress?" *Legislative Studies Quarterly* 4: 53–61.

Tufte, Edward R. 1975. "Determinants of the Outcomes of Midterm Congressional Elections." *American Political Science Review* 69: 812–26.

Chapter 2

Did the Media Do it?

The Influence of News Coverage on the 2006 Congressional Elections[1]

Edward G. Carmines, Jessica C. Gerrity, and Michael W. Wagner

Elections are notoriously blunt instruments. As such, it is often difficult to interpret what the results mean or why the elections favored the winners in the first place. In an era where competitive elections are increasingly scarce, the 2006 midterm elections turned a 232–201 Republican advantage in the House of Representatives to a 233–202 Democratic majority. Similarly, and in some ways more remarkably, the Senate narrowly slipped out of the GOP's hands as well, giving the Democrats a majority in both chambers of the legislative branch of the federal government for the first time since 1994.

Despite the fact the results of the 2006 midterms comport nicely with traditional explanations of a midterm loss in elections occurring during the "sixth-year itch"[2] of twoterm presidential administrations, times of war,[3] and years of economic tumult, political pundits have been quick to point the finger at another source: the news media. A November 13, 2006 *Washington Times* op-ed from former Sen. Robert Dole's press secretary Douglass MacKinnon claimed that "the remnants of objectivity in the mainstream media were all but exterminated by some on the left" because "many in the media have worked in concert with the Democratic spin doctors to indoctrinate the American voter into believing this election had to be a referendum on President Bush and the 'failed' war in Iraq." *National Review Online* editor Jonah Goldberg wrote in the November 9, 2006 *USA Today* that though the Democrats' victory was hardly impressive, it occurred, in part, "because Democrats—with the help of a transmission-belt media—convinced a lot of voters that they could simply change the channel on the war by voting for 'change.'"

Do these claims have merit? Or, are they the excuses and accusations of the electorally vanquished? In this chapter, we examine these issues by asking, first, did the news media cover Republicans more negatively than the Democrats in the 2006 elections by tying negative coverage issues such as the war in Iraq and congressional scandals to Republican congressional candidates? Second, we ask the following about media coverage of the 2006 congressional elections: did it help the Democrats?

To answer these questions, we present the results of content analyses of broadcast news coverage of Congress by NBC and FOX News during the fall 2006 election season.[4] Using that analysis as a starting point, we turn to more formal analysis, using data from the 2006 Congressional Elections Study (CES) to explore questions regarding the news media's role in affecting the 2006 midterms. In particular, we examine how media use among survey respondents affect public attitudes toward congressional partisans and citizens' vote choice.

The analysis suggests a more complicated story than those told in the *Washington Times* and *USA Today*. Depending on the source, coverage toward congressional partisans and partisan congressional challengers varied during the final months before the election, typically in response to newsworthy events or institutional factors. Regarding the media's real political consequences in 2006, we demonstrate that when being a television news watcher independently affected items such as vote choice, attitudes toward congressional partisans and attitudes toward specific candidates, use of television news as one's main source of information about Congress slightly *helped* Republican candidates. On the other hand, when we *interact* variables measuring television viewers and political knowledge, the Democrats gained the advantage at the ballot box. Indeed, the finding that it is the interaction of one's preferred source for news and one's political knowledge that affects vote choice improves our understanding about how voters make decisions in contemporary American politics.

Congressional Elections and the News Media

Typically, studies of House and Senate races focus on local radio, television, and newspaper campaign coverage (Cook 1989). If there are any general truths that stem from work in this area, they are that television coverage is hard to come by and incumbents have the advantage in grabbing the few morsels of attention local television provides (Cook 1989; Schaffner 2006). Examining local coverage makes sense as many congressional campaigns turn on community issues rather than national tides (Fenno 1978).

As with the elections of 1994, though, many congressional candidates in 2006 focused on a national issues strategy, centering campaign messages on the Iraq War, the War on Terror, congressional scandals, and the election-as-referendum on President Bush. While local news pays scant attention to congressional candidates, we demonstrate that stories about Congress and the midterm elections were regularly covered on national network television news during the 2006 election season.

The mass media are a crucial intermediary between elite actors and the public. What is more, the news media's institutional structure regularly requires giving attention to both Republicans and Democrats in political news coverage. Professional norms of journalistic objectivity regularly lead the news media to cover "both sides" of an issue[5] (Gamson and Modigliani 1989; Downie and Kaiser 2002; Graber 2002; Schudson 2003). Because political parties provide institutional structure for American political debate (Schattschneider 1942; Wright and Schaffner 2002; Sniderman and Bullock 2004), they are often key players in media stories that provide two "sides" to an issue (Hershey 1999).

Naturally, elite partisans make up a clear majority of the "official sources" that are routinely relied upon in political news stories (Cook 1989).

With respect to congressional elections, media consumers bemoan the regular occurrence of Republican vs. Democrat "horserace journalism" that focuses on campaign strategy and survey numbers even as reporters often prefer covering the horserace as they can more readily defend themselves from charges of bias by claiming that they are merely reporting the polls (Graber 2002). Specifically regarding television coverage, there is reason to explore whether often dramatic storytelling style and vivid pictures resonate with viewers during an election season. Zaller (1992) argues that people tend to resist the persuasive attempts often found in campaigns, as reported by the news media, to the extent that people can apply their predispositions to the relevant information, suggesting important roles for the content of information and the political awareness of the individual. We argue that the interaction of these two items can have an important, independent influence on vote choice and attitudes toward congressional partisans.

The Mediated Context of the 2006 Midterm Elections

In order to more fully understand what television news viewers were seeing with respect to the midterm elections, we examined congressional elections coverage from the *NBC Nightly News with Brian Williams* and *FOX News' Special Report with Brit Hume* from mid-September through Election Day.[6] We coded the transcripts for every story that mentioned any of the following terms: "Congress," "congressional," "House," "Senate," "Senator," or "Representative" for a variety of factors.[7] For this chapter, the crucial coding categories include the issues present in the news stories and tone of the coverage aimed at the institution of Congress, Republicans in Congress, and Democrats in Congress. We coded for the possibility of 17 different issues (see Coding Appendix) present in the stories. For each story containing one or more of the search terms, we recorded up to four issues. The most prominent coverage focused on the Iraq War, the War on Terror, congressional scandals, and stories related to the 2006 horserace.

We coded the category of Congress as an institution when all or part of the story dealt with Congress, the House, or the Senate and not specific members of the legislative branch. The stories were coded as being generally negative about Congress, generally neutral/equally positive or negative about Congress, or generally positive about Congress. The categories relating to the tone of coverage about congressional Republicans and congressional Democrats were coded when all or part of a story specifically referred to a partisan member of the House or Senate *or* when a story referred to congressional partisans as a group. Once again, the stories are coded as being generally negative, neutral/equally positive and negative, or positive about congressional partisans.

Coders determined whether the stories were mostly positive, mostly negative or neutral by categorizing each statement referring to the subject in question (congressional Republicans, for example) as positive, negative, or neutral. The coder then assessed whether, on balance, the story was mostly positive, negative, or neutral toward that source.[8] For example, a story on the October 12, 2006 *NBC Nightly News* that focused on the U.S. Senate race in Montana included several mentions of Republican Sen. Conrad Burns' ties to disgraced lobbyist Jack Abramoff, his dwindling support among many Montana Republicans, and criticisms of his position on the Iraq War. The story also included a sound bite from Burns in which he claimed that he had "weathered the worst of the attacks"; it also mentioned how the national Republican Party was supporting Burns by sending GOP "all-stars" to campaign for him. On balance, the information was more negative than positive and the story was categorized as mostly negative.

On the Democratic side, the same story aired a sound bite from Democratic challenger Jon Tester which explained his beliefs about the important issues in the campaign, mentioned how one of those issues (honesty and integrity) was a big benefit to his Senate bid, noted how Democrats were making significant gains in Montana more generally, and quoted a long-time Republican voter as saying he would not be voting for the Republicans in the election. The story did air a snippet of a negative advertisement about Tester claiming that while his haircut was conservative, his behavior was not. In the main, though, the information was much more positive about Tester and his chances to win than it was neutral or negative, so the story was categorized as mostly positive for congressional Democrats.

Special Report with Brit Hume aired 46 stories mentioning Congress or congressional partisans between mid-September and Election Day while the *NBC Nightly News* aired 71 stories.[9] Figure 2.1 highlights week by week measures of the tone of the *NBC Nightly News* and the FOX News program *Special Report with Brit Hume*'s nightly coverage of Republican candidates and members of Congress during the midterm election season. With respect to congressional Republicans, late September and early October were weeks of decidedly bad news as the GOP's Mark Foley made headlines when it was revealed that he had sent sexually explicit electronic messages to male congressional pages. The Republican leadership, notably Speaker Dennis Hastert, was also the target of negative coverage in the fallout of the Foley revelations as allegations surfaced that complaints about Foley had been made to Speaker Hastert long before ABC News first broke the story of Foley's inappropriate instant messages to pages. Republicans also endured negative coverage about the party's dealings with convicted lobbyist Jack Abramoff (for further discussion of these scandals, see Chapter 5 of this volume).

As Figure 2.1 highlights, NBC's reports that included congressional Republicans were decidedly negative during the two weeks that the Foley scandal erupted. However, once the scandal passed and no new information became available to report, NBC's coverage of Republican candidates for and members

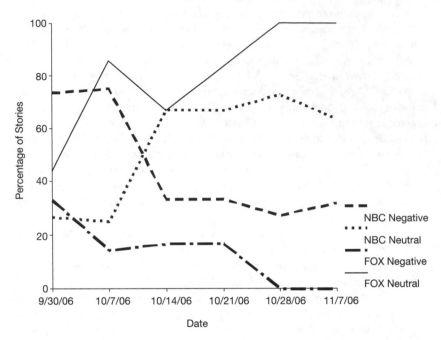

Figure 2.1 NBC and FOX News Coverage of Republican Congressional Candidates.

of Congress was mostly neutral. Indeed, between 64 and 73 percent of NBC stories mentioning congressional Republicans were neutral while no more than 36 percent were negative. NBC did not air a single story that treated GOP congressional hopefuls in a mostly positive manner.

On the other hand, the coverage that FOX News provided during *Special Report with Brit Hume* was decidedly different. When the Foley scandal broke, FOX coverage of Republicans often presented the Foley story as an anomaly, one in which most Republicans were not involved; FOX also took time to point out similar indiscretions from the past made by congressional Democrats. During the two weeks when approximately 75 percent of NBC's stories about Republicans in Congress were decidedly negative, reflecting the Foley scandal and its fallout, between 16 and 33 percent of FOX coverage of GOP congress members was negative. Remarkably, though not shown in Figure 2.1, during the first week of the Foley scandal, 25 percent of FOX stories about Republicans were purely positive in tone.

After the Foley scandal, both FOX and NBC's coverage of congressional Republicans was predominantly neutral, though NBC was slightly more likely to air negative stories than was FOX News. During the last weeks of the campaign, all of FOX's stories treated Republicans with a neutral tone; meanwhile, the negatively toned stories broadcast by NBC typically dealt with horserace coverage, showing polls suggesting trouble was in store for the GOP on Election Day.

Figure 2.2 reports the tone of the coverage NBC and FOX gave to Democratic congressional candidates and representatives. In the main, Democrats escaped negative coverage during the time when the Mark Foley scandal was most prominent; notably, however, they were not able to generate positive coverage in response to the scandals from either NBC or FOX. Indeed, the Abramoff scandal touched Democrats as well, but not as severely as it did Republicans in NBC's coverage. This resulted in congressional Democrats receiving relatively equal amounts of positive and negative coverage in stories about legislative scandals while Republicans took more negative heat from NBC.

From mid-October to Election Day, congressional Democrats received predominantly neutral coverage from NBC. As was the case with NBC's coverage of congressional Republicans, coverage of congressional Democrats and Democratic hopefuls saw a notable rise in neutral coverage during the last week of the campaign. While the coverage during the final push was relatively equal for congressional partisans, Democrats still received less negative coverage than Republicans on NBC. Typically, negative coverage about congressional Republicans centered on public dissatisfaction with the war in Iraq, poll numbers predicting a Democratic victory in the midterms, and congressional scandals with a Republican face.

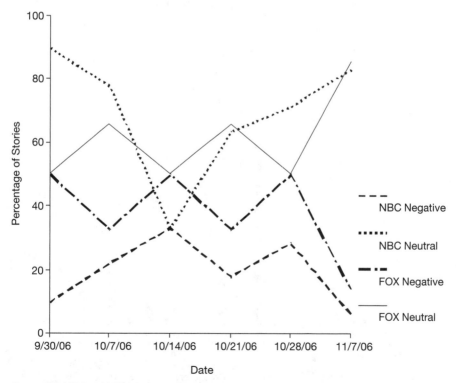

Figure 2.2 NBC and FOX News Coverage of Democratic Congressional Candidates.

Even a quick glance at Figures 2.1 and 2.2 reveal strong differences between the coverage choices of NBC and FOX's flagship news programs. During the time that the Foley scandal broke, FOX actually aired more negative stories about congressional Democrats than Republicans, while simultaneously airing some positive stories about GOPers in Congress. During the time period coded, FOX never aired a positive story about congressional Democrats. However, FOX's coverage of Democrats was still more likely than not to be neutral as well. As was the case with NBC, the percentage of stories that were either neutral or equally positive and negative about partisans on both sides of the aisle rose during the final weeks of the campaign in FOX's coverage.

It is particularly interesting that neither network aired a story that was generally positive in tone towards the Democrats even though poll numbers predicted that the majorities of both houses of Congress could shift in their favor. Stories mentioning this possibility were quick to point out items such as Democratic culpability in the Abramoff scandal, the possibility that voter turnout would favor Republicans, and suppositions that the Democrats' advantage in the polls was related to President Bush's unpopularity, and not due to any resonant campaign messages from the minority party.

Figure 2.3 breaks down the tone of congressional partisans' coverage by issue. With the exception of the coverage NBC gave Republicans on congressional scandals, both parties had more neutral stories about the war in Iraq,

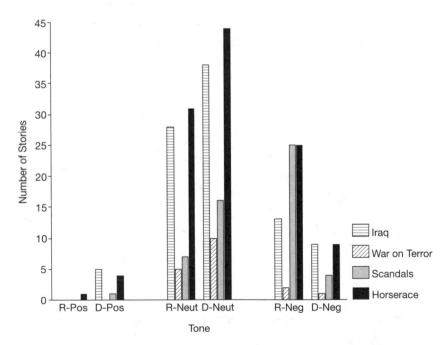

Figure 2.3 Tone of NBC Coverage about Prominent Issues, September 30–November 7, 2006.

the War on Terror, and the horserace than positive or negative stories. However, in many cases, NBC coverage of Republicans on these issues consisted of more stories that were negative in tone compared to the negative coverage of the Democrats. NBC aired 44 stories about campaign numbers and/or strategy that treated the Democrats in a neutral manner; nine stories treated Democrats negatively and four were positive in tone. For the Republicans, a majority (31) of the horserace coverage was neutral, but another 25 stories were negative while only one was positive.

Turning to NBC's coverage of scandals, Democratic coverage that was neutral in nature appeared four times more than negative coverage and 16 times more than positive coverage. NBC's coverage of Republicans and scandals was decidedly more downbeat, with 25 stories treating congressional Republicans negatively compared to seven even-handed stories and no positive coverage. Most of the negative stories appeared in late September and early October, when the Mark Foley scandal was at its height, while the lion's share of the neutral offerings from NBC were in the final weeks of the campaign.

Coverage of the Iraq War was more even-handed, though NBC's coverage was less favorable to congressional Republicans. The Democrats were covered in more stories than were congressional Republicans as the minority party was often used as a counterpoint to President Bush's positions on the war. Thirty-eight stories treated Democrats in a neutral way while nine stories had a negative tone. In five stories, the Democrats came off positively; in three of those cases the positive nature of the coverage reflected how the war was helping the Democrats' chances in the midterm elections.

Congressional Republicans received more neutral treatment than anything else from NBC (28 stories), but they still received more negative treatment (13 stories) than the Democrats, even though congressional Democrats found their way onto the evening news more frequently than GOP lawmakers with respect to the Iraq issue. NBC coverage of the war in Iraq that dealt with congressional Republicans yielded no positive stories. NBC's treatment of the War on Terror focused on the President; when congressional partisans were brought into the mix, the coverage tended to be neutral for both parties.

Even though *Special Report with Brit Hume* is an hour-long program and the *NBC Nightly News with Brian Williams* is 30 minutes, NBC had more coverage about Congress than their FOX counterparts. Figure 2.4 illustrates the tone of the issue coverage congressional partisans received for the four most frequently covered issues. Twenty-three horserace stories treated the Democrats in a neutral fashion while 14 had a negative view of Democratic campaign strategy, their chances for taking the House and the likelihood that they would win back the Senate. No FOX News horserace stories had a positive take on congressional Democrats. On the GOP side, 19 stories were neutral while six were negative and three were positive.

Nearly all of the positively toned stories came during discussions of the FOX "All-Star Panel," typically consisting of pundits Fred Barnes, Mort Kondracke, Charles Krauthammer, and Mara Liasson. Many of the negatively toned

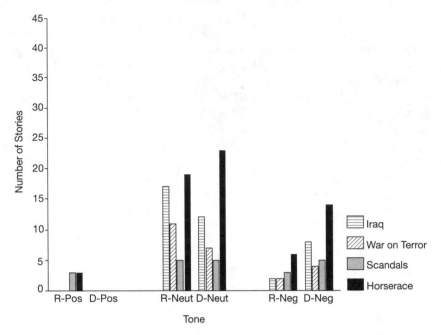

Figure 2.4 Tone of FOX News Coverage about Prominent Issues, September 30–
November 7, 2006.

Democratic stories also came from these discussions rather than conventional news reporting. FOX's coverage of the Iraq War and the War on Terror were overwhelmingly neutral to Republicans while slightly more neutral than negative for congressional Democrats. Regardless of both the issue and the network, congressional Democrats received more coverage in every instance save for scandals on NBC and the War on Terror on FOX.

Taken together, our review of the news media's coverage suggests that, in the main, Democrats and Republicans were treated neutrally by the television media. However, in most instances, Republicans in Congress received more negative coverage than Democrats did on NBC, the most watched network, while Democrats received more negative coverage on FOX News, the most watched cable station. What role, if any, did this coverage play in evaluations of Congress and citizens' congressional vote choices?

In the week following the highest level of negative stories about Republicans broadcast on both NBC and FOX (the week after the breaking of the Foley scandal), 64.5 percent of respondents surveyed on the 2006 CES reported their intent to vote Democrat in the midterm House elections. As network and cable news coverage treated congressional partisans with increasingly neutral gloves, the percentage of voters siding with the minority party dropped back to "pre-Foley" scandal levels of just under 60 percent.[10] Of course, in order to understand what systematic role media coverage of Congress and congressional partisans may have had in the 2006 election season, it is crucial to conduct more sophisticated analyses.

We suggest that congressional attitudes and citizens' voting behavior in the 2006 midterms is, in part, affected by the news media's coverage of Congress and its members. Of course, there is reason to believe that the news coverage will not influence all people equally (Hibbing and Theiss-Morse 1998; Graber 2002). We believe that one's source of information about Congress, the information that source provides about Congress, and one's political knowledge (Huckfeldt *et al.* 2007) should independently and jointly influence congressional vote choice. Specifically, congressional evaluations should be higher for those citizens with a high degree of political knowledge and a high level of media use. As Mondak *et al.* (2007) argue, there is nothing that should automatically suggest that the politically knowledgeable disapprove of Congress.

However, this does not mean that negative coverage about Congress or congressional partisans automatically translates into disapproval of Congress. Hibbing and Theiss-Morse (1998) demonstrate that the news media differentially influence cognitive and emotional evaluations of Congress. The questions in the CES do not allow us to make this distinction; indeed, the dependent variables we explore are cognitive evaluations, the precise process in which we traditionally should not expect the specific contents of media coverage to bring influence.

Media Coverage, Congressional Approval, and Voting in the 2006 Midterms

We examine these expectations by utilizing data from the CES. The CES expands the effort initially made by the Center on Congress at Indiana University's 2002 midterm election survey. As was the case in 2002, survey interviews were conducted by telephone by the Center for Survey Research at Indiana University. The CES draws respondents from 100 randomly selected congressional districts and an additional set of districts the developers of the CES identified as competitive (a total of 72 districts, 17 of which were already in the random sample) for a total of 155 districts in the sample (for additional discussion of the properties of the 2006 CES, see Chapter 1 of this volume).

Four different interviews were conducted as part of the 2006 CES. First, 1,023 pre-election interviews were completed between September 28, 2006, and the November 7 election. The reasonably comprehensive interviews lasted an average of 33 minutes. Second, a "past-tense" version of the full pre-election survey was completed by an additional 174 respondents later in November, after the elections. Next, 766 of the pre-election survey respondents also completed a 22-minute post-election survey in the weeks following the November 7 elections. In this chapter, our analysis is restricted to those who participated in both the pre- and post-election surveys, to maximize the amount of questions available to us for analysis. The CES does not distinguish what type of national television news program respondents generally watch, so it is impossible to isolate independent effects, if any, that exist for NBC and FOX's coverage of the midterm elections.

First, we turn our attention to the determinants of the 2006 midterm vote among CES respondents. Among the major independent variables of interest are *TV*, which is coded 1 if the respondent uses television as her or his main source of news about Congress and 0 otherwise; *Knowledge*, coded from 0–3 based on the number of questions about American politics answered correctly; *TV × Knowledge*, an interaction which multiplies the *TV* and *Knowledge* (see below) variables together to help us determine their joint effect; and *Newspaper*, which is coded 1 if the respondents name newspapers as their top source for congressional news and 0 otherwise. Likewise, *News × Knowledge* multiplies the *Newspaper* and *Knowledge* variables. *Competitive* is a dichotomous variable coded 1 if the respondent's congressional district was deemed competitive before the 2006 elections and 0 otherwise.[11] *TV × Competitive* and *Newspaper × Competitive* interact respondents' favored source for information about Congress and the closeness of the House races in the respondents' congressional districts.

Party is coded 1 for Republican and 0 for Democrat (including "independent leaners"), *Age* is the respondent's age, *White* is coded 1 for a white respondent and 0 otherwise, *Date of Interview* is coded on a 6-point scale based on the week the survey was completed (higher scores indicate a survey completed closer to the election). *Bush Approval* is coded 1–4 from strongly approve to strongly disapprove of the job George W. Bush is doing as president. *Iraq* is a 5-point scale moving from 1 for most unfavorable to 5 for most favorable with respect to the respondent's views about the war in Iraq. *Age* and *Income* are 5-point scales that range from lowest to highest. *Scandals* reports a numeric value for the letter grade respondents give Congress for behaving in an ethical manner coded 1–6 (grades of A-F). *Congressional GOP Evals* and *Congressional Dems Evals* are coded 1–5 (most favorable to least favorable).

Table 2.1 reports the coefficients and standard errors for a logistic regression model seeking to predict the factors that affect vote choice in the 2006 midterms. The dependent variable is coded 1 for a vote for the Democratic House candidate and 0 for a vote for the Republican candidate. On its own, the *TV* and *Newspaper* coefficients are negatively signed, suggesting that both mediums breed support for Republican House candidates, but the variables ($p < .13$, $p < .28$) do not approach statistical significance. Political *Knowledge* also fails to have an independent influence on the 2006 congressional vote. Still, the direction of these variables suggests that the chorus of complaints about how the nature of news coverage propelled the Democrats to office are ill-conceived as, *ceteris paribus*, the seeking of information about Congress from the television or the newspaper seemed to help the GOP, albeit to a degree that falls short of a statistically meaningful effect.

On the other hand, the interaction of *Television × Knowledge* significantly predicts support ($p < .05$) for the Democratic House candidate. Similarly, but to a lesser degree of significance, *Newspaper × Knowledge* has the same effect

Table 2.1 Determinants of Congressional Vote

Independent Variables	Democratic Vote
TV	−1.734
	(1.17)
Newspaper	−1.503
	(1.4)
Knowledge	0.865
	(0.549)
TV × Knowledge	0.78**
	(0.395)
Newspaper × Knowledge	0.776*
	(0.471)
Competitive District	0.362
	(1.395)
TV × Competitive	0.156
	(1.111)
Newspaper × Competitive	0.141
	(1.2)
Knowledge × Competitive	−0.378
	(0.409)
Party	−3.292**
	(0.466)
Ideology	−0.007
	(0.213)
Congressional Approval	−0.573**
	(0.286)
Congressional Evals of GOP	−0.969**
	(0.22)
Congressional Evals of Dems	0.318
	(0.217)
Bush Approval	0.764**
	(0.278)
Age	−0.000
	(0.000)
Scandals	0.05
	(0.182)
Iraq	−0.328
	(0.17)
Income	−0.293**
	(0.113)
White	−1.633
	(1.31)
Date of Interview	0.0636
	(0.123)
Constant	5.789**
	(2.148)

Note: N = 547, LR chi^2 = 527.30**, Pseudo R^2 = .70, **p < 0.05, *p < 0.10

Table 2.2 Determinants of Evaluations of Congressional Partisans and Candidates

	Congressional Republicans Evaluation	Congressional Democrats Evaluation	Democratic Candidate Evaluation	Republican Candidate Evaluation
TV	1.296**	0.233	−0.286	0.204
	(0.461)	(0.445)	(0.441)	(0.441)
Newspaper	0.352	0.010	−0.604	−0.57
	(0.638)	(0.633)	(0.632)	(0.657)
Knowledge	0.318	0.234	0.236	0.288
	(0.344)	(0.321)	(0.201)	(0.273)
TV × Knowledge	−0.428**	0.017	0.239	−0.003
	(0.155)	(0.149)	(0.151)	(0.151)
Newspaper × Knowledge	−0.944	0.176	0.184	0.216
	(0.217)	(0.213)	(0.213)	(0.225)
Competitive District	−0.208	1.334**	0.988	0.408
	(0.632)	(0.615)	(0.635)	(0.681)
TV × Competitive	−0.606	−0.511	−0.303	−0.418
	(0.469)	(0.458)	(0.483)	(0.489)
Newspaper × Competitive	−0.225	−0.329	0.415	−0.115
	(0.485)	(0.476)	(0.5)	(0.504)
Knowledge × Competitive	0.201	−0.443**	−0.449**	−0.135
	(0.193)	(0.188)	(0.19)	(0.2)
Party	1.203**	−0.774**	−1.527**	0.995**
	(0.247)	(0.24)	(0.247)	(0.246)
Ideology	0.248**	−0.178**	−0.267**	0.359**
	(0.091)	(0.086)	(0.089)	(0.09)
Congressional Approval	−0.525**	−0.385**	−0.323**	−0.234**
	(0.121)	(0.116)	(0.119)	(0.117)
Bush Approval	−0.785**	0.742**	0.437**	−0.576**
	(0.132)	(0.13)	(0.128)	(0.13)
Age	−0.000	0.000	0.000	−0.000
	(0.000)	(0.000)	(0.000)	(0.001)
Scandals	−0.222**	−0.150*	−0.141*	−0.282**
	(0.083)	(0.081)	(0.082)	(0.087)
Iraq	0.265**	0.038	0.08	0.095
	(0.09)	(0.086)	(0.086)	(0.867)
Income	0.076	−0.004	0.03	0.075
	(0.049)	(0.046)	(0.048)	(0.051)
White	−0.012	−0.743**	−0.261	−0.239
	(0.385)	(0.353)	(0.338)	(0.354)
Date of Interview	0.000	−0.272	−0.018	−0.014
	(0.051)	(0.049)	(0.051)	(0.051)

Notes:
Model 1: N = 621, LR chi² = 507.55**, Pseudo R^2 = .28, **p < 0.05, *p < 0.10
Model 2: N = 623, LR chi² = 221.99**, Pseudo R^2 = .12, **p < 0.05, *p < 0.10
Model 3: N = 561, LR chi² = 218.01**, Pseudo R^2 = .12, **p < 0.05, *p < 0.10
Model 4: N = 563, LR chi² = 323.85**, Pseudo R^2 = .18, **p < 0.05, *p < 0.10

(p < .10). Citizens who get their information about Congress from the television saw coverage that highlighted Republican scandals and the war in Iraq while still providing, more often than not, neutral coverage of congressional partisans and candidates. Nonetheless, the negative information about the Republican financial and moral scandals, and steady news about an unpopular war was especially influential when interacted with high degrees of political knowledge. Knowing about politics and learning about contemporary issues combined to give Democrats an advantage in 2006. Interestingly, *Competition* and the various interactions with that variable in Table 2.1 have no effect in the model.

Aside from the interactions of the media use and knowledge variables, the only other factors in the model that affect the midterm vote are *Congressional GOP Evals, Congressional Approval, Party, Income,* and *Bush Approval.* As disapproval of the president increases, so does the likelihood of a Democratic congressional vote. When evaluations of congressional Republicans increase, the likelihood of a Republican ballot rises as well. Wealthier respondents were also more likely to vote Republican, as were folks who were already GOP identifiers. As operationalized here, hot-button issues such as congressional scandals and the war in Iraq did not have a statistically significant effect on vote choice in the 2006 midterms. One's ideology is also notably absent from the statistically significant variables in the model.

Table 2.2 reports the coefficients and standard errors for four different ordinal logistic regression models relating to determinants of the public's evaluation of both congressional partisans and the actual candidates seeking the CES respondents' votes in the 2006 elections. The left-hand column of results explores the factors predicting positive evaluations of congressional Republicans. As was the case in Table 2.1, the *Television* coefficient is positive, suggesting a benefit for Republicans; this time the variable is also statistically significant (p < .05). Getting one's information about Congress from the tube has a positive, independent effect on evaluations of congressional Republicans. *Newspaper* has a positive coefficient, but does not come close to achieving statistical significance.

Similar to the case with vote choice, *Television × Knowledge* negatively affects (p < .05) favorability ratings of congressional GOPers. *Newspaper × Knowledge* has a negative coefficient, but is not significant. While scandals did not affect vote choice, they did take their toll on Republicans in the House. *Scandals* has a significant (p < .05), negative coefficient. Republicans and self identified conservatives (*Party* and *Ideology*) are more likely to positively evaluate congressional conservatives. Positive evaluations of the progress of the Iraq War bred support for House Republicans as well (*Iraq*, p < .05). As disapproval of Congress and the president increased, negative evaluations of Republicans in the House of Representatives did too (p < .05). Living in *Competitive* districts has no systematic effect on the dependent variable.

The next column to the right illustrates that evaluations of Congressional Democrats did not come from the news media. None of the media variables and their interactions affected evaluations of congressional Democrats. Indeed, living in a *Competitive* district led to more positive evaluations of the Democrats already in Congress while the interaction between one's congressional district and *Knowledge* led to less favorable takes on the minority party (p < .05). While conservative editorialists were quick to blame the media for harping on GOP scandals, those who gave bad grades to Congress' ethical behavior were also more likely to negatively evaluate congressional Democrats (*Scandals*, p < .05). The same is true for *Congressional Approval.* As disapproval of the body of Congress increases, so do negative evaluations of House Democrats. However, disapproval of the president led to improved favorability toward the president's Democratic opponents in the House. Non-whites (p < .05) had more positive evaluations of Congress than whites while Republican and conservative identifiers were more likely to have less favorable appraisals of congressional Democrats.

Thus, media coverage of Congress seemed to influence evaluations of congressional Republicans more than their Democratic counterparts. Meanwhile, Democrats in Washington were not immune to the ill-effects of scandal and negative evaluations of the institution of Congress more generally. Living in a competitive electoral environment affected assessments of Democratic congress members, but did not have a similar independent effect on public views about Republican representatives.

The third column from the right examines the factors that affect evaluations of the individual Democratic candidates running for the House in the CES respondents' districts. *TV × Knowledge* once again had a positive coefficient, suggesting more favorable views toward Democratic candidates, but the variable falls short of conventional levels of statistical significance (p < .11). The other media variables fall well short of statistical significance, though the direction of the *TV*, *Newspaper*, and *Newspaper × Knowledge* coefficients are in directions equal to their position in the other models.

The coefficient for living in a *Competitive* district also has a positive, but non-significant (p < .12) effect on Democratic candidate evaluations. However, *Knowledge × Competition* negatively and significantly (p < .05) affected public views of Democratic candidates for the House. Indeed, *Party* (Republican) and *Ideology* have negative effects on the dependent variable, as does increasing disapproval of Congress. Negative assessments of President Bush benefit the standing of individual Democratic candidates while Congress' ethical lapses hurt the candidates of the minority party.

The far-right hand column assesses determinants of positive evaluations of Republican candidates for the House. None of the media variables, competition variables, and knowledge variables affects evaluations of individual GOP candidates for the House. As is often the case in midterm elections, assessments of the president and Congress as an institution led to more negative evaluations of GOP candidates. Variables representing Republican and conservative identifiers show positive and significant independent effects (p < .05) on the dependent variable.

Discussion

The 2006 elections swept the Democrats back into the legislative majority in both houses of Congress for the first time in 12 years. After the election, explanations for the GOP loss centered on a familiar tune, "blame the media." Our analysis here suggests a more complicated story. On the one hand, interacting television coverage, which did aggressively cover the war in Iraq and congressional scandals, with citizens' knowledge about politics, helped the Democrats in 2006. On the other hand, we demonstrate an independent effect in favor of GOP votes for those who chose television as their main source of news about Congress during the election season. Public views about scandals and about the institution of Congress consistently led to negative evaluations of Republicans *and* Democrats. Meanwhile, the vast unpopularity of President Bush was consistently associated with negative views of Republicans and positive views of Democratic office seekers. Explanations of the 2006 results should start by examining public evaluations of the president (for one such examination, see Chapter 7 of this volume).

Our content analysis of television news coverage of Congress and its members allows us to suggest three broad conclusions. First, NBC and FOX treated congressional partisans differently. FOX paid less attention to congressional scandals and chose to cover them in ways that were more negative about Democrats than Republicans. NBC's coverage focused on the more explicit nature of the scandals and prominent Republicans involved in the stories, such as former Representative Mark Foley. NBC's reporting of the horserace was generally neutral to the poll leaders (the Democrats) but negative to the party trailing in public surveys (Republicans). FOX was nearly the opposite. Second, both television news outlets covered congressional news in a more even-handed manner as Election Day drew near. It is possible that both outlets wanted to avoid charges that they were trying to sway an election in the final week, but it is equally possible that the information they were reporting did not lend itself as well to positive or negative coverage.

Interestingly, the competitiveness of the district mattered only when considering evaluations of congressional Democrats or when interacting it with political knowledge. Much as pork barrel spending only helps congress members when people are aware that their district is receiving the benefits of the government trough, living in a district with a close congressional race matters for the politically knowledgeable—the precise people likely to be aware that the election is a competitive one.

While the story is not as simple as "the media did it," we believe that the sketch that we supply here suggests that the national broadcast media's coverage of Congress and congressional partisans is a factor that ought to be more carefully considered in studies seeking to understand how congressional elections work and how American political institutions are evaluated by the citizenry.

Appendix: Content Analysis Coding Procedures

A. The Search Process. Coders conducted the search for news stories using the following directions

TV search terms:

- Using Lexis-Nexis, click the "news" button
- Select "Transcripts" in the drop-down box
- For NBC Only
- Then choose "NBC Transcripts"
- Type "NBC Nightly News" (in quotes)
- For FOX Only
- Then choose "FOX News Transcripts"
- Type "Special Report with Brit Hume" (in quotes)
- For both NBC and FOX
- Then type the word—"and"—and then type the following (no quotes): Congress or congressional or house or senate or Republican or Democrat or senator or representative
- Search from September 1, 2006–November 7, 2006
- Coders code the following categories in an Excel spreadsheet provided by the authors:

Note: You should code *anything* that refers to "Congress," "the House of Representatives/the House," or "the Senate"—the same is true for things such as "House members," "Senators" etc.

B. Information Recorded. Upon identifying relevant stories, coders recorded the following information

Date: The date of the story (e.g. 11/1/2006)

Source: The source of the story:

NBC = 1
FOX = 2

Length: Number of words in the story

Congressional Prominence: Would you say that Congress is one of the central features of the news article or a peripheral part of the news article/story?

1 = Central
0 = Peripheral

Congress Tone:
In regards to how the institution of Congress is treated, would you say that the article/story is:

Mostly Negative = 1
Equally Positive and Negative/Neutral = 2
Mostly Positive = 3
Not Applicable = .

Republican Tone: In regards to Republicans in Congress, would you say the article/story is:

Mostly Negative = 1
Equally Positive and Negative/Neutral = 2
Mostly Positive = 3
Not Applicable = .

Democrats Tone: In regards to Democrats in Congress, would you say the article/story is:

Mostly Negative = 1
Equally Positive and Negative/Neutral = 2
Mostly Positive = 3
Not Applicable = .

Use "Not Applicable" only if that particular category is not present in the story. If Democrats in Congress, for instance, are mentioned, you must choose a value from 1 to 3.

Coders noted the first four issues considered in each story from the following list:

 1 = War in Iraq
 2 = War on Terror/national security issues/Patriot Act
 3 = Healthcare
 4 = Economy/taxes/budget
 5 = Gun Control
 6 = Environment
 7 = Abortion
 8 = Gay Marriage
 9 = Stem Cell Research
10 = Katrina/hurricanes
11 = Education
12 = Racial issues
13 = Immigration
14 = Scandals

15 = Judicial Appointments
16 = Horserace/election
17 = Other

Notes

1   The authors would like to thank Joanna Follman, Rachel Beeson, Allie Scheer, Courtney Ruwe, and Amanda Crook for research assistance on various pieces of our project. We would also like to thank Jeff Mondak, Scott McClurg, and an anonymous referee for Routledge for their helpful comments on the chapter. All interpretations of the data and any errors remain our own.

2   Presidents Eisenhower, Johnson, and Nixon lost over 45 fellow partisans in the House in each of their sixth-year midterm elections. On the other hand, the last two "sixth-year itch" elections resulted in President Reagan's Republicans losing a mere five seats in the House in 1986 and President Clinton's fellow Democrats *gaining* five seats there in 1998.

3   Interestingly, however, public opinion just before the 2006 elections with respect to whether voters believed the war in Iraq has been worth it (53 percent claiming the war has not been worth it) looks strikingly similar to public beliefs about the war in September of 2004 (51 percent claiming the war has not been worth it) (ABC News/*Washington Post* polls). Of course, in 2004, President Bush won re-election and gained a small number of seats in both the House and the Senate.

4   NBC generally had the number one rated network newscast while FOX News was the number one rated cable news source for the time period analyzed.

5   This, to the dismay of some media critics, occurs even when an issue has more than two sides. Typically, only two sides of an issue are reported; just as typical, these sides are Republican and Democrat.

6   We call all coverage related to Congress or the congressional elections "congressional elections coverage." Our content analysis validated this choice as the vast majority of stories mentioning Congress during the time period analyzed tied the coverage to the elections.

7   Of course, if a story containing the word "house," for example, was about the White House or how a tornado destroyed a person's house, the story was not coded. In other words, the search terms led us to the possible universe of stories to code and our coders made judgments from there as to whether the story was mentioning Congress, congressional Republicans, or congressional Democrats in some way.

8   Initially, we tried to have our coders categorize the stories as mostly negative, somewhat negative, neutral, somewhat positive, or mostly positive. Inter-coder agreement ranged between 62–77 percent; most of the disagreements were with respect to the degree of the tone (e.g. somewhat positive or very positive). Thus, we had the coders collapse the categories relating to the degree of positive or negative messages in the stories.

9   One of the authors and four advanced undergraduates completed the coding. Inter-coder reliability was never below 91 percent for any category. All inter-coder disputes were settled through discussion between the coders and one of the authors.

10   Aside from the week following the highest level of negativity in congressional Republican reports on NBC.

11   The scholars involved in creating the 2006 CES jointly determined which districts were likely to be competitive, using, among other sources, the *Cook Political Report*, *Congressional Quarterly*, and Larry Sabato's "Crystal Ball" website.

References

Cook, Timothy E. 1989. *Making Laws and Making News: Media Strategies in the U.S. House of Representatives*. Washington, D.C.: The Brookings Institution.

Downie, Leonard, Jr. and Robert G. Kaiser. 2002. *The News About the News: American Journalism in Peril*. New York: Alfred A. Knopf.

Fenno, Richard F., Jr. 1978. *Home Style: House Members in Their Districts*. Boston: Little, Brown.

Gamson, William A. and Modigliani, Andre. 1989. "Media Discourse and Public Opinion on Nuclear Power: A Constructionist Approach." *American Journal of Sociology* 95: 1–37.

Graber, Doris A. 2002. *Mass Media and American Politics*. Sixth Edition. Washington D.C.: CQ Press.

Hershey, Marjorie Randon. 1999. "If the Party's in Decline, Then What's Filling the News Columns?" in Nelson Polsby and Raymond Wolfinger, eds., *On Parties*. Berkeley: University of California.

Hibbing, John R. and Elizabeth Theiss-Morse. 1998. "The Media's Role in Public Negativity Toward Congress: Distinguishing Emotional Reactions and Cognitive Evaluations." *American Journal of Political Science* 42: 475–98.

Huckfeldt, Robert, Edward G. Carmines., Jeffery J. Mondak., and Eric Zeemering. 2007. "Information, Activation, and Electoral Competition in the 2002 Congressional Elections." *Journal of Politics* 69: 798–812.

Mondak, Jeffery J., Edward G. Carmines, Robert Huckfeldt, Dona-Gene Mitchell, and Scot Schraufnagel. 2007. "Does Familiarity Breed Contempt? The Impact of Information on Mass Attitudes toward Congress." *American Journal of Political Science* 51: 34–48.

Schaffner, Brian F. 2006. "Local News Coverage and the Incumbency Advantage in the U.S. House." *Legislative Studies Quarterly* 31: 491–511.

Schattschneider, E.E. 1942. *Party Government*. New York: Rinehart.

Schudson, Michael. 2003. *The Sociology of News*. New York: W.W. Norton and Company.

Sniderman, Paul M. and John Bullock. 2004. "A Consistency Theory of Public Opinion and Political Choice: The Hypothesis of Menu Dependence" In *Studies in Public Opinion*, eds. Willem E. Saris and Paul M. Sniderman. Princeton, NJ: Princeton University Press.

Wright, Gerald C. and Brian F. Schaffner. 2002. "The Influence of Party: Evidence from the State Legislatures." *American Political Science Review*, 96: 367–79.

Zaller, John R. 1992. *The Nature and Origin of Mass Opinion*. New York: Cambridge University Press.

Chapter 3

Polarization, Attribution, and Communication Networks in the 2006 Congressional Elections

Matthew Buttice, Robert Huckfeldt, and John Barry Ryan

During the last several election cycles, a widespread sentiment shared by many voters might have been expressed as a question: "what were they thinking?" In this context, "they" refers to individuals who voted for the opposite candidate in the election. The sentiment and the question may have arisen most frequently among supporters of the losing candidates who were unable to understand the attraction of the victor, but many of the successful candidate's supporters might well have posed the same question. In the aftermath of closely contested elections, many voters on both sides are unable to understand or even conceive the logic and motivation behind the opposite side's voting choice.

The question thus arises, what are the factors that make it difficult for voters to conceive the preferences of the other side? A number of answers have been provided to this question, and most revolve around arguments related to political polarization within the electorate. A particularly popular argument is that citizens in red (Republican) states are different from citizens in blue (Democratic) states. They have different values, different styles of life, and consistently different political preferences. These differences, in turn, serve to heighten the incomprehensibility of the political preferences held by the other side.

Other analyses point out that Democratic and Republican states include substantial levels of internal heterogeneity—there are blue counties in red states and red counties in blue states. The principal argument remains, however, that citizens tend to be sorted by their political preferences, even if the segregation occurs at levels of aggregation more proximate than state boundaries. Indeed, the argument has been made that Republicans reside among Republicans and Democrats reside among Democrats, sometimes as a direct consequence of individual choice.

An underlying problem in this discussion is that analyses of political polarization in the American electorate are sometimes complicated by a lack of clarity regarding what, exactly, qualifies as polarization among voters. In a compelling analysis that focuses on the distribution of policy preferences among politicians and citizens, Fiorina (2005) argues that polarization only exists among politicians, not within the electorate. Democratic politicians tend to be clustered together on one end of the continuum, and Republican politicians together on the other end of the continuum. In contrast, the electorate tends to be clustered in the middle, and even the strong Democrats and strong Republicans are likely to be more moderate than the politicians. This analysis poses genuine problems for many of the red state–blue state accounts of polarization within the electorate, calling into question the apocalyptic language of the developing cultural chasm in American politics.

In contrast, a different definition of polarization focuses on the frequency of communication among and between citizens who hold different preferences. According to this definition, polarization is not simply a matter of relative preference locations on some underlying scale, but rather the frequency with which people at one end of the scale communicate with citizens at the opposite end of the scale. What is the justification for this alternative definition? This chapter's argument is that the frequency of communication among citizens holding different preferences is responsible for differential levels of conflict, compromise, and accommodation within the electorate. To the extent that communication occurs among citizens with divergent political preferences, these citizens are more likely to acquire information about one another's preferences—they are more likely to comprehend the political motivation of the other side.

The goal of this chapter is first to assess the levels of political polarization in the 2006 congressional elections, defined as the frequency of communication between citizens holding different viewpoints, and second to assess the effects of polarization for voters' conceptions of one another. We base this analysis on the 2006 Congressional Elections Study (CES) that was undertaken with support from the Center on Congress at Indiana University, and particularly on the social network data collected as part of the study. Our analysis addresses several questions:

1   How frequently did communication occur between citizens who held different political preferences?
2   How is the frequency of heterogeneous communication related to conditions in congressional races, and particularly the level of competitiveness within congressional districts?
3   What are the implications of varying patterns of cross-preference communication for the perceptions of political parties in Congress?

The Problem

Public attention has increasingly focused on problems related to political polarization in American politics. These concerns are quite understandable in the aftermath of two closely fought presidential elections, a closely and often rancorously divided U.S. Congress, campaign strategies that forsake the median voter in favor of fully mobilizing core partisans, and spatial distributions of voters that seem to assure the existence of Republican and Democratic strongholds within particular regions, states, and congressional districts. In this context, the red state–blue state divide has become an object of concern among those who believe that a polarized electorate threatens the viability of democratic politics.

Indeed, the level of polarization among party elites has increased dramatically since the 1960s, particularly in terms of the ideological distance between Democrats and Republicans in Congress (Rohde 1991; Jacobson 2000). As House and Senate delegations from the south steadily migrated toward the Republican party, the national Republican party became correspondingly more conservative, and northern states began electing Democratic (and typically more liberal) representatives to the House and Senate (see Brewer, Mariani, and Stonecash 2002). This increased polarization among elites has led, in turn, to increased polarization within the electorate (Levine, Carmines, and Huckfeldt 1997; Abramowitz and Saunders 1998). When elites polarize, voters are better able to differentiate the parties' positions and hence support the party that best represents their own political orientations, thereby producing more ideologically homogeneous parties (Abramowitz and Saunders 2006). In short, these changes in party ideology produce polarization in voters' evaluations of the parties (Hetherington 2001), polarization in voters' attitudes on issues (DiMaggio, Evans, and Bryson 1996; Evans 2003; Brewer 2005), and increased levels of party-line voting (Bartels 2000).

The problem made clear by Fiorina's analysis (2005) is that political polarization within the electorate is less pronounced than political polarization among elites. Indeed, he argues that, when polarization is defined in terms of divergent political preferences within the American electorate, the so-called cultural divide largely disappears. And hence the important issue in the Fiorina analysis is the set of institutions and circumstances that give rise to polarized politicians in the context of moderate citizens. According to this conception, the red state–blue state problem is a chimera, stimulated by the attributions made by journalists and others that Democratic voters are as liberal as the Democratic candidates for whom they vote, and Republican voters are as conservative as the Republican candidates for whom they vote.

This chapter does not take issue with the main thrust of the Fiorina argument. Voters *are* typically more moderate than the candidates they support, and attributing the policy preferences of candidates to the voters who support them is thus a risky undertaking. At the same time, such attributions are not limited to journalists. Citizens also form judgments regarding the politics of the other side, and our argument is that (1) these attributions enhance and sustain the reality of political polarization; and (2) the partisan composition of political communication networks is crucial to these attributions.

Reality vs. Perception: The Importance of Attribution

In this context, the analysis of Brady and Sniderman (1985) becomes particularly helpful. Using national survey data, they show that citizens sometimes attribute excessively extreme views to those who hold preferences that are different from their own. In particular, conservatives tend to believe that liberals are more liberal than the liberals' own aggregated self-reports, and well educated liberals tend to believe that conservatives are more conservative than the conservatives' own aggregated self-reports. Brady and Sniderman point toward the importance of several explanatory factors that lie behind these attributions: (1) how much the individual knows about liberals and conservatives; as well as (2) the individual's level of affect for the opposite group—the extent to which conservatives, for example, dislike liberals. On this basis they construct their likeability heuristic—a decision-making short-cut in which people attribute political preferences to groups based on the extent to which they like or dislike the group in question (also see Sniderman, Brody, and Tetlock 2001).

Brady and Sniderman offer insight into the polarization of American politics because they explicitly focus *both* on the perception *as well as* the reality of preference distributions within the electorate. Even if voters are, in reality, clustered toward the moderate middle of the distribution on most issues, these same voters may not attribute moderate views to the opposite party, to the opposite ideological stance, and to the other groups to which they do not belong. As Brady and Sniderman suggest, an important factor in explaining this attribution process is how much voters *know* about the positions of various groups in American politics. The question thus arises, how and from where is such knowledge acquired?

Locating Attribution in Context

This chapter's analysis looks to several sources of information that citizens employ when forming judgments regarding the likely preferences of various groups and individuals (Huckfeldt, Johnson, and Sprague 2004). First, if you are a member of a group, you might infer that your own preferences provide information to use in forming an assessment of the group's preferences. Thus, if you are a self identified Democrat, you are more likely to believe that Democratic politicians hold preferences similar to your own. In contrast, you are more likely to believe that Republican politicians hold preferences dissimilar to your own.

Second, you are likely to infer that the preferences of a group are represented by public figures who represent the group. Hence, you might infer that the preferences of conservatives are represented by participants in the larger public discussion—President Bush and Republican leaders in Congress. Similarly, you might infer that the preferences of liberals are represented by Nancy Pelosi and other Democratic leaders in Congress (Carmines and Kuklinski 1990; Mondak 1993).

Finally, and most importantly for this analysis, you are likely to infer that the preferences of a group are represented by preferences held among the group members with whom you are acquainted. Thus, you might infer that the preferences of conservatives are similar to the preferences of those conservatives with whom you are acquainted, and that the preferences of liberals are similar to the preferences of those liberals with whom you are acquainted (Huckfeldt *et al.* 1998). Moreover, you may even form judgments regarding the positions of Democratic and Republican politicians based on the preferences of the corresponding partisans with whom you are acquainted.

Returning to the red state–blue state problem, our analysis thus relies on a different definition of polarization that focuses on the frequency of communication among and between citizens who hold different preferences. According to this definition, it is not simply the location of preferences on some underlying scale, but rather the frequency with which citizens on one side of the political continuum communicate with citizens at the opposite side of the political continuum. What is the justification for this alternative definition? Our argument is that the frequency of communication among citizens holding divergent preferences is responsible for citizens' conceptions of the political process. Lacking real-life experience with members of the opposite political grouping, citizens form impressions and perceptions based on images and symbols they take from the media regarding the political leadership of the group. What are the implications for levels of polarization in democratic politics?

Polarization is most likely to occur in circumstances when the members of different political groups fail to encounter one another on a recurring basis. Thus, Republican partisans who do not communicate with Democrats must base their perceptions on reports taken from the media and other remote sources, as well as from the accounts of other Republican partisans. In such a situation, the perceived gap between Democrats and Republicans is likely to be exaggerated. In contrast, Republicans who *do* communicate with Democratic partisans might construct more moderate expectations regarding the distribution of preferences among Democrats. In short, communication with the opposition is likely to enhance understanding, while communication with fellow partisans is likely to reinforce attributions of extremity.

Heterogeneity within Communication Networks

Respondents to the post-election interview of the CES answered the following question:

> From time to time, people discuss government, elections and politics with other people. I'd like to ask you about the people with whom you discuss

these matters. These people might or might not be relatives. Can you think of anyone?

Interviewers only asked for the discussants' first names. In response, 20 percent of the post-election respondents failed to provide any names, 17 percent provided one, 18 percent provided two, 15 percent provided three, and 30 percent provided four. After compiling the list of first names, interviewers asked a single question regarding each of the identified discussants—the respondent's perception regarding each of their discussants' congressional votes in 2006. The discussants were not identified or interviewed, and hence all information regarding the discussants is based on the respondent's perceptions.

The consequence of heterogeneity within political communication networks is central to this analysis, and we are intentionally adopting a strict standard for the definition of political heterogeneity. A network is defined to be heterogeneous if either (1) the respondent and at least one of her discussants supported different major party candidates; or (2) the respondent voted for neither of the major party candidates, but the members of the network were perceived by the respondent to vote for opposite major party candidates.

Section A of Table 3.1 demonstrates levels of political heterogeneity within communication networks that increase quite dramatically as a function of network size.[1] In the sample as a whole, 28.4 percent are located in heterogeneous networks. This summary percentage includes individuals who do not name political discussion partners and hence cannot, by definition, experience political heterogeneity. Among the respondents with one or more discussants, the percentage in heterogeneous networks increases from 14 percent to 49 percent as a monotonically increasing function of network size. In short, the experience of heterogeneous networks is driven, perhaps first and foremost, by the size of the network, and those individuals located in large networks are equally probable to reside in homogeneous or heterogeneous networks.

In this context, it becomes important to consider the factors that drive not only network size, but also the intensity of the partisan signal that is communicated through the networks. The first model in section B of Table 3.1 considers two different predictors for network size—partisan extremity and education. Education is defined in terms of the respondents' years of schooling, and partisan extremity is defined as the number of steps removed from the midpoint of independence on a seven point party identification scale. In the present context, education serves as a proxy for social and civic involvement more generally defined. People with higher levels of education are more likely to be engaged in a range of participatory activities—not only political activities but communal activities as well (Verba and Nie 1972). In contrast, partisan extremity serves as a measure of partisan political engagement, where strong partisan identifiers with either of the major parties are at one extreme (coded 3) and independent non-identifiers are located at the opposite extreme (coded 0).

Table 3.1 Sources of Political Heterogeneity in Communication Networks

A. Percent of Respondent Networks that include Disagreement

Network Disagreement?	0	1	2	3	4	Total
No	100.00	85.7	72.7	62.6	50.9	71.6
Yes	0.00	14.3	27.3	37.4	49.1	28.4
Weighted N =	188	186	183	146	331	1034
Actual N =						1049

B. Number of Discussants and Number of Partisan Discussants by Main Respondent's Partisanship and Education (Least Squares)

	Number of Discussants		Number of Partisan Discussants	
	Coefficient	t-value	Coefficient	t-value
Years of School	0.11	(5.05)	0.12	(5.87)
Partisan Extremity	0.25	(4.61)	0.30	(6.01)
Constant	0.10	(0.29)	−0.47	(1.56)
N =	1140		1138	
R^2	0.06		0.08	
s.e. of est.	1.46		1.37	

C. Network Heterogeneity by Main Respondent's Partisanship and Education, District Victory Margin, and Number of Partisan Discussants. (Logit Model)

	Coefficient	t-value
Partisan Extremity	-0.33	(3.01)
District Victory Margin	-0.03	(2.33)
Years of School	-0.01	(0.32)
Partisan Discussants	0.70	(8.11)
Constant	-0.97	(1.29)

N = 778
χ^2, df, p = 71, 4, .00

D. Predicted Probability of Heterogeneous Network (Part C estimates; Δ = predicted change in probability)

Partisan Extremity	Number of Partisan Discussants	Percentage for Winning Candidate			
		50.01%	75%	90%	Δ
Independent	4	0.86	0.77	0.69	0.17
Independent	3	0.75	0.62	0.53	0.23
Independent	2	0.60	0.45	0.36	0.25
Independent	1	0.43	0.29	0.22	0.22
	Δ	0.43	0.48	0.47	
Strong Partisan	4	0.70	0.55	0.45	0.24
Strong Partisan	3	0.53	0.38	0.29	0.24
Strong Partisan	2	0.36	0.23	0.17	0.19
Strong Partisan	1	0.22	0.13	0.09	0.13
	Δ	0.48	0.42	0.36	

Two different network measures are addressed as criterion variables in the two models of Table 3.1B. The first model addresses the total number of political discussion partners identified by the respondent. The second model considers the number of partisan discussants—discussants perceived to support a major party candidate in the House race. Both models show that the volume of political discussion, measured both by numbers of discussants and by numbers of partisan discussants, is strongly associated both with education and with partisan extremity. In short, there are strong positive relationships among the size of networks, the levels of partisan activation in networks, and the education and partisanship of the individuals who are located in these networks.

Indeed, the two measures of political activation within networks respond very similarly to the two predictor variables. The primary difference in the two models relates to the size of the constants, which suggest that, on average, the number of political discussants is about six-tenths higher than the number of discussants perceived to support a major party congressional candidate, controlling for education and partisan extremity. While not all political discussion carries a discernible partisan signal, relatively few discussants fail to transmit a partisan preference in the House race. The overall sample means for numbers of discussants and numbers of discussants with two-party House candidate preferences are 2.2 and 1.8 respectively.

Finally, section C of Table 3.1 provides simultaneous consideration to several predictors of network heterogeneity. Network size has a direct relationship that *increases* the probability of heterogeneous networks, partisan extremity has a direct relationship that *decreases* the probability of network heterogeneity, and education demonstrates no direct relationship. This distinction between direct and indirect relationships is particularly important in the present context. As we have seen, people with higher levels of education who demonstrate higher levels of partisanship are more likely to be located in larger communication networks, and larger networks enhance the likelihood of network heterogeneity. But when we control for network size, the nature of the direct relationships becomes clear.

The model in section C also includes a homogeneity measure for the district's two-party vote, measured as the distance between the winning candidate's vote percentage and a dead heat. In a district where the two-party vote is equally divided, the vote is maximally heterogeneous (scored 0 on the measure). In contrast, if everyone votes for the winner, the vote is maximally homogeneous (scored as 50 on the measure). This measure of district homogeneity produces a negative effect on the probability of heterogeneous networks. That is, respondents who reside in districts that are more homogeneous in terms of their support for the winning candidate are less likely to be located within politically heterogeneous communication networks.

We do not mean to suggest that congressional districts are meaningful communities that translate directly into networks of social relationships among district residents. To the contrary, vast and complicated layers and patterns of political structure, social structure, and individual engagement lie between the district populations and patterns of communication among district residents. Rather, this model does suggest that, net of all these other complex factors, highly heterogeneous and hence competitive congressional districts tend to be populated by residents who are more likely to be located in heterogeneous communication networks. In contrast, residents of homogeneous and hence less competitive districts are less likely to be surrounded by heterogeneous preferences.

How important are these various effects? The estimates of Table 3.1C are employed in section D to calculate the probabilities of heterogeneous networks as a function of the winning candidate's percentage of the two-party vote and the number of partisan discussants, for independents and strong partisans.[2] Network size stands out as the most important predictor, with probability differences that vary from .36 to .48 across the range of 1 to 4 partisan discussants. The effects of the district vote are less pronounced, being very comparable to the differences between independents and strong partisans. In conclusion, this analysis shows non-trivial levels of political heterogeneity within networks that vary as a function of network size, partisan extremity, and the district vote. The analysis now turns to the implications of network composition for political preference and perception.

Network Composition and Polarized Attitudes toward Congress

What difference does the composition of communication networks make for the political polarization of attitudes toward Congress? The respondents on the 2006 survey were asked to evaluate the political parties in the Congress on a 5-point scale from most unfavorable to most favorable. We construct a polarization measure by taking the absolute differences in the evaluations of the Democrats and the Republicans in the Congress. If the respondent evaluates the Democratic and Republican parties at identical points on the scale, the difference is 0, indicating no polarization. In contrast, if the respondent evaluates one party at the low extreme (1) and the other at the high extreme (5), the difference is 4, or a high level of polarization.

Table 3.2 uses an ordered logit model to regress these five-point polarization measures on partisan extremity, partisan identification, the number of Democratic and Republican discussants, and the product of the number of Democratic and Republican discussants.[3] These models are estimated separately for the entire sample, for self identifying Democrats, and for self identifying Republicans.

As we would expect, all the models in Table 3.2 show consistently higher levels of polarization regarding the congressional parties among individuals who are more extreme in their partisan orientations. In the model for the entire sample, we see some evidence of a partisan asymmetry in which Republicans are less likely to hold polarized attitudes after controlling for partisan extremity. The measure for network heterogeneity only produces a statistically discernible effect among Democrats, and the effect is positive.

In the models for the entire sample, the effects due to network composition are always positive and at least marginally discernible. That is, respondents with more discussants tend to have polarized attitudes, regardless of the partisan preferences of the discussants. This pattern shifts dramatically when the models are estimated separately for self identified Democrats and Republicans. Partisan respondents are more likely to hold polarized attitudes to the extent that their communication networks mirror their partisan preferences, but discussants who hold opposite preferences produce effects on polarization that are at most marginally discernible and even lie in a negative direction. Hence, this evidence suggests that political communication with fellow partisans tends to enhance attitude polarization, while communication with the other side either has no effect or a negative effect.

This asymmetry is particularly consequential to the extent that we view the volume of communication as fixed—to the extent that respondent communication with individuals holding contrary preferences comes at the expense (or benefit) of foregoing opportunities to communicate with people holding

Table 3.2 Polarized Evaluations of Democrats and Republicans in Congress by Partisanship and Political Discussion (Coefficient t-values are in parentheses)

	Entire Sample	Democrats	Republicans
Partisan Identification	−0.05		
	(1.52)		
Partisan Extremity	0.72	0.58	0.84
	(8.57)	(5.50)	(5.70)
Democratic Discussants	0.24	0.26	−0.08
	(3.73)	(3.19)	(0.84)
Republican Discussants	0.17	−0.32	0.21
	(1.82)	(1.79)	(1.93)
Dem. Discs. × Rep. Discs.	−0.04	0.27	−0.02
	(0.65)	(2.13)	(0.17)
1st Cut Point	−0.13	−0.37	0.19
	se = 0.19	se = 0.29	se = 0.30
2nd Cut Point	1.64	1.33	2.12
	se = 0.19	se = 0.27	se = 0.34
3rd Cut Point	3.25	2.89	3.85
	se = 0.20	se = 0.31	se = 0.37
4th Cut Point	4.35	3.95	5.12
	se = 0.23	se = 0.34	se = 0.41
N	1102	560	495
χ^2, df, p =	137, 5, 0.00	61, 4, 0.00	63, 4, 0.00

Table 3.3 Predicted Probabilities of Polarized Attitudes toward Democrats and Republicans in Congress

Number of Discussants Supporting Local Candidate of Respondent's Party

	0	1	2	3	4	Δ
Among:						
Democrats	0.15	0.18	0.23	0.27	0.33	0.18
Republicans	0.10	0.12	0.15	0.17	0.21	0.10

Number of Discussants Supporting Local Candidate of Opposition Party

Among:						
Democrats	0.15	0.11	0.08	0.06	0.05	−0.10
Republicans	0.10	0.10	0.10	0.10	0.10	0.00

Note: Attitudes are defined to be polarized when the respondent's evaluations of the related attitude objects are 3 or 4 points different on a 5-point scale.

coincidental preferences. We can see this in Table 3.3, where the estimates for partisan respondents in Table 3.2 are used to predict the probability of holding polarized attitudes. In producing these probabilities, the value of partisan extremity is held constant at 2 (not a strong identifier), the heterogeneity measure and the count of discussants with the opposite preference are set to 0, and the count of discussants with corresponding preferences is varied from 0 to 4. As the table shows, the probability of polar attitudes regarding the parties increases from 10 to 18 points across the range of variation in the sympathetic discussant count, where polar attitudes are defined as being separated by 3 or 4 points on a 5-point scale.

In summary, communication networks dominated by fellow partisans produce individually held attitudes that are more polarized along partisan lines. This is not to say that partisans are easily recruited to the opposite party's candidate if they come into contact with individuals who support that candidate. Instead, the strength of their preference tends to be enhanced by communication with others who share the preference, where strength is defined relative to the distance that separates their evaluation of the relevant alternatives.

Network Effects on Party Placements

Finally, we are concerned with network effects on the ways that citizens think about politics—the categories and labels they attach to political actors and objects, and the ways in which these categorizations respond to the partisan mix of their communication networks. The respondents to the survey were asked to place the "Democrats in Congress" and the "Republicans in Congress" on 5-point scales regarding ideology. The ideology scale identified one end of the scale as "very conservative" and the other as "very liberal."

Part A of Table 3.4 addresses the ideological placements made by Democratic respondents regarding congressional Democrats and congressional Republicans. The scales are adjusted to reflect common understandings—that Republicans are more conservative and Democrats more liberal. The question thus becomes, how does network composition affect the extent to which the Democratic respondents perceive Republicans as conservative and Democrats as liberal? The

Table 3.4 Ideological Placements of Congressional Parties by Partisanship and Network Composition

A. Democratic Placements of Congressional Parties on Ideology Scale

	Republicans are More Conservative		Democrats are More Liberal	
	Coefficient	t-value	Coefficient	t-value
Years of School	0.16	4.97	0.08	1.89
Partisan Extremity	0.20	1.86	−0.08	0.70
Democratic Discussants	0.32	3.93	0.03	0.39
Republican Discussants	0.10	0.60	0.43	1.74
Dem. Discs. × Rep. Discs.	0.05	0.31	−0.17	1.09
1st Cut Point	0.97	se = 0.46	−2.07	se = 0.67
2nd Cut Point	1.85	se = 0.47	−0.64	se = 0.68
3rd Cut Point	2.93	se = 0.50	1.83	se = 0.70
4th Cut Point	4.21	se = 0.51	3.66	se = 0.77
N =	571		572	
χ^2, df, p =	71, 5, 0.01		7, 5, 0.22	

B. Republican Placements of Congressional Parties on Ideology Scale

	Republicans are More Conservative		Democrats are More Liberal	
	Coefficient	t-value	Coefficient	t-value
Years of School	0.04	0.75	0.11	2.35
Partisan Extremity	0.07	0.53	0.51	3.37
Democratic Discussants	0.38	1.73	0.05	0.27
Republican Discussants	0.17	1.62	0.35	3.02
Dem. Discs. × Rep. Discs.	−0.20	1.54	−0.04	0.27
1st Cut Point	−3.39	se = 0.94	−1.22	se = 0.78
2nd Cut Point	−1.57	se = 0.90	0.07	se = 0.67
3rd Cut Point	1.01	se = 0.82	2.06	se = 0.68
4th Cut Point	3.45	se = 0.86	3.67	se = 0.68
N =	512		512	
χ^2, df, p =	6, 5, 0.31		60, 5, 0.00	

first model in Part A suggests that Democrats are more likely to view Republicans as conservative if they are in networks dominated by Democrats, and the second model suggests, in a relationship that is only marginally discernible, that they are more likely to view Democrats as liberals to the extent that their networks include more Republicans. Additionally, more highly educated Democratic respondents are more likely to view Democrats as liberals and Republicans as conservatives.

Part B of Table 3.4 addresses the same ideological placements made by Republican respondents. In a way that is consistent with the Democratic placements, the Republicans are more likely to view Republicans as conservative to the extent that they interact with Democrats, and they are more likely to view Democrats as liberals to the extent that they interact with Republicans. In a marginally discernible effect, their perceptions of Republicans as conservatives are also enhanced by interaction with other Republicans. And their perceptions of Democrats as liberals are also enhanced by education and partisan extremity.

The magnitude of the network effects are examined in Table 3.5.[4] The table shows that both Democrats and Republicans are substantially more likely to

Table 3.5 Predicted Probabilities of Ideological Placements for Congressional Parties

Probability that Democrats believe:

		a. Republicans are Conservative Number of Democratic Discussants					b. Democrats are Liberal Number of Democratic Discussants				
		0	1	2	3	4	0	1	2	3	4
Number of	0	0.35	0.42	0.50	0.58	0.66	0.29	0.30	0.31	0.32	0.32
Republican	1	0.37	0.46	0.55	0.64		0.39	0.36	0.33	0.30	
Discussants	2	0.39	0.50	0.60			0.49	0.42	0.34		
	3	0.42	0.53				0.60	0.48			
	4	0.44					0.70				

Probability that Republicans believe:

		a. Republicans are Conservative Number of Democratic Discussants					b. Democrats are Liberal Number of Democratic Discussants				
		0	1	2	3	4	0	1	2	3	4
Number of	0	0.27	0.35	0.44	0.53	0.62	0.56	0.57	0.59	0.60	0.61
Republican	1	0.30	0.34	0.38	0.42		0.64	0.65	0.65	0.65	
Discussants	2	0.34	0.33	0.33			0.72	0.71	0.71		
	3	0.38	0.33				0.78	0.77			
	4	0.42					0.84				

view Republicans as conservatives if they interact with Democrats. Moreover, both Democrats and Republicans are substantially more likely to view Democrats as liberals if they interact with Republicans. In summary, *perceptions of the opposite party are frequently driven by communication with fellow partisans, and perceptions of one's own party are often driven by communication with supporters of the opposite party.*

These results are qualified by the fact that Republicans are more likely to reside in networks populated by Republicans, and Democrats in networks populated by Republicans (Huckfeldt, Mendez, and Osborn 2004). In the unweighted sample, 25.1 percent of self identified Democrats[5] report three or four Democratic discussants, but only 2.5 percent of self identified Republicans report three or four Democratic discussants. Similarly, 16.9 percent of self identified Republicans report three or four Republican discussants, but only 1.8 percent of self identified Democrats report three or four Republican discussants. Hence, we see the most variation in the concentration of fellow partisans within the communication networks. Indeed, 37.4 percent of the Republicans report no Republican discussants, and 29.8 percent of the Democrats report no Democratic discussants.

What are the implications for levels of polarization in the perceptions of the opposition? First, consider the perceptions when networks are held constant at no partisan content—neither Democrats nor Republicans. Democrats are somewhat more likely to view congressional Republicans as conservatives than congressional Democrats as liberals, and Republicans are much more likely to view congressional Democrats as liberals. The Republicans are, however, as likely as Democrats to view congressional Republicans as conservatives. In short, absent communication effects, the Republicans carry more polarized perceptions.

Second, consider Democrats in large homogeneous Democratic networks and Republicans in large homogenous Republican networks. Under these circumstances, the Democrats are very likely to view congressional Republicans as highly conservative and they are much less likely to view congressional Democrats as highly liberal. In contrast, Republicans in large homogeneous Republican networks are highly likely to view Democrats as liberal, and much less likely to view Republicans as conservative. In short, *the highest levels of polarization are generated in settings where partisans are imbedded in homogeneously supportive networks.*

Finally, citizens who believe that the parties in Congress are polarized can hardly be criticized for holding inaccurate views. Hence one might plausibly argue that the politically homogeneous network configurations that produce these perceptions are, in fact, conveying accurate views of contemporary politics. The problem with this interpretation is that it ignores the fact that asymmetries in communication produce asymmetric views of polarization. Democrats in homogeneously Democratic networks view polarization in the context of polarized Republicans, while Republicans in homogeneously Republican networks view polarization in the context of polarized Democrats. In short, asymmetric patterns of communication produce corresponding asymmetries regarding the perceived locus of responsibility for polarized politics—polarized views regarding the source of polarization!

Summary and Conclusion

This chapter has shown several things. First, citizens in competitive congressional districts are more likely to be imbedded in communication networks characterized by higher levels of political diversity. Hence, at a personal and immediate level, they are more likely to encounter divergent political perspectives and positions. Second, citizens located in communication networks that more homogeneously reflect their own partisan preferences are more likely to hold polarized preferences and attitudes regarding the parties in Congress. Finally, their conceptions of political parties—particularly the party in opposition to their own—are often affected by the composition of their own communication networks. Republicans in homogeneously Republican networks are more likely to view Democrats as more extremely liberal, and Democrats in homogeneously Democratic networks are more likely to view Republicans as extremely conservative.

What are the consequences of these results for the analysis of American politics, and particularly for the analysis of citizens, Congress, and congressional elections? First, the composition of congressional districts may be important in ways that extend beyond seat safety and partisan advantage. To the extent that Democratic districts tend to be homogeneously Democratic and Republican districts homogeneously Republican, we run the risk of creating district electorates that less frequently encounter, at a human and social level, contrary opinions.

As a consequence, these voters are more likely to develop strongly held preferences toward candidates and parties. The gap in affections for their own party over the opposite party can, indeed, reach epic proportions. Moreover, they are fully prepared to believe the worst, at least in their own eyes, regarding the opposite side. These are the districts where the dominant Republicans are more likely to believe that Democrats are hopeless liberals, and where the dominant Democrats are more likely to believe that Republicans are hopeless conservatives. Their representatives are not only assured of easy re-election, but they also respond to an electorate that supports and encourages their movement to the extreme of their own parties.

In this context, we offer a somewhat revisionist view of the Fiorina (2005) argument. Along with Fiorina, we believe that politicians' actual positions are,

in general, more polarized than the positions held by citizens. But, if they are to be successful, politicians' policy preferences must ultimately receive support from electorates. As we have seen, politicians located in politically homogeneous, noncompetitive districts are constructing political appeals for an audience that is less likely to have communicated with other citizens who support the opposition. That lack of experience would appear to support exaggerated views regarding the extremity of the opposition, thereby encouraging viewpoints that sometimes take on an apocalyptic flavor. If we expect politicians in a democracy to reflect the views of their constituents, it should come as no surprise that the rhetoric and actions of some politicians often reflect these views. The important point is that the consequences that arise are not only due to the *actual* positions of opponents, but also to the *perceptions* held by each side regarding the positions of their opponents.

Notes

1 The CES is based on a complex sampling design in which respondents are randomly sampled within selected congressional districts. One hundred of those districts were selected randomly, and an additional 72 districts were selected because they were identified as open or competitive. Seventeen of these 72 purposefully selected districts were also included in the random sample, and thus respondents were randomly chosen from 155 congressional districts (for additional discussion, see Chapter 1 of this volume). All analyses employ sample weights as well as estimation procedures that take account of clustered respondents within districts (Rogers 1993).
2 In section D of Table 3.1, other explanatory variables are held constant at typical values, and only discernible effects are considered.
3 This final measure ranges from 0 for no heterogeneity (or no discussants) within networks to 4 for maximal heterogeneity—two Democrats and two Republicans. This heterogeneity measure, in combination with the other two network composition measures, provides an opportunity to consider the consequences that arise due to both the volume and the heterogeneity of partisan signals that are communicated through political communication networks.
4 Due to the interdependence of the network composition variables, we calculate the predicted probabilities based on the coefficients for all three variables, regardless of their t-values, in Table 3.5. The table entries are the probabilities of perceiving the Republicans at either of the two most conservative positions on the scale, or the Democrats at either of the two most liberal positions.
5 For these purposes, self identified partisans are defined as independents leaning to the party, those who self identify as weak identifiers, and those who identify as strong identifiers.

References

Abramowitz, Alan I. and Kyle L. Saunders. 1998. "Ideological Realignment in the U.S. Electorate." *Journal of Politics* 60: 634–52.

Abramowitz, Alan I. and Kyle L. Saunders. 2006. "Exploring the Bases of Partisanship in the American Electorate: Social Identity vs. Ideology." *Political Research Quarterly* 59:175–87.

Bartels, Larry M. 2000. "Partisanship and Voting Behavior, 1952–1996." *American Journal of Political Science* 44: 35–50.

Brady, Henry E. and Paul M. Sniderman. 1985. "Attitude Attribution: A Group Basis for Political Reasoning." *American Political Science Review* 79: 1061–78.

Brewer, Mark D. 2005. "The Rise of Partisanship and the Expansion of Partisan Conflict within the American Electorate." *Political Research Quarterly* 58: 219–29.

Brewer, Mark D., Mack D. Mariani, and Jeffrey M. Stonecash. 2002. "Northern Democrats and Party Polarization in the U.S. House." *Legislative Studies Quarterly* 27: 423–44.

Carmines, Edward G. and James H. Kuklinski. 1990. "Incentives, Opportunities, and the Logic of Public Opinion in American Political Representation," in John A. Ferejohn and James H. Kuklinski (eds.), *Information and Democratic Processes*. Urbana: University of Illinois Press, pp. 240–68.

DiMaggio, Paul, John Evans, and Bethany Bryson. 1996. "Have American's Social Attitudes Become More Polarized?" *American Journal of Sociology* 102: 690–755.

Evans, John H. 2003. "Have Americans' Attitudes Become More Polarized?—An Update." *Social Science Quarterly* 84: 71–90.

Fiorina, Morris P. with Samuel J. Abrams and Jeremy C. Pope. 2005. *Culture War? The Myth of a Polarized America*. New York: Pearson Longman.

Hetherington, Marc J. 2001. "Resurgent Mass Partisanship: The Role of Elite Polarization." *American Political Science Review* 95: 619–31.

Huckfeldt, Robert, Paul Allen Beck, Russell J. Dalton, Jeffrey Levine, and William Morgan. 1998. "Ambiguity, Distorted Messages, and Nested Environmental Effects on Political Communication." *Journal of Politics* 60: 996–1030.

Huckfeldt, Robert, Paul E. Johnson, and John Sprague. 2004. *Political Disagreement*. New York: Cambridge.

Huckfeldt, Robert, Jeanette Morehouse Mendez, and Tracy Osborn. 2004. "Disagreement, Ambivalence, and Engagement: The Political Consequences of Heterogeneous Networks," *Political Psychology* 25: 65–96.

Jacobson, Gary C. 2000. "Party Polarization in National Politics: The Electoral Connection." In *Polarized Politics: Congress and the President in a Partisan Era*, eds. Jon R. Bond and Richard Fleisher. Washington, D.C.: Congressional Quarterly Press.

Levine, Jeffrey, Edward G. Carmines, and Robert Huckfeldt. 1997. "The Rise of Ideology in the Post-New Deal Party System, 1972–1992." *American Politics Quarterly* 25: 19–34.

Mondak, Jeffery J. 1993. "Source Cues and Policy Approval: The Cognitive Dynamics of Public Support for the Reagan Agenda." *American Journal of Political Science* 37: 186–212.

Rogers, William. 1993. "Regression Standard Errors in Clustered Samples." *Stata Technical Bulletin* 13: 19–23.

Rohde, David. W. 1991. *Parties and Leaders in the Postreform House*. Chicago: University of Chicago Press.

Sniderman, Paul M., Richard A. Brody, and Philip E. Tetlock. 1991. *Reasoning and Choice*. New York: Cambridge.

Verba, Sidney and Norman Nie. 1972. *Participation in America: Social Equality and Political Democracy*. New York: Harper and Row.

Chapter 4

Candidate Entry, Voter Response, and Partisan Tides in the 2002 and 2006 Elections[1]

Walter J. Stone, Nathan J. Hadley,
Rolfe D. Peterson, Cherie D. Maestas,
and L. Sandy Maisel

The results of the 2006 elections marked the end of 12 years of Republican control of the House of Representatives, and almost as long in control of the U.S. Senate. Congressional elections that take place in years when there is no presidential contest—they are often referred to as "midterm elections" because they occur half way through a president's four-year term—provide the opportunity to study the push and pull of national and local factors at work on voters. U.S. House elections necessarily involve a mix of national policy and partisan concerns, combined with the variation one finds across 435 districts of vastly different geographical size and demographic makeup. While local concerns and the politics of the district are often important in explaining House elections, the simple fact that candidates affiliate with the Democratic or Republican party in virtually every district can shift attention away from local interests to concerns that resonate in similar ways across all district races. Our focus in this chapter is on how the decisions by candidates to run reflects and shapes the forces at work in district races, and how these factors ultimately play out in the decisions voters make on Election Day.

When individuals who would make strong U.S. House candidates decide not to enter the race in their district, voters cannot respond to the campaigns they would have mounted. The effect of strategic non-entry is most obvious when the challenger's party does not field a candidate at all, because voters cannot evaluate or cast a ballot for a candidate who does not run. The same problem affects a great many House elections to a lesser degree since the challengers who run are low in quality, under-skilled, and under-funded. While the literature recognizes the general importance of strategic entry on voter response to the candidates (Krasno 1994; Kahn and Kenney 1999; Gronke 2000; Jacobson 2004), our understanding of how voters respond to *variation* in challenger quality is limited. Moreover, the effect of incumbent quality is almost completely ignored in the literature (McCurley and Mondak 1995 is a notable exception). This is an important oversight because high-quality incumbents are likely to deter strong challengers (Mondak 1995; Stone, Maisel, and Maestas 2004). Because strategic potential challengers are sensitive to incumbent quality, their entry may trigger responses by constituents that otherwise would not occur

(Gordon, Huber, and Landa 2007). This raises the question of whether voter response in House elections is anticipated and explained by the entry decisions of strategic politicians, or whether voters respond to the dominant cues in the election independent of candidate entry.

We investigate the relationship between candidate entry and voter response in U.S. House elections by comparing two midterm elections in which the structure of opportunity for potential candidates and the pattern of voter response are very different. The dimension of comparison is defined at one extreme by a focus on local district and candidate-centered concerns, and by national partisan interests on the other. This comparison will highlight the simple fact that House candidacies potentially contain information of very different types. In some campaigns, House challengers may signal to voters the opportunity to react to the quality and performance of the incumbent. In others, House candidates may be vessels of their national political parties, presenting opportunities for voters to register dissatisfaction with the president and/or the party in control of the government.

Former Speaker Tip O'Neill's aphorism that "all politics is local" is often quoted in reference to U.S. House elections, and it is fair to say that in most years House races emphasize local concerns. In such elections, incumbents are evaluated by how well they respond to their constituency's needs and interests; the political complexion of the district shapes the fortunes of incumbent and challenger alike; and voters are moved to support particular candidates based on the skills, resources, and qualities they bring to bear in their campaigns. The vast literature attesting to the importance of incumbency in determining the vote adopts an essentially local perspective because incumbents tailor their careers to their district by cultivating a "personal vote" based on their home style and their personal relationship with their constituents. Perhaps another way of characterizing Speaker O'Neill's observation is that "all (congressional) politics is personal."

Embedded in this perspective on House elections is the view that candidates' electoral fortunes are largely in their own hands. Incumbents' re-election depend on their ability to deliver particularized benefits to their constituencies, to build up their name recognition and personal following in their districts, and to avoid scandal or voting in ways egregiously contrary to dominant district interests (Mayhew 1974; Fenno 1978; Canes-Wrone *et al.* 2002). Potential challengers control their electoral fates through their strategic calculations about whether to enter the race. If the incumbent appears to be unbeatable, strong potential challengers look to venues other than their local House race to advance their political ambitions, or they wait for the incumbent to retire. Incumbents' quality affects their prospects for victory, which in turn motivates strong potential challengers to enter or refrain from running (Stone, Fulton, Maestas, and Maisel, 2006). And, as noted, strong-challenger entry has the potential to energize the electorate by stimulating competition and offering a visible choice.

A highly partisan election should produce a different pattern of responses, both by potential challengers and by voters. In an election characterized by a partisan tide, incumbents in the party hurt by the tide become vulnerable while the favored party attracts high quality challengers in greater numbers than the disadvantaged party (Jacobson 1989). Voters likewise respond in a more partisan way, with greater percentages voting with their party identification and fewer defecting from party for local reasons, including incumbency. The effect of party in such elections may be complex. On the one hand, the salience of partisan cues may encourage voters to rely more heavily on partisan predispositions in reacting to the choice they face in their districts. Thus, there may be less defection by challenger partisans, enhancing the effect of party (relative to the incumbent and challenger) on vote choice. At the same time the visibility of national partisan issues and cues systematically favor one party over the other, regardless of whether the party is represented by an incumbent or a challenger in any given district.

A Model of Local and National Effects

Our expectations about the importance of strategic entry and voter choice in district- and party-centered elections can be illustrated with a simple model. Quality-challenger entry (QC) depends on a combination of local (L) and national (N) conditions:

$$QC = f(L, N) \tag{1}$$

When "all politics is local," the weight of L in explaining quality-challenger entry is greater and the weight of N is reduced; when a national partisan tide shapes the opportunity structure in House districts, things are reversed as the impact of L is reduced and N is enhanced.

Likewise, voting choice by individual constituents for or against the incumbent (V) reflects some combination of local and national considerations as well as voters' individual predispositions (IP), such as their partisanship and ideological or issue preferences:

$$V = f(L, N, IP) \tag{2}$$

When the structure of opportunity in House districts is oriented to local factors, the weight of L in explaining voting choice should increase consistently with the cues that voters receive; when national partisan concerns dominate, N and IP should more strongly affect voter choice.

The general nature of equations (1) and (2) ignores the similarities and differences between them. Challenger and incumbent quality (QC and QI respectively) are part of L in the voting-choice model, which captures the effect of quality-challenger entry on voter choice. We can expand Equation 1 to get:

$$QC = f(QI, \textit{District Predispositions, Party, Open Seat}) \qquad (1')$$

District predispositions include the partisan and ideological makeup of the district; party is the party affiliation of the incumbent. Local factors are captured by incumbent quality, district partisanship, and district ideological predispositions, because the quality of incumbents and the predispositions of districts vary across House races. National factors are reflected in the incumbent's party affiliation, which reflects any national sentiment favoring one party over the other. The open-seat variable may reflect local or national factors, if incumbents retire strategically.[2] Differences between an election in which the structure of opportunity is district centered and one where partisan tides characterize the opportunity structure should be apparent, especially in the effects of incumbent quality and party. In localized elections, quality challengers are deterred by high quality incumbents and encouraged to enter when the incumbent's quality is low. To the degree that district partisan and ideological predispositions favor the incumbent, the local context is inhospitable to a strong challenger from the out party. In nationalized elections, incumbent quality should have weaker effects on quality-challenger entry, while the party affiliation of the incumbent is strengthened as strong potential challengers enter or sit the election out, depending on whether they are in the favored party.[3]

$$V = f(QI, QC, IP, \textit{Party, Open Seat}) \qquad (2')$$

In Equation (2'), incumbent and challenger quality are local and party is national. By logic similar to the discussion of quality-challenger entry, candidate quality should more strongly affect voting choice in localized elections and party should be enhanced in nationalized elections. Individual predispositions in the form of party and ideological identifications relative to the incumbent may also be enhanced in nationalized elections to the extent that the campaign elevates the salience of partisan and issue cues.[4]

The presence of challenger quality in the voting-choice equation poses the question of how much voter response to the local vs. national context of the election is mediated by challenger quality. One possibility is that the emergence of a high quality-challenger signals to voters what the election is about and stimulates responses by voters consistent with the structure of opportunity that shapes prospective challengers' entry decisions. Thus, in a localized election, strong-challenger entry signals to voters that the incumbent is weak on some dimension, and cues them to respond in a "localized" fashion because of what is motivating strong challengers to run (Gordon, Huber, and Landa 2007). In some districts, a strong Democrat emerges to challenge a vulnerable Republican incumbent; in other districts, the reverse is true. In most districts, strong incumbents receive weak, half-hearted challenges or none at all. Variation in the emergence of strong challengers, then, might mediate the impact of incumbent quality, such that QI has no direct effect on voter choice. Across districts, voter engagement and behavior would be explained by the district differences that draw high quality challengers into the race. In a nationalized election, entry by high quality challengers is driven by party, which likewise could explain most or all of voters' responses, leaving little additional effect of party on voter choice. It is possible, in other words, that challengers' strategic-entry decisions anticipate the reactions of voters sufficiently to account fully for the localized or nationalized nature of their choices, depending on the election.[5]

Although George W. Bush was president at the time of both the 2002 and 2006 elections, he had become a far more polarizing and partisan figure by 2006 than he was in 2002. Thus, the stage was set in 2006 for a nationalized election, in which voters could be expected to reward or punish President Bush. Jacobson (2007, 9) found substantially greater percentages of voters who said their vote in the congressional race was a vote for or against the president than in 2002, or in any midterm election since 1982.[6] The 2002 election certainly was not one in which local district concerns rendered partisanship irrelevant and 2006 was not an election in which partisanship and the evaluation of President Bush completely dominated local district considerations, but the difference between the two elections along these lines was clear.

Our goal is to sketch in a descriptive way the effects of election context on candidate entry and voter choice. We demonstrate that the structure of opportunity in the election affects quality-challenger entry. At the same time, the district and national-partisan components of our analysis suggest that voters react to appropriate cues independent of quality-challenger entry. Thus, although strategic entry is an important mechanism of popular control as potential challengers anticipate how their candidacy will be received, citizens retain the capacity to react independently to the quality of incumbents when national partisan conflicts do not dominate. Moreover, even when the electoral context is nationalized and voting choice is dominated by party considerations, voters react in reasonable ways to variation in challenger quality.

Candidate Quality Reconsidered

The importance of candidate quality in the relationship between challenger entry and voter response prompts us to revisit the standard measure. Elected office-holding experience has provided powerful insights into the logic and effects of challenger entry in congressional elections. We see the measure as limited, however, not so much by the usual criticism that it fails to differentiate among prior offices held, as by its failure to distinguish between strategic and personal dimensions of candidate quality. We define strategic quality as the skills, resources, and attributes necessary to wage a strong campaign. This is what Jacobson and Kernell argued their office-holding indicator was measuring:

Our discussion of the opportunity structure suggests that the quality of candidates can be measured by their prior office-holding experience. The base office itself is an important resource. Intuitively, we assume that people who previously managed to get elected to public office at least once should be more effective campaigners than those who have not.

(Jacobson and Kernell 1983, 30)

In contrast, personal quality is composed of qualities and attributes such as competence, integrity, and dedication to public service (Mondak 1995). The distinction is important because ordinary citizens intrinsically value the characteristics and qualities in candidates and office holders that we define as personal quality (Miller 1990). Although winning elections may depend on the ability to wage an effective campaign, voter evaluations of candidates should ultimately depend on the skills and qualities they would bring to their job as representative.

A further limitation of the office-holding measure is that it cannot distinguish among incumbents' quality, since all incumbents running for re-election meet the standard. But incumbents surely vary on both strategic and personal dimensions of quality. Squire (1992) developed a measure of campaign prowess for U.S. Senators to explain voter evaluation and choice, and Jeffery Mondak (1995) used indicators of House incumbents' personal integrity and competence to explain electoral outcomes such as vote share and whether incumbents were challenged by experienced candidates. Both studies demonstrate the value of extending the concept and measurement of candidate (incumbent) quality.

Both the strategic and personal dimensions capture important aspects of what we normally mean by candidate quality. The personal characteristics, abilities, and traits that define personal quality are intrinsically desirable to voters, contributors, and activists because candidates and office holders aspire to wield power as agents of their constituents. Trust is essential to the relationship between constituents and representatives because constituents cannot hope to monitor every action, and candidates high in personal quality will be more trustworthy than those low in these qualities (Bianco 1994; Stone and Maisel 2003; Stone, Fulton, Maestas, and Maisel 2006). Likewise, candidates high in personal qualities who lack the skills necessary to wage effective campaigns are less likely to win office, which is essential to completing the electoral bargain with their supporters. Strategic quality is likely to be especially important to challengers because they are usually well behind incumbents in their visibility and experience. Personal quality of incumbents may be important to voters because of the implications of this dimension for representation.

Drawing the distinction between personal and strategic quality does not mean they are unrelated empirically. Both should contribute to candidates' electoral prospects (Stone and Maisel 2003; Stone, Fulton, Maestas, and Maisel 2006). If voters value the personal qualities of candidates, so also should contributors and others who control the resources candidates need to mount effective campaigns. Thus, strategic qualities such as fund-raising ability should depend on personal qualities because integrity and competence make candidates more electable as well as intrinsically more attractive.

Design and Measurement

This chapter employs data from the 2002 and 2006 elections on both citizens and district informants. Data gathered from district informants provide indicators of the strategic and personal quality of incumbents and challengers. The citizen survey data enable us to observe voter response to variation in incumbent and challenger quality along with the partisan bases for their voting choice.

The citizen survey data were collected by Indiana University's Center for Survey Research in telephone surveys of approximately consistent designs in the two years. Both years' studies included a pre-election survey followed by a post-election wave. The 2002 Congressional Elections Study (or 2002 CES) sample was based on a national RDD cross-section, supplemented by a targeted over-sample from 50 congressional districts judged during the summer of 2002 as likely to be competitive in the election. The 2006 Congressional Elections Study (or 2006 CES) was also an RDD cross-section drawn from pre-selected U.S. House districts in the lower 48 states. Like the 2002 study, the 2006 cross-section was supplemented with additional interviews taken in 72 districts identified in the summer of 2006 as open or likely to be competitive (some of these districts were also included in the random sample, yielding a total of 155 districts included as part of the 2006 CES; for additional discussion of the survey's properties, see Chapter 1 of this volume). Analyses from both years' surveys are weighted to adjust for the probability of selection in the national cross-section and over-sampled competitive districts.

The informant surveys in both elections were conducted by mail during September and October immediately before the November election. The 2002 informant survey was part of the Candidate Emergence Study begun in 1998 and involved contacting Democratic and Republican party activists, former national convention delegates, county chairs, and others likely to be knowledgeable about their House district and its politics.[7] In 2006, we identified a fresh sample of district informants composed of 2004 Democratic and Republican national convention delegates and state legislators. The 2006 study has the advantage of being based on exactly the same districts used in the CES, whereas the 2002 data rely on overlap between the districts sampled in the informant study and respondents interviewed in the CES that year.[8] In 2002 we had a larger sample of informants, and ended up with 12.1 informant respondents per district; in 2006 the study yielded 6.2 informants per district.

In each year's survey, we put a battery of questions to informants designed to tap the strategic and personal quality of the Democratic and Republican

House candidates in the respondent's district. The items asked respondents to rate the candidates on 7-point scales ranging from "Extremely Weak" (coded –3) through "Extremely Strong" (+3). Items tapping strategic quality in 2002 were: name recognition in the district, ability to raise money from others to fund his/her campaign, and overall strength as a campaigner. The 2006 strategic-quality items were: ability to attract attention, ability to raise funds, name recognition, ability to be persuasive in public, ability to run a professional campaign, and overall strength as a campaigner. The 2002 personal-quality items asked informants to rate candidates' personal integrity, dedication to serving the public, and overall strength as a public servant; the 2006 items were personal integrity, ability to work well with other leaders, competence, grasp of the issues, ability to find solutions to problems, qualifications to hold office, and overall strength as a public servant. In both years, the distinction between the personal- and strategic-quality dimensions was confirmed by principal components analyses of all individual items; reliabilities within each dimension averaged well over .80.

Because there is consistent evidence of partisan bias in the ratings informants give to candidates, especially the ratings on the personal-quality dimension, we adjust all candidate ratings by whether the candidate and informant are in the same party (Stone and Maisel 2003). We aggregated adjusted scores to the district level as attributes of the incumbent or challenger, depending on which party holds the seat in the district.

We have explored the validity and reliability of the informant-based approach to measuring characteristics of House candidates and districts by comparing aggregated district informant perceptions and evaluations with comparable variables from other sources (Stone, Fulton, Maestas, and Maisel 2006; Stone and Simas 2007). For example, in the 2006 study the correlation between informants' placements of incumbents on the liberal–conservative scale and the same incumbents' first-dimension DW-NOMINATE scores is .94, while informant perceptions of district partisanship and liberalism correlate at .72 and .68 with district-level estimates of the same variables from the CES common-content survey. In previous years, we find similar relationships.

Addressing the distinction between the strategic and personal quality of incumbents and challengers is difficult. One obvious comparison is with the office-holding variable commonly used to measure challenger quality. In the 2006 study, the correlation between the informant-based challenger strategic-quality score and the office-experience indicator is .48, whereas the correlation between the personal-quality scores of challengers and the office-holding dummy is .32.[9] The modestly stronger correlation with strategic quality suggests that the elective office-holding experience is tapping campaign skills, much as Jacobson and Kernell (1983) originally intended. When we "predict" challenger office holding using the two dimensions of challenger quality, the effect of strategic quality is highly significant, while there is no significant effect of personal quality.

Finally, in the 1998 version of the study, we replicated the Mondak (1995) procedures for measuring incumbents' competence and integrity, a dimension of quality closely related to our concept of personal quality. The 1998 inform-ant survey included a battery of personal-quality items about incumbents similar to those employed in 2002 and 2006 (Stone, Maisel, and Maestas 2004). The comparison between the two measures of incumbent quality is complicated by the fact that the Mondak approach appears to be sensitive to the number of descriptors of incumbent quality published in the relevant sources. Of 200 incumbents in the sample, 33 (16.5 percent) do not have any descriptive words or phrases that could be culled from either the *Almanac of American Politics* or *CQ's Politics in America* for purposes of rating their competence or integrity. The correlation between the informant-based indicator of personal quality and the Mondak measure rises monotonically with the number of descriptors recovered from these sources, from a low of .23 with only one descriptor to .55 for incumbents with seven or more descriptors. However, only 30 incumbents (15 percent) in the sample had seven or more descriptors.[10]

These results do not settle questions about the reliability and validity of an informant-based approach, but they do seem to provide enough support for proceeding with our measures, provided we do so with caution. Although there are undoubtedly problems with measuring challenger and incumbent quality based on informants' ratings, our goal is to provide a broad-gauged perspective on the questions we have posed. For these purposes, the approach seems at least provisionally adequate.

Challenger Entry, Partisanship, and Incumbent Deterrence

The differences in electoral conditions between 2002 and 2006 have important potential implications for challenger entry. We expect challengers to be strategic in their entry decisions in years that experience a partisan tide and in years when the election is district centered, but that the conditions that make for a vulnerable incumbent differ in the two scenarios. In 2002, the structure of opportunity should reflect local conditions, including the quality of the incumbent. An incumbent who is strong in strategic resources should deter strong challengers; a relatively weak incumbent should be more likely to attract strong opposition. In 2006, quality challengers should be more likely to emerge against Republican incumbents due to the national tide, because the incumbent's party, more than her quality as a candidate per se, is what makes her vulnerable.

We test these expectations by modeling the strategic quality of challengers in both elections. Strategic quality is a consistently important dimension of challenger quality because the principal difficulty challengers confront is becoming visible enough to attract attention from voters in the district. The independent variables are coded in the same way between the two elections and are included in the analysis to capture local and partisan influences on the entry of high quality challengers.[11]

Consistent with expectations, Table 4.1 shows that incumbent strategic quality had a strong and significant negative effect on the strategic quality of the challenger in 2002, while there was no effect of incumbent quality in 2006. Another difference between the two years also fits our expectations: whereas the party of the incumbent does not have a statistically significant effect on challenger quality in 2002, it has a strong effect in 2006. Comparing the effects of incumbent strategic quality and party between the two years reveals the difference between a year without much national partisan structure to the opportunities strong potential challengers faced and a year when there was a clear partisan structure of opportunity. In 2002, strong challengers ran in districts where incumbents were relatively weak, regardless of party. In 2006, the party of the incumbent, rather than his or her personal strategic qualities, defined the incumbent's vulnerability and correspondingly stimulated or deterred strong-challenger entry.[12]

Most of the other variables in the model, with one exception, have consistent effects on quality challenger entry in both years. In neither year is there evidence that the personal quality of incumbents deters strong challengers independent

Table 4.1 Determinants of Challenger Strategic Quality, 2002 and 2006 (Ordinary Least Squares)

	2002	*2006*
Incumbent Strategic Quality	−0.653***	−0.257
	(0.157)	(0.182)
Incumbent Personal Quality	0.202	0.129
	(0.145)	(0.131)
Republican Incumbent	0.333	0.817***
	(0.204)	(0.204)
District Partisanship (coded to favor incumbent)	−0.229**	−0.114
	(0.010)	(0.012)
Open Seat	0.824***	0.856***
	(0.296)	(0.247)
Incumbent's Vote Share, Previous Election	−0.039***	−0.036***
	(0.009)	(0.013)
Constant	3.944***	2.531***
	(0.758)	(0.660)
F	12.74***	10.66***
Adjusted R^2	0.348	0.315
N	133	127

Notes:
Standard errors in parentheses.
*** $p < 0.01$, ** $p < 0.05$, * $p < 0.1$
The dependent variable is the mean informant rating of challengers in sample districts.

of strategic quality; an open seat attracts stronger challengers equally in both years; and in both years incumbents with a higher vote share in the previous election deter strong challengers more than their colleagues whose winning margins in the previous election were lower. Note, however, that district partisanship has a strong deterrent effect in 2002, but no impact on challenger strategic quality in 2006.

The absence of an effect of district partisanship in 2006 is consistent with the expectation that local district factors had a decreased impact. In a district-centered election constituencies favorable to the incumbent in their makeup deter strong challenges from the minority party; districts less favorable to the incumbent encourage such challenges. When national partisan concerns dominate as they did in 2006, the effect of district partisan makeup is reduced. In Republican-held districts strong Democratic challengers would be encouraged to run in districts marginally predisposed against them in 2006 because of the national tide in their favor, while they would be discouraged by the partisan predisposition of their district in the absence of a national tide favoring their party.

The results in Table 4.1 confirm our expectations about the difference between the 2002 and 2006 elections with respect to strong-challenger entry. In 2006, the national partisan tide against the Republicans stimulated Democratic challengers relatively strong in strategic resources and skills to enter and deterred strong Republican challengers. In 2002, the impact of incumbent quality and district makeup is apparent, which shows that challenger entry in that year was responsive to local conditions. The strength of national party in 2006 reflects the national partisan structure of opportunity in that year compared with 2002.

Incumbency, Partisanship, and Voting Choice

Having established that challenger entry responded to the different structures of opportunity in the two elections, two primary questions remain about how voters made their voting choices: (1) Did voters react to the differences between 2002 and 2006 by responding more to candidate quality in 2002 and to partisanship in 2006?; and (2) Were voter responses fully explained by candidate entry? The first question addresses possible differences between the two types of elections in the cues that voters respond to in making their voting choice. The second speaks to their capacity to respond to different contexts beyond the entry decisions of strong challengers that shape differences in the campaigns to which voters react.

In the absence of national tides favoring one party over the other, we know that strong prospective challengers are sensitive to the strength of the incumbent in deciding whether to enter. The question is whether voters also respond to variations in incumbent quality. It is perhaps easier to believe that voters' choices are motivated by partisanship when the election is nationalized, and our model is designed to assess the impact of party in both years as well. The purpose of the voting-choice models in Table 4.2 is to compare how voters differ in what motivates their choices in the two elections. The dependent variable is whether the voter voted for the incumbent. The model includes individual predispositions in the form of partisanship and ideology (both coded relative to the incumbent), the party of the incumbent, and the quality of the incumbent and challenger. We also include a control for whether the seat is open.

The results in Table 4.2 reflect the expected differences between the two elections, especially with respect to partisanship. The most dramatic difference between 2002 and 2006 is in whether or not the incumbent was a Republican. In 2002, this variable had no significant effect on voting choice. In other words, all else equal, Republican incumbents did as well among voters in 2002 as Democratic incumbents. In 2006, however, Republican incumbents suffered a direct hit because of their party affiliation.

Table 4.2 Determinants of Voting for the Incumbent, 2002 and 2006 (Logistic Regression)

	2002	2006
Party ID (coded to favor incumbent)	0.408***	0.770***
	(0.108)	(0.100)
Ideology (coded to favor incumbent)	0.243**	0.839***
	(0.108)	(0.122)
Republican Incumbent	0.184	−3.423***
	(0.462)	(0.476)
Incumbent Strategic Quality	−0.044	0.130
	(0.441)	(0.641)
Incumbent Personal Quality	0.520*	−0.062
	(0.273)	(0.387)
Challenger Strategic Quality	−0.444***	−0.510**
	(0.15)	(0.206)
Challenger Personal Quality	0.421	0.210
	(0.263)	(0.190)
Open Seat	−0.202	−0.132
	(0.502)	(0.494)
Constant	−0.492	2.184***
	(0.936)	(0.744)
Pseudo R^2	0.231	0.609
N	258	511

Notes:
Robust standard errors in parentheses
*** $p < 0.01$, ** $p < 0.05$, * $p < 0.1$
Dependent variable is vote for the incumbent (1) or challenger (0).

Figure 4.1 illustrates the marginal effect on the probability of the incumbent's party on voting choice in 2002 and 2006 for a range of values of respondents' combined partisan and ideological predispositions. The flat dashed line for 2002 is close to 0, indicating that the party of the incumbent had no impact on voting choice, no matter the degree of partisan and ideological affinity of the respondent for the incumbent. In 2006, however, the effect of incumbent party is dramatically different. As we would expect, its effect is strongest among respondents whose partisanship and ideology did not strongly predispose them for or against the incumbent. Among those inclined for or against the incumbent by their party identification and ideology, the loss by Republican incumbents declines, but remains substantial, except among voters whose predispositions commit them most strongly.[13] Note that these effects of party are independent of quality-challenger entry, which motivated strong candidates to challenge Republican incumbents, as we have seen. Thus, voters expressed their dissatisfaction with the GOP beyond the push against the Republican Party they received from the greater strategic strength of Democratic compared with Republican challengers.

The contrast in party effects between the two years is partially mirrored in the effects of incumbent and challenger quality. In 2002, incumbents stronger in their personal quality received a boost in voting support, while voters were less likely to support weaker incumbents. In contrast to the personal-quality effect, incumbent strategic quality did not directly influence voting choice.

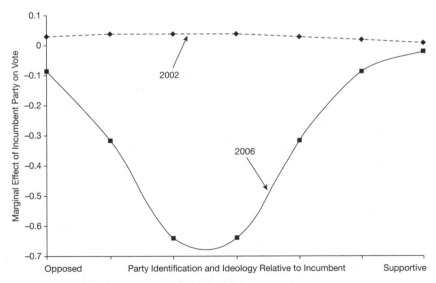

Figure 4.1 Estimated Marginal Effects of Republican Incumbent on Vote Choice by Respondent Party Identification and Ideology.

Figure 4.2 displays the magnitude of the incumbent personal-quality effect. The positive effect of incumbent personal quality on voting choice in 2002 is consistent with previous work on 1998 and 2002 in which we found positive effects of incumbent quality on a variety of incumbent evaluation items as well as vote choice (Stone, Hadley, Peterson, Maestas, and Maisel 2006). High quality incumbents appear to benefit from voter evaluation of their personal quality, perhaps because the average incumbent is visible enough so that quality differences affect voter response (cf. McCurley and Mondak 1995).

Note also that variations in incumbent strategic quality do not evoke a response among voters, independent of challenger quality. However, because incumbent strategic quality affected the willingness of quality challengers to run, and because challengers stronger in strategic quality depress voting for the incumbent, there is an indirect effect of incumbent strategic quality.

These candidate-quality effects, along with those we reported more extensively on 1998 and 2002 (Stone, Hadley, Peterson, Maestas, and Maisel 2006),

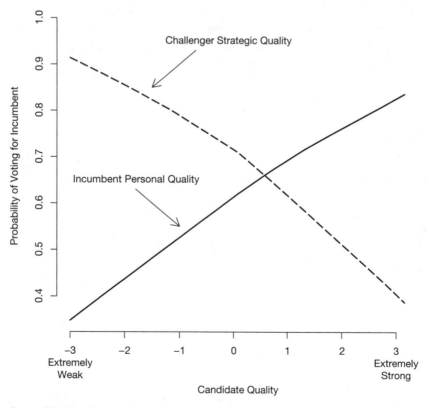

Figure 4.2 Vote for the Incumbent by Candidate Quality, 2002.

suggest that variations in candidate quality can affect voter support of incumbents in elections not characterized by a strong partisan tide. The fact that incumbent personal quality evokes a response independent of the strength of the challenger further suggests that voters can discern differences in the personal quality of their representatives in ways not directly dependent on strong-challenger entry.

Although national partisan effects on voting choice were strong in 2006, they do not obliterate the effects of challenger strategic quality. Even in the face of a strong partisan tide, challengers strong in strategic quality generate significant voting support (reduce the probability of voting for the incumbent). By no means could it be said that "all politics were local" in 2006, but local variation in the strength that challengers brought to their campaigns nonetheless mattered beyond the party differences in challenger entry in that year. Of course, the strategic strength of challengers in 2006 is explained more by the partisan structure of opportunity in that year than by local concerns. Thus, in responding to challengers who were stronger in their strategic quality, voters also reacted to the effects of the national partisan opportunity structure that motivated challengers, in addition to their own strong partisan preferences.

The greater strength of individual voters' party identification and ideological preferences in 2006 than in 2002 is notable, especially in light of the stronger effect of district makeup on challenger entry in 2002 than in 2006 (Table 4.1). For individual voters, it makes sense that a nationalized election would elevate the salience of partisan and ideological predispositions in explaining voting in House elections. As a result of the charged national context, voters assess the candidates in their districts based upon the greater salience of partisan and national issues or ideological concerns, and we find a correspondingly stronger effect of these variables on voting choice in 2006 than in 2002.[14] Thus, a nationalized election elevates the salience of voters' partisan and ideological commitments, while these same factors at the district level have a reduced effect on quality-challenger entry (see Table 4.1).

A Further Exploration of Challenger Quality Effects

We interpret the effects of challenger strategic quality in both years as evidence that entry by strong candidates has the potential to affect voter response even in a campaign heavily dominated by national partisan conflict. The fact that it is challenger *strategic* quality that affects voting choice does not seem surprising given the barriers of inertia challengers must overcome in House elections. The skills and resources necessary to run a viable campaign are a necessary condition for challenger success. Moreover, voter response to challenger strategic quality in 2006 did not negate the strong partisan effect that caused strong challengers to run in the first place.

The results raise the question of whether challenger *personal* quality matters in any way. The 2006 design is well suited to monitor change in the evaluation of candidates through the course of the campaign because there was a pre-election wave followed by a post-election re-interview, and appropriate questions were posed in both waves. Table 4.3 presents analysis of the post-election favorability of the incumbent and challenger as a function of pre-election favorability, and of the strategic and personal qualities of both candidates. As we might expect, most of incumbent favorability after the campaign was completed was accounted for by pre-election favorability. However, challenger strategic strength does reduce incumbent favorability

Table 4.3 Determinants of Post-Election Favorability toward House Candidates, 2006 (Ordered Logit Regression)

	Incumbent	Challenger
Pre-Election Favorability	0.656***	0.493***
	(0.118)	(0.125)
Republican Incumbent	−0.252	0.246
	(0.187)	(0.177)
Incumbent's Personal Quality	0.162	−0.023
	(0.181)	(0.162)
Incumbent's Strategic Quality	−0.302	−0.094
	(0.237)	(0.241)
Challenger's Personal Quality	−0.051	0.379**
	(0.114)	(0.169)
Challenger's Strategic Quality	−0.171*	0.094
	(0.093)	0.109
Party Identification (coded to favor Incumbent)	0.232***	−.316***
	(0.059)	(0.056)
1st Cut Point	−2.873	−2.225
	(0.263)	(0.366)
2nd Cut Point	−1.665	−0.891
	(0.229)	(0.342)
3rd Cut Point	−0.201	0.994
	(0.226)	(0.321)
4th Cut Point	1.684	2.703
	(0.275)	(0.328)
χ^2	72.24	77.57
N	497	435

Notes:
Robust standard errors in parentheses
*** $p < 0.01$, ** $p < 0.05$, * $p < 0.1$
Open seats excluded from analysis; dependent variable is favorability rating of incumbent and challenger in post-election interview.

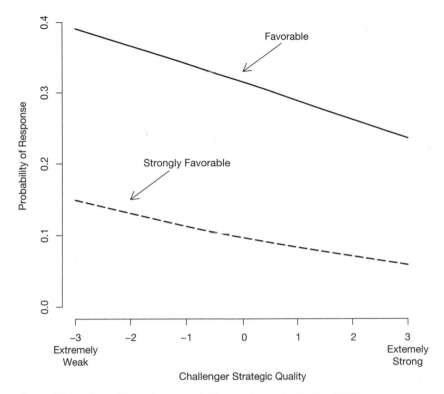

Figure 4.3 Ratings of Incumbent by Challenger Strategic Quality, 2006.

(see Figure 4.3).[15] This is in keeping with our argument about the importance of the challenger's ability to wage an effective and visible campaign. Overall, the continuity of incumbent favorability—voters who liked or disliked the incumbent at the beginning of the campaign remained steadfast in their attitudes—reflects the visibility of incumbents and the limited effects on voter evaluation that result from the campaign period.

The challenger favorability equation offers intriguing evidence that voters respond to challenger *personal* quality as a result of the campaign. As we would expect, the continuity effects from the pre-election wave are weaker in the case of challenger favorability because challengers are less well known than incumbents. But there is quite a strong increase in favorability toward the challenger tied to challenger personal quality. As Figure 4.4 demonstrates, the probability of favorable evaluations of the challenger is sensitive to challenger personal quality ratings. Here, then, is an instance of challenger personal quality affecting voters' evaluations, even in the context of a campaign in which national partisan concerns strongly shaped both challenger entry and voter reaction to local candidates.

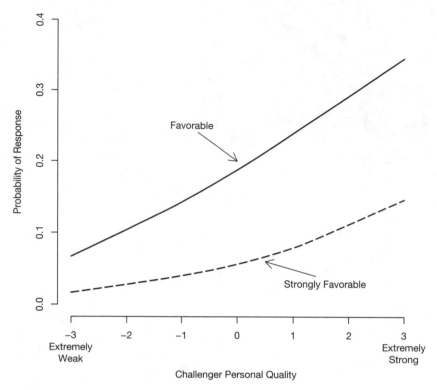

Figure 4.4 Ratings of Challenger by Challenger Personal Quality, 2006.

Conclusion

Our purpose has been to sketch the broad consequences of differences between a midterm election characterized by a national partisan tide and one more typically focused on local concerns. Our interest is in how the context of the election shapes candidate entry and how, in turn, voters respond. Challenger and incumbent quality figures prominently in our account, and our approach has relied on the distinction between strategic and personal quality for both challengers and incumbents.

Our key findings with respect to challenger entry are simple: challengers strong in strategic quality responded to the strategic quality of the incumbents they would have to unseat in 2002, with relatively weak incumbents drawing stronger challengers than their colleagues more skilled in the art of campaigning. We interpret this result as consistent with the local structure of opportunity in that year, when national partisan concerns did not strongly invade local House races. In contrast, strong-challenger entry in 2006 was explained not by incumbent quality but by party, with stronger challengers emerging to challenge Republican incumbents, and weaker Republican challengers running against Democratic incumbents.

The second question we took up—voter response to candidate entry and to the context of the two elections—is more complex. The effects of the national party context in our models of voting choice run deep in 2006 and are nonexistent in 2002. Although party motivated strong-challenger entry in 2006, voters' strongly partisan response to House candidates did not depend on strong challengers to be activated. Further analysis in 2006 shows that approval of President George W. Bush and evaluations of the Iraq War were more tightly bundled by voters' partisanship in 2006 than they were in 2002. The voters' inclination to rebuke the president in 2006, anticipated by strong Democratic challengers prior to 2006, did not require activation by those challengers to affect voting choice.[16]

The deeply partisan nature of the 2006 election was about punishing President Bush and the GOP majority in Congress, primarily for their Iraq policy. This was evident both because Republican incumbents drew strong challengers in 2006, and by the anti-Republican component of the vote. A secondary effect of nationalizing the election along party lines was to raise the salience of partisan and ideological concerns among voters in their House voting choice. At the same time, it is in a localized election such as 2002 that the partisan makeup of the district has the greater impact on quality-challenger entry, as district predispositions help define the opportunity challengers have in their districts. In a national partisan election, the party makeup of the district is less important, especially for the challenger in the party favored by the national tide.

Our results reinforce the value of a two-dimensional understanding of candidate quality. Strategic quality is captured by the office-holding experience indicator, but employing the traditional measure would not allow us to observe that strong challengers are deterred by incumbents strong in strategic quality in an election dominated by local concerns because the measure would not allow us to differentiate among incumbents. Our conclusions about challenger strategic quality fit with previous work on the electoral impact of challenger quality, and with the intuition that the primary goal of challengers must be to build the visibility of their candidacy. In particular, challenger strategic quality appears to matter in an election characterized by a national tide as well as one focused on district concerns by boosting votes for high quality challengers.

Candidates are judged, however, not only by their skills and the resources they have to mount effective campaigns. In 2002 incumbent personal quality affected vote about as much as challenger strategic quality did, which suggests that in localized elections, incumbents are visible enough to voters to be judged on their personal qualities independent of challenger entry. We also found challenger personal quality affected favorability ratings of challengers through the 2006 campaign, although it did not have a direct effect on voting choice.

Voting behavior in House elections reflects a complex mix of the motivations for challenger entry in each district, the signals that voters pick up from the national and local context, and the quality of the candidates. A highly partisan year such as 2006 when the election is a referendum on the president and his policies structures the opportunity of potential challengers and voter choice along partisan lines. Voter partisan response in 2006 did not depend in any significant way on the presence of a strong challenger, so candidate entry in a nationalized election may be more about anticipating the opportunity created by the national election than it is about mediating and informing voter reaction. In a localized election, weaker incumbents draw strong challengers, regardless of party. Thus, strong challenger entry reflects the opportunity created by a weak incumbent and in turn directly affects voter response in House campaigns.

Voter capacity to respond to variations in the quality of incumbents and challengers on both the strategic and personal-quality dimensions warrants further investigation. While our results challenge a view of voters as inert recipients of candidate (principally, incumbent) manipulation, we do agree with the view that voters depend on the quality of campaigns run by challengers and incumbents to provide them the information they need to assess candidate quality. These assessments are most likely activated through personal discussion networks, media-borne signals, and campaign contacts. Voters need not have high levels of information when quizzed about what they know about the candidates or the election in order to react sensibly to variations in candidate quality. But the evidence that they do react by whatever means to differences in candidate quality suggests an electorate more engaged and capable than is often portrayed in the congressional elections literature.

Notes

1 We are grateful to the Carnegie Corporation for a grant to support the 2002 phase of the Candidate Emergence Study and to the College of Letters and Science at UC Davis for funding the 2006 district informant survey. Gary Jacobson generously provided some of the data and Elizabeth N. Simas collaborated in conducting the 2006 informant survey.

2 In a district-oriented election, strategic incumbent retirement should reflect local factors such as the incumbent's quality and vulnerability and the predispositions of the district. In a nationalized election, incumbents in the party hurt by the national tide may disproportionately retire.

3 Incumbent vulnerability lurks in the background here. In localized elections, incumbents are more or less vulnerable depending on their quality and the makeup of their district; in nationalized elections their vulnerability is directly related to their party. We do not address incumbent prospects in this chapter, but we have shown elsewhere that they are a powerful factor in explaining both incumbent retirement and challenger entry (Stone, Fulton, Maestas, and Maisel 2006).

4 2006 offered a visible example in the Rhode Island senate campaign of moderate Republican Lincoln Chaffee, who was well liked personally by Rhode Island voters

(a majority of whom are Democrats). However, he was unseated by a Democratic challenger who emphasized the consequences for control of the Senate of re-electing a Republican, however moderate and likeable the individual incumbent. www. boston.com/news/local/rhode_island/articles/2006/11/09/chafee_unsure_of_staying_with_gop_after_losing_election/

5 Incumbent quality seems more likely to be mediated by challenger entry than national partisanship, given the salience of such party-centered factors as partisan polarization and presidential performance. Incumbent quality, by comparison, is probably much less visible to the average voter.

6 According to Jacobson's (2007) Figure 9, 54 percent said their house vote in 2006 was for/against the president, whereas the comparable percentage in 2002 was 46 percent, and in most previous midterm elections it was less than 40 percent. Jacobson also reports that 58 percent of the public in 2006 said that which party controls Congress was a factor in how they voted, while only 43 percent said party control was a factor in 2002.

7 The 2002 informant sample was composed of individuals who had responded to an earlier survey of informants conducted in the early summer of 2001.

8 We have found no significant differences on a number of district-level indicators between the districts that overlapped between the two studies with those that were in the CES sample but did not include respondents in the IU sample. However, there are some significant differences between IU survey respondents included in the CES districts and those not included. Because of the over sample of competitive districts in 2002, challenger visibility was higher among respondents in the overlapping districts, and support for the incumbent was significantly lower (Stone, Hadley, Peterson, Maisel, and Maestas 2006).

9 The corresponding correlations in the 2002 study are .42 and .31.

10 A possible problem with the informant-based approach is that the number of informants who respond per district varies, but the correlation between the informant and Mondak measures is much less sensitive to the number of informants than it is to the number of descriptors.

11 The district-partisanship measure is based on the presidential vote share in the district in the previous election.

12 A simple comparison of mean strategic-quality scores makes the partisan differences in the two years apparent. In 2002, Democratic and Republican challengers were rated negatively, with Republicans slightly more negative than Democrats (−.71 and −.51 respectively). In contrast, Democratic challengers in 2006 averaged a positive rating on their strategic quality (+.12), while Republican challengers were rated negatively (−.69).

13 The asymmetry in the figure (weaker effects of party among those predisposed toward the incumbent than among those predisposed by party and ideology to the challenger) results from the different effects of party on incumbents and challengers along with the partisan composition of the sample. The national partisan tide against the Republicans in 2006 had a stronger impact on challengers than on incumbents because Republican and Democratic incumbents were about equal in their quality. Because of the party effects on entry, in contrast, Democratic challengers were significantly stronger than Republican challengers. Thus party-induced defection from incumbents whom voters were predisposed to support was lower than the effect of party on defection from challengers because the quality difference favored the Democrats. The asymmetry shows up in the figure because there are more Republican incumbents in the sample owing to the fact that we

over sampled competitive districts, which were disproportionately Republican-held seats.

14 Pooled analysis between the two years (not shown) demonstrates that the effects of party identification, ideology, and the party of the incumbent are all significantly higher in 2006 than in 2002 ($p < .01$).

15 We calculated the probabilities for strict independents with all other variables set at their means.

16 Although it is possible that turning a district from Republican to Democratic hands did require a strong challenger, we do not address that question in this chapter.

References

Bianco, William T. 1994. *Trust: Representatives and Constituents.* Ann Arbor: University of Michigan Press.

Canes-Wrone, Brandice, David W. Brady, and John F. Cogan. 2002. "Out of Step, Out of Office: Electoral Accountability and House Members' Voting." *American Political Science Review* 96: 127–40.

Fenno, Richard F., Jr. 1978. *Home Style: House Members in their Districts.* Boston: Little Brown.

Gordon, Sanford C., Gregory A. Huber, and Dimitri Landa. 2007. "Challenger Entry and Voter Learning." *American Political Science Review* 101: 303–20.

Gronke, Paul. 2000. *The Electorate, the Campaign, and the Office: A Unified Approach to Senate and House Elections.* Ann Arbor: University of Michigan Press.

Jacobson, Gary C. 1989. "Strategic Politicians and the Dynamics of U.S. House Elections, 1946–1986." *American Political Science Review* 83: 773–93.

———. 2004. *The Politics of Congressional Elections.* 6th ed. New York: Longman.

———. 2007. "Referendum: The 2006 Midterm Congressional Elections." *Political Science Quarterly* 122: 1–24.

Jacobson, Gary C. and Samuel Kernell. 1983. *Strategy and Choice in Congressional Elections.* 2nd ed. New Haven: Yale University Press.

Kahn, Kim Fridkin and Patrick J. Kenney. 1999. *The Spectacle of U.S. Senate Campaigns.* Princeton, NJ: Princeton University Press.

Krasno, Jonathan S. 1994. *Challengers, Competition, and Re-election: Comparing Senate and House Elections.* New Haven: Yale University Press.

Mayhew, David. 1974. *Congress: The Electoral Connection.* New Haven, CT: Yale University Press.

McCurley, Carl and Jeffery J. Mondak. 1995. "Inspected by #1184063113: The Influence of Incumbents' Competence and Integrity in U.S. House Elections." *American Journal of Political Science* 39: 864–85.

Miller, Arther H. 1990. "Public Judgments of Senate and House Candidates." *Legislative Studies Quarterly* 15: 525–42.

Mondak, Jeffery J. 1995. "Competence, Integrity, and the Electoral Success of Congressional Incumbents." *Journal of Politics* 57: 1043–69.

Squire, Peverill. 1992. "Challenger Quality and Voting Behavior in U.S. Senate Elections." *Legislative Studies Quarterly* 17: 247–63.

Stone, Walter J., Sarah A. Fulton, Cherie D. Maestas, and L. Sandy Maisel. 2006. "Incumbency Reconsidered: Prospects, Strategic Entry, and Incumbent Quality in U.S. House Elections." Unpublished Manuscript, UC Davis.

Stone, Walter J., Nathan J. Hadley, Rolfe D. Peterson, Cherie D. Maestas, and L. Sandy Maisel. 2006. "Candidate Quality and Voter Response in U.S. House Elections." Paper presented at the Annual Meeting of the American Political Science Association, Philadelphia.

Stone, Walter J. and L. Sandy Maisel. 2003. "The Not-So-Simple Calculus of Winning: Potential House Candidates' Nomination and General Election Prospects." *Journal of Politics* 65: 951–77.

Stone, Walter J., L. Sandy Maisel, and Cherie Maestas 2004 "Quality Counts: Extending the Strategic Politician Model of Incumbent Deterrence" *American Journal of Political Science* 48: 479–95.

Stone, Walter J. and Elizabeth N. Simas. 2007. "Candidate Valence and Ideological Positions in the 2006 House Elections." Unpublished Manuscript, UC Davis.

Chapter 5

Abramoff, Email, and the Mistreated Mistress

Scandal and Character in the 2006 Elections

David J. Hendry, Robert A. Jackson, and Jeffery J. Mondak

> In Don Sherwood's seat, that would have been overwhelmingly ours if his mistress hadn't whined about being throttled.
>
> (Grover Norquist)[1]

In the aftermath of the 2006 elections, many Republicans engaged in finger-pointing in efforts to assign or escape blame for the party's failure to retain control of Congress. With numerous factors possibly in operation—among them, the Iraq War, President's Bush's lagging popularity, and the historic tendency of the incumbent president's party to lose seats in midterm congressional elections, all coupled with the Republicans' narrow pre-election margins in the House and Senate—there was no shortage of possible accounts of the Republican defeat. Two especially popular storylines held, first, that the elections signaled a tactical failure on the part of Bush adviser and political strategist Karl Rove, and, alternately, according to Rove supporters, such as Grover Norquist, that the Republican defeat traced in large part to the ethical stumbling of a few scandal-plagued Republican incumbents.[2] This chapter explores the latter thesis. We seek to assess to what extent, if any, allegations of impropriety affected the outcomes of the 2006 elections.

Recall that Democrats captured control of Congress in 2006 by picking up 30 seats in the U.S. House and six seats in the U.S. Senate. Charges of corruption and incidents of scandal were prominent in some of these campaigns, and also in a few other races in which the incumbent party narrowly retained the seat. However, scandal was a direct factor in fewer than half of the elections in which Democrats made gains. Among Republicans defeated in the Senate, only Conrad Burns (R-MT) was hurt by charges of possible wrongdoing. The margin of victory in that race was less than one percent, suggesting that Burns could have survived had ethics not been a factor in the election. In this scenario, the Senate would have been split 50–50, leaving Republicans in control via Vice President Dick Cheney's tie-breaking vote. In the House, 22 Republican incumbents lost in 2006, and Democrats also won in eight Republican-held open seats. Of these 30 races, it appears that scandal and ethics exerted possible influence in as many as 14,[3] with scandal playing a role in ten of the campaigns in which Republican incumbents were defeated,[4] and in three of the open seats where Democrats scored gains.[5]

These numbers suggest that scandal was an important, but perhaps not a decisive, factor in the 2006 House elections. As a thought experiment, we might speculate that, absent scandal, the Republicans conceivably could have retained all 14 House seats identified here. In this scenario, the Democrats still would have gained 16 seats, one more than the 15 needed to secure a majority in the House. But perhaps this view of the effect of scandal is too restrictive. In 2006, exit poll data revealed that 41 percent of voters viewed corruption as an extremely important issue, slightly more than for issues such as terrorism and the war in Iraq.[6] With so many voters concerned with corruption, the possibility of a spillover effect must be entertained. That is, perhaps even in states or districts in which Republican incumbents were not charged with impropriety, the salience of scandal in 2006 led some voters to opt for Democrats. This may have occurred either because voters were receptive to the Democrats' claim that Republicans had instilled a "culture of corruption,"[7] or, less generously, because uninformed voters thought that their own incumbents were involved in scandals even when they were not. Either way, it is conceivable that ethics matters influenced voting in 2006 beyond the districts and states with scandal-plagued incumbents. With several House Republicans defeated by margins narrower than 52–48, including Rob Simmons' 83-vote loss in Connecticut, even a very slight scandal spillover could have proved decisive. Additionally, absent charges of wrongdoing, Republicans would not have been placed on the defensive and would not have had to divert resources to those otherwise safe Republican seats that apparently were made competitive by scandal.

In this chapter, we explore the impact of scandal both on vote margins in the 2006 House elections and on voters' perceptions and judgments. In the first portion of the analysis, we devise simple aggregate models similar to those offered by Welch and Hibbing (1997). This exercise will permit us to gauge whether scandal did, in fact, correspond with discernible electoral effects in 2006, and whether any such effects may have spelled defeat in particular districts. We then draw on data from the 2006 Congressional Elections Study (CES) to examine the possible impact of scandal and corruption on voters' perceptions and decisions. We focus specifically on effects pertaining to incumbents in the 2006 U.S. House races. Several questions are considered. First, did the presence of a scandal-plagued incumbent actually matter for the individual citizen's vote choice? The fact that so many of these incumbents were defeated suggests that the answer is yes, but individual-level vote choice must be examined for this point to be demonstrated more conclusively. Second, what mechanisms underlie the effects of scandal? Did scandal matter for voters' assessments of House incumbents? If so, did scandal operate in a discriminate or indiscriminate fashion? Third, is there any evidence suggestive of a spillover effect? For instance, might it be that the reputations of even those Republicans not directly implicated in ethics matters were tarnished? If so, might such effects have been large enough to topple those incumbents in the most closely-fought districts? As a prelude to these analyses, we first provide additional information regarding those incumbents associated with the most prominent ethics and corruption charges in 2006, and then review what prior research has suggested regarding the electoral significance of scandal.

The Salience of Ethics Charges in 2006

Leading up to the 2006 elections, allegations of wrongdoing on the part of congressional incumbents—mostly Republicans—abounded. Two factors made these allegations especially problematic for the Republican effort to maintain control of Congress. First, seemingly there was a scandal to suit every taste. Although the most widespread involved charges of corruption, we will see below that other stories concerned a variety of racier matters. Second, news of scandals continued to emerge throughout 2006, including in the weeks immediately prior to Election Day. This steady news stream made it difficult for Republicans seeking to move past scandal and return the focus to substantive policy considerations.

Well before 2006 campaigning hit full stride, scandal took down long-time House member Duke Cunningham (R-CA). Cunningham was charged with illegally steering military expenditures to defense contractor Mitchell Wade. Wade was convicted of providing over $1 million in bribes to Cunningham, and Cunningham pled guilty to multiple felony counts in the matter, ultimately receiving a prison sentence of over eight years. Cunningham resigned from Congress in late 2005. He was succeeded by a former House member, fellow Republican Brian Bilbray, who won a special election to replace Cunningham in June 2006. Bilbray went on to be re-elected in November.

The largest and most complex scandal in 2006 centered on the actions of Jack Abramoff. Abramoff was a political activist and lobbyist with strong ties to many prominent Republican officials, including some in the Bush administration. Indeed, Abramoff was part of George W. Bush's 2001 transition advisory team and, as a lobbyist, participated in several hundred meetings with Bush officials during the first years of the administration.[8] Many of Abramoff's practices seemed ethically questionable, and Abramoff eventually became the focus of an extensive Justice Department investigation. In January 2006, Abramoff pled guilty to several felony counts on charges of conspiracy, fraud, and tax evasion, and admitted as part of his plea agreement that he had bribed public officials. Abramoff was sentenced to almost six years in prison. He was assigned to a prison in Maryland so that he would be accessible to investigators exploring possible criminal links between himself and members of Congress and their staffs, and between himself and members of the Bush administration.

Because Abramoff had been a highly active lobbyist, he had developed ties to numerous public officials. Further, Abramoff interacted almost exclusively with Republicans. As a result, multiple Bush administration officials and Republican congressional incumbents eventually were caught in the wake of the Abramoff scandal. In some instances, these individuals had what appears to have been only minor contact with Abramoff, whereas in others the involvement was much more substantial.

Two members of the Bush administration were convicted of felonies and sentenced to prison for their involvement with Abramoff. The first is David Safavian, appointed by President Bush to a top post in the Office of Management and Budget, who was found guilty on four felony counts, including lying and obstruction of justice. The second is Steve Griles, once the second-ranking official in the Department of Interior, and a member of Vice President Dick Cheney's energy task force, who received a ten-month prison sentence following his conviction for obstruction of justice.

The two members of Congress most adversely affected by the Abramoff affair were House members Tom DeLay (R-TX) and Bob Ney (R-OH). DeLay, the House Majority Leader, had maintained a close relationship with Abramoff for years, and two former DeLay aides, Tony Rudy and Michael Scanlon, were convicted on charges related to the Abramoff investigation. Although DeLay ran in, and won, the Republican primary in his House district in 2006, the combination of the Abramoff matter and DeLay's own 2005 indictment by a Texas grand jury led DeLay to resign. Under Texas law, the Republicans were not permitted to replace DeLay on the 2006 ballot. Republican Shelley Sekula-Gibbs, who served the last weeks of DeLay's term, ran as a write-in candidate in the general election, but was defeated by Democrat Nick Lampson. Bob Ney, who entered the House as part of the Republican Revolution in 1994, had been named in the Abramoff-related indictments of several figures, including Abramoff himself, former DeLay aide Michael Scanlon, and Ney's own former chief of staff, Neil Volz. Like DeLay, Ney won the Republican primary in his district in 2006, but withdrew from the race in August and, on October 13, just weeks before the November election, pled guilty to two criminal counts stemming from the Abramoff investigation. Democrat Zack Space easily defeated Republican Joy Padgett in Ney's former district on Election Day, garnering 62 percent of the vote.

Numerous other Republicans running in 2006 were tainted by financial connections to Abramoff or by links to DeLay or Ney. These include several incumbents who were defeated in 2006, among them former Senator Conrad Burns (R-MT), and former House members J.D. Hayworth (R-AZ), Richard Pombo (R-CA), Jim Ryun (R-KS), Charles Taylor (R-NC), Charlie Bass (R-NH), and Michael Fitzpatrick (R-PA). In Pombo's case, former Republican House member Pete McCloskey challenged him in the Republican primary, running on the slogan "Restore Ethics to Congress." When Pombo won the primary, McCloskey threw his support to Pombo's Democratic challenger, Jerry McNerney. Republicans linked to Abramoff or DeLay who were re-elected in 2006 include House members Roy Blunt, John Doolittle, Tom Feeney, Dennis Hastert, and Deborah Pryce. In early 2007, Feeney was ordered by the House Ethics Committee to pay $5,600 to cover the cost of an Abramoff-sponsored 2003 trip to Scotland. Pryce was re-elected in her Ohio district with only 50.2 percent of the vote, and she declined to defend her seat in 2008.

Apart from the Abramoff matter, most of the additional scandals that made news in 2006 involved individual House members. Among Democrats, Patrick Kennedy (D-RI) entered rehab and pled guilty to driving under the influence of prescription drugs following a late-night car crash at the Capitol in May 2006. Alan Mollohan (D-WV) has been under scrutiny since early 2006 for a variety of possible financial irregularities. William Jefferson (D-LA) was videotaped accepting $100,000 in cash from a Virginia investor in 2005, and most of the cash later was found in Jefferson's freezer. In June 2007, Jefferson was indicted on 16 counts by a federal grand jury. Although the Jefferson matter made news throughout 2006, and despite the fact that two of his former aides pled guilty to corruption charges earlier in the year, Jefferson won re-election. On Election Day, he was one of the top two finishers in a multi-candidate contest, and Jefferson then defeated his fellow Democrat Karen Carter in a December run-off.

During the 2006 campaign, various additional allegations of wrongdoing played prominent roles in races involving three Republican incumbents. The most senior of these was Curt Weldon (R-PA), a 20-year veteran of Congress. On October 13, less than four weeks before Election Day, the story broke that the FBI was investigating Weldon on the grounds that he possibly had been using his influence to steer business to his daughter's political consulting firm.[9] A few days later, the FBI conducted a search of the home of Weldon's daughter. Negative publicity from this matter likely contributed to Weldon's defeat. In 2007, the FBI launched an internal investigation to determine whether the leak of the Weldon story and the subsequent raid on the home of Weldon's daughter were timed so as to influence the outcome of the election.[10]

Another Republican House member from Pennsylvania, Don Sherwood, was rocked by the news story that he had had a five-year extra-marital affair with a woman, Cynthia Ore, who was 35 years younger than Sherwood. Ore had placed a 911 call in 2004, claiming that Sherwood had attempted to strangle her. Ore later sued Sherwood, alleging that he had been physically abusive toward her on multiple occasions. Sherwood settled the suit, purportedly agreeing to pay Ore $500,000. During the 2006 campaign, Sherwood ran a television ad in which he apologized for the affair, but also denied having abused Ore. Sherwood's challenger, Democrat Chris Carney, capitalized on news of Sherwood's affair and defeated Sherwood on Election Day.

The final noteworthy scandal in 2006 concerned Florida Republican Mark Foley. News broke in late September 2006 that Foley had exchanged sexually-explicit emails and instant messages with teenage boys who were part of the Congressional page program, and that Foley perhaps even had sought liaisons with some of the pages. The story quickly dominated the national news. In the space of just a few days, Foley resigned from Congress, said that he was an alcoholic and entered rehab, and his lawyer announced that Foley was gay and had been molested by a priest as a youth. Republicans selected state legislator Joe Negron to run in Foley's place. Negron had only a few weeks to campaign, and, under Florida law, Foley's name remained on the November ballot. Negron was defeated on Election Day by Democrat Tim Mahoney.

The Foley scandal is one that may have had broader effects, influencing voting behavior in other House races. The Foley matter is an especially good example in this regard because it was revealed that several Republican House members, including some in key leadership positions, had known of concerns over Foley's interactions with congressional pages well before news of the story broke. One Foley staff member alleged that he had warned House Speaker Dennis Hastert about concerns with Foley three years earlier. This development led to charges that the Republican leadership had tried to cover up the story, resulting, in turn, in calls for Hastert to resign as Speaker.[11] Several other Republican House members were criticized for their handling of the Foley incident, including Tom Reynolds (R-NY), the chair of the National Republican Congressional Committee. Reynolds narrowly won re-election in 2006.

The numerous scandals detailed here are summarized in Table 5.1. These scandals generated a considerable amount of adverse publicity. As noted above, these incidents likely contributed to the electoral defeat of Republican Senator Conrad Burns, and to the outcomes in many of the 30 House seats that shifted from the Republicans to the Democrats in 2006. But the evidence of an electoral effect is, to this point, merely circumstantial. To assess more systematically the link between scandal and voting in 2006, we next review what past research has found regarding the electoral significance of scandal, followed by an examination of aggregate vote returns and survey data from the 2006 CES.

Perspectives on the Impact of Scandal

Political scientists previously have considered whether how incumbents perform in office, and especially whether those incumbents have been accused of wrongdoing, matters for subsequent electoral success. Three approaches have been used in these past works. First, some research has examined incumbent quality in broad form, with scandal merely representing one facet of the record. Second, and somewhat more narrowly, other research has explored the general impact of scandal and corruption, typically with evidence on U.S. House incumbents from across multiple electoral cycles. Third, and most specifically, the significance of particular scandals has been studied, especially those incidents that affected large numbers of incumbents. Methodological approaches and

Table 5.1 U.S. House Incumbents Linked to Scandal in 2006

A. Incumbents Running for Re-election

Don Young (R-AK 1st)	Implicated in Abramoff scandal
J.D. Hayworth (R-AZ 5th)*	Linked to DeLay and Abramoff
John Doolittle (R-CA 4th)	Implicated in Abramoff scandal
Richard Pombo (R-CA 11th)*	Implicated in Abramoff scandal
Jerry Lewis (R-CA 41st)	Justice Department investigation of defense appropriations
Ken Calvert (R-CA 44th)	Federal investigation of profits from a land deal
Ginny Brown-Waite (R-FL 5th)	Opponent accusations of covering up for Mark Foley
Tom Feeney (R-FL 24th)	Implicated in Abramoff scandal
Dennis Hastert (R-IL 14th)	House Ethics Committee investigation of possible role in covering up Foley scandal as Speaker and controversy over campaign receipts from Abramoff
Jim Ryun (R-KS 2nd)*	Receipt of campaign contributions from DeLay's ARMPAC and financial ties to organization funded by Abramoff
Roy Blunt (R-MO 7th)	Leadership PAC received contributions from Abramoff
Charlie Bass (R-NH 2nd)*	Receipt of financial contributions from DeLay's ARMPAC; painted as a hypocrite by media after calling for DeLay's resignation
Heather Wilson (R-NM 1st)	Accused by a U.S. attorney fired in the Justice Department scandal of attempting to expedite the indictment of a Democratic state senator in a public corruption case
Sue Kelly (R-NY 19th)*	Previously served on page board and questioned about Foley scandal
John Sweeney (R-NY 20th)*	Implicated in questionable lobbying activities and report of domestic disturbance incident
Tom Reynolds (R-NY 26th)	Public disagreement with Hastert about whether he passed on to the Speaker information about Foley's improprieties
Charles Taylor (R-NC 11th)*	Receipt of campaign contributions from Abramoff
Deborah Pryce (R-OH 15th)	Implicated in Abramoff scandal
Jim Gerlach (R-PA 6th)	Receipt of campaign contributions from DeLay's ARMPAC
Curt Weldon (R-PA 7th)*	Justice Department investigation of improper use of influence to win contracts for daughter's lobbying firm
Michael Fitzpatrick (R-PA 8th)*	Receipt of campaign contributions from the PACs of Ney, DeLay, and Duke Cunningham
Don Sherwood (R-PA 10th)*	Acknowledgement of 5-year extra-marital affair involving charges of abuse and resulting in an out-of-court settlement
Patrick Kennedy (D-RI 1st)	Pled guilty to driving under the influence of prescription medicines following accident outside House office buildings
Pete Sessions (R-TX 32nd)	Implicated in Abramoff scandal
Alan Mollohan (D-WV 1st)	Investigations into questions about ethics and personal finances

B. Open Seats

Joe Negron (R-FL 16th)*	District of Mark Foley (R), who had exchanged sexually-explicit emails and instant messages with teenage male pages and resigned on September 29
Joy Padgett (R-OH 18th)*	District of Bob Ney (R), who was implicated in Abramoff scandal and resigned on November 3
Shelley Sekula-Gibbs (R-TX 22nd)*	District of Tom DeLay (R), who was under indictment in Texas on campaign finance charges and implicated in Abramoff scandal and resigned in June

Note: * Designates candidate of the incumbent party lost the general election.

data sources have varied within these research traditions. Some studies have gauged the aggregate consequences of scandal for election margins and outcomes, whereas others have focused on individual-level vote choice. In some instances, laboratory experiments have been conducted in efforts to generate insight regarding how and why voters respond to information about scandal. Despite these differences in approach, the clear consensus emerging from these various works is that when congressional incumbents are charged with misconduct, their electoral prospects are harmed. In short, scandal matters.

Broad evaluations of incumbent quality have been formed in three manners. First, some works have relied on a content analysis of descriptions of House incumbents in sources such as *The Almanac of American Politics* and *Politics in America*. Numerical values are assigned to the words and phrases used to describe each incumbent, and then combined into measures of competence, integrity, and overall quality. Research using this approach reveals effects of incumbent quality on aggregate indicators—including election margins, challenger spending, and the incumbent's length of tenure—and also on individual-level vote choice (e.g., McCurley and Mondak 1995; Mondak 1995; Mondak, McCurley, and Millman 1999). Differentiating between incumbents' levels of competence and integrity, it appears that voters respond directly to information pertinent to integrity, whereas the electoral effects of competence are driven largely by elite actors, and especially by prospective challengers.

Walter Stone and his colleagues (Stone, Maisel, and Maestas 2004) have employed a second approach for the measurement of incumbent quality, a technique that involves surveying activists and informants within the congressional district, and asking them, among other things, to assess the skill and integrity of the district's U.S. House member. Stone and his colleagues also survey potential candidates in each district, and gauge the impact of incumbent quality on the potential candidate's likelihood of entering the race. Very strong effects are identified, establishing that incumbent quality functions as a critical factor in elite-level strategic considerations. These considerations, in turn, matter for electoral behavior by influencing the choice set available to voters on Election Day (e.g., Stone and Maisel 2003; Maestas *et al.* 2006).

Incumbent quality also has been studied in the laboratory (e.g., Kulisheck and Mondak 1996; Canache, Mondak, and Cabrera 2000; Mondak and Huckfeldt 2006). In these works, descriptions of candidates' traits are varied as a means to determine whether information about incumbent quality resonates directly with voters. In each of these studies, competence and integrity were shown to be accessible and influential as bases of candidate evaluation. Coupled with the work of Stone and his colleagues on candidate entry, their results suggest that incumbent quality exerts both direct and indirect effects on the voter's decision calculus.

As an alternate to studying the general attributes of competence and integrity, other scholars have examined the specific matter of charges of corruption. The most prominent works in this tradition are a pair of studies co-authored by Susan Welch—one focuses on 81 incidents of scandal relevant to U.S. House elections in the period 1968 to 1978 (Peters and Welch 1980), and a second considers 88 charges raised against incumbents during the 1982 to 1990 elections (Welch and Hibbing 1997).[12] Both studies assess the aggregate consequences of scandal. Results reveal an inverse relationship between implication in scandal and electoral survival. In the latter study, for instance, nine of the 88 incumbents in question resigned or opted against running for re-election, and 22 were defeated. In both studies, charges of corruption and misconduct were shown to correspond with a loss of approximately 10 percentage points in an incumbent's vote margin. Although most scandal-plagued incumbents win re-election, the evidence reveals that scandal does place an incumbent at greater electoral peril.

Among specific incidents of alleged legislator misconduct, the one that sparked the greatest scholarly interest was the 1992 House banking scandal. News emerged in early 1992 that House members who made use of the House bank were permitted overdrafts without repercussion provided that the amount of the overdrafts did not exceed the amount of their next paycheck. Although these overdrafts did not violate bank rules, the sheer magnitude of the practice made it newsworthy. A large number of House members had recorded at least some overdrafts; the total number of overdrafts in the previous year numbered in the thousands, and a dozen House members had more than 400 overdrafts. Several teams of researchers sought to determine whether implication in this scandal was consequential for incumbents' retirement decisions and for voting in the 1992 elections (e.g., Alford *et al.* 1994; Banducci and Karp 1994; Groseclose and Krehbiel 1994; Jacobson and Dimock 1994; Dimock and Jacobson 1995).

The research on the effects of the bank scandal includes a mix of works regarding district-level outcomes and individual-level vote choice. Collectively, the lesson emerging from these studies is that involvement in the bank scandal did matter, although some analysts suggest that the overall effects were modest in magnitude (e.g., Alford *et al.* 1994). Consistent with findings from the Welch studies, it appears that some House members entangled in the bank scandal engaged in strategic retirement rather than face what likely would have been difficult re-election bids (Groseclose and Krehbiel 1994; Jacobson and Dimock 1994). Likewise, involvement in the scandal dampened both the likelihood that individual voters would opt to re-elect the incumbent (Dimock and Jacobson 1995) and that scandal-plagued incumbents would win re-election (Jacobson and Dimock 1994).

Whether viewed in terms of summary measures of incumbent quality, charges of corruption, or the specific events surrounding the 1992 House bank scandal, past research reveals that questions regarding congressional incumbents' honesty and integrity adversely affect their prospects for re-election. As we have seen, numerous House incumbents faced allegations of misconduct in 2006. Moreover, unlike the mostly idiosyncratic incidents studied by Welch and her colleagues and the bipartisan 1992 House banking scandal, the vast majority of scandal-plagued incumbents in 2006 were from one party. Consequently, voter response to scandal may partially account for why the Republicans lost their congressional majorities.

Scandal and Vote Margins

The analysis begins with assessment of the possible impact of scandal on vote margins in the 2006 House races. In districts with incumbents running for re-election, the vote share in the prior election cycle offers a strong baseline from which to predict the vote share in the present election. Hence, in the current case, we use the incumbent's vote share from 2004 as a predictor of the corresponding 2006 vote. The logic here is that, all else equal, an incumbent who, for example, won with 65 percent of the vote in 2004 would be predicted to fare similarly in 2006. However, because 2006 was, for various reasons, a bad year for Republicans, our model also will include a dummy variable identifying Republican incumbents. Lastly, to gauge the impact of scandal, we include a dummy variable singling out those incumbents who faced allegations of wrongdoing in 2006.

Results of three models are depicted in Table 5.2. The first model includes coefficient estimates for districts with incumbents who ran for re-election in 2006; following Welch and Hibbing (1997), the analysis is limited to incumbents who faced major-party competition in 2004.[13] As expected, the lagged vote exerts a powerful structuring influence. Further, the results confirm that 2006 was a bad year for Republicans, as, on average, Democratic incumbents finished 8.5 percentage points higher than did their Republican counterparts. Most noteworthy for present purposes is that being implicated in a scandal on average directly cost incumbents an additional 4.8 percentage points. The second model in Table 5.2 restricts the analysis to districts with Republican incumbents. Only two of the incumbents implicated in scandal were Democrats, Patrick Kennedy and Alan Mollohan.[14] With the analysis limited to Republican incumbents, a scandal effect of 5.4 percentage points is identified. Nine Republican incumbents[15] implicated in scandal lost in 2006, while receiving more than 45 percent of the vote, suggesting that scandal was a decisive force in these races. A tenth Republican, Pennsylvania's Curt Weldon, lost his election receiving just below 44 percent of the vote. However, rather than suggesting that Weldon still would have been defeated absent allegations of misconduct, the more plausible account is that scandal produced a greater than average effect in Weldon's district due to the flurry of critical last-minute news coverage regarding the FBI's October investigation. Thus, of the 22 Republican incumbents defeated in 2006, present evidence indicates that the fate of as many as ten turned on scandal.

The third model in Table 5.2 reports estimates for open seat contests. Three Republicans in these contests had to overcome not only Democratic opponents,

Table 5.2 Linear Regression Models of the Impact of Scandal on the Two-Party Vote Proportion in 2006

	All Incumbents, Seats with Major Party Opposition in 2004	Republican Incumbents, Seats with Major Party Opposition in 2004	Open Seats
Constant	0.176*** (0.029)	0.103* (0.044)	0.150*** (0.040)
Incumbent Party Vote Proportion in 2004	0.787*** (0.040)	0.769*** (0.066)	
Republican Party Vote Proportion in 2004			0.568*** (0.075)
Republican Incumbent	−0.085*** (0.0061)		
Scandal	−0.048** (0.014)	−0.054*** (0.014)	−0.074* (0.036)
N	293	165	27
R^2	0.77	0.50	0.73

Notes:
The dependent variable in the first two models is the incumbent's proportion of the 2006 district-level U.S. House vote. The dependent variable in the third model is the Republican candidate's proportion of the vote. Unopposed races are not considered.
Robust standard errors are in parentheses.
*** $p < .001$, ** $p < 0.01$, * $p < 0.05$

but also the aftermath of a scandal involving a Republican incumbent—Tom DeLay, Mark Foley, and Bob Ney—who had resigned in the weeks or months prior to Election Day. The estimates reveal that scandal cost the Republicans over 7 percentage points in these races, a mark greater than the margin of victory for the Democratic candidates in the districts previously held by Foley and DeLay. Further, as with Curt Weldon's unsuccessful bid for re-election, we suspect that scandal produced a greater than average effect in Ohio's eighteenth district following Bob Ney's mid-October guilty plea on two felony counts.

The analyses reported here corroborate our previous speculation regarding the impact of scandal in 2006. Scandal contributed to the defeat of many Republicans, and our results suggest that scandal may have been decisive in as many as 13 contests. It follows that, absent scandal, the Democrats most likely still would have captured control of the House, probably winning 17 seats, two more than the 15 required to take the House. A Democratic win in this scenario is not a certainty, however, because scandal put Republicans on the defensive in 2006, and drained campaign resources that could have been directed elsewhere. But for scandal, party control of Congress would have gone down to the wire in 2006, and, at best, the Democrats would have chiseled out a narrow victory. Because of their involvement in scandal, the Republicans discussed here unwittingly combined to provide Democrats with a much more comfortable margin of victory.

Voters and Scandal in the 2006 U.S. House Elections

As argued above, aggregate patterns and anecdotal accounts indicate that incumbents implicated in scandal did in fact suffer for their alleged transgressions on Election Day 2006. However, thus far we have not evaluated this claim in the context of individual-level vote choice. The 2006 CES is geocoded to allow us to place individual respondents within congressional districts, and thus facilitates an examination of responses in the context of district-level characteristics.[16]

To investigate whether scandal was indeed a factor in individual vote choice in 2006, Table 5.3 presents a simple logistic regression model of vote choice among respondents to the CES. The dependent variable is whether the respondent voted for the candidate of the same party as the incumbent (in non-open seat races, this is simply a vote for the incumbent). In addition to the presence of scandal (coded dichotomously: 1 = Yes), we have included an indicator of the respondent's strength of identification with the party of the incumbent. Respondents were asked about their identification with one of the two major parties and the strength of that identification in two separate questions. Combining the two questions forms a 7-point indicator, with independents falling in the middle category. This indicator was recoded to reflect, for each respondent, identification with the party of the incumbent. Strength of identification with the incumbent's party ranges from 0 to 6, with higher values indicating stronger identification. Additionally, dummy variables indicate the party of the incumbent (1 = Republican) and whether the seat was open (1 = Yes). The model presented in Table 5.3 shows all posited relationships to be statistically significant and in the expected direction. Most important for the discussion presented thus far, the presence of a scandal in a district significantly lowered the probability that a respondent reported having voted for the incumbent (or, in the case of open seats, for the candidate of the same party as the incumbent). And this relationship persists even after controlling for strength of party identification. Interestingly, the dummy variable for the party of the incumbent shows an exceedingly strong independent effect. In fact, the model indicates that the very presence of a sitting Republican in the district lowered the probability of the incumbent (or candidate of the incumbent's party) receiving electoral support even more so than the presence of scandal.

Table 5.3 Logistic Regression Model of the 2006 House Vote for Party of Incumbent

	Coefficient	Robust S.E.	z-score
Constant	−1.98***	(0.263)	−4.55
Strength of Identification with Incumbent Party	0.999***	(0.074)	13.46
Scandal	−1.038*	(0.454)	−2.29
Party of Incumbent	−1.579***	(0.301)	−5.25
Open Seat	−0.779*	(0.263)	−2.46

N = 866
Log-Pseudolikelihood = −272.101
Wald χ^2, 4 d.f. = 183.50***
Pseudo R^2 = 0.509

Notes:
Entries in column 1 are logistic regression coefficients. Robust standard errors are in parentheses. Dependent variable is reported vote choice. Respondents in the panel sample were first asked a Yes/No question about whether they voted in the House race. Those answering "Yes" were asked a follow-up question about whom specifically they voted for. Additionally, about 15% of our sample consists of respondents in the pool for the pre-election wave who were actually interviewed after the election. For this portion of the sample, a pre-election question tapping vote intention was changed to a simple retrospective, "For whom did you vote?" Model is weighted to reflect oversampling of competitive congressional districts.
***p < 0.001, **p < 0.1, *p < 0.05

To ease interpretation, predicted probabilities based on the vote model are presented in Figure 5.1. Panels (a) and (b) present the results of selected covariate profiles for races in which the incumbent candidate was running and for open seats, respectively. And the results are remarkably similar. Each panel presents the results for Republicans in scandal districts, Republicans in non-scandal districts, and Democrats in non-scandal districts. The remaining category, Democratic candidates in scandal districts, is excluded because such cases were relative rarities in our sample.[17] Several aspects of the plots are striking. First is the stark increase in the probability of voting for the incumbent candidate across the range of strength of identification with the incumbent's party (obviously, this result is to be expected). More interesting for the purposes of examining the effects of scandal is the clear separation between Democratic incumbents and both categories of Republicans. Particularly from the low to

(a) Incumbents Running for Re-election

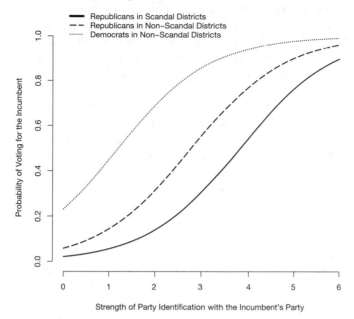

(b) Open Seats

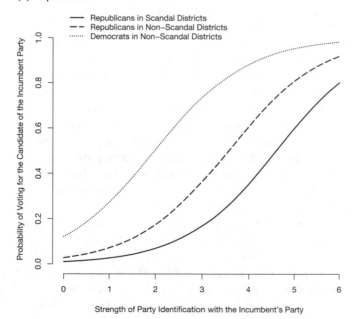

Figure 5.1 Predicted Probability of Voting for Party of Incumbent.

middle range of the strength of identification scale, non-scandal-plagued Democratic candidates fared exceptionally well compared to their non-scandal-plagued Republican counterparts, and even more so relative to Republicans tainted by scandal. Specifically, between the values of 2 and 4 on the strength of party identification scale, the gap between the likelihood of voting for Democrats in non-scandal districts and Republicans in scandal districts ranges between about 40 and 60 percentage points.

These findings provide a sense of the impact of scandal on the vote choice; however, in itself, evidence that scandal mattered tells us nothing definitive regarding how or why this effect came to operate. One fundamental question concerns whether information about allegations of misconduct actually entered the consciousness of the voter. The occurrence of scandal shapes elite behavior. If a scandal causes an incumbent to appear vulnerable, party leaders, campaign donors, and strategic challengers all may respond. In the extreme case, a scandal's eruption therefore could matter at the polls even if voters are wholly unaware of, or unconcerned about, the allegations. In this scenario, the effects of scandal would trace to the presence of a high-quality, well-funded challenger.

Although we cannot provide a full delineation of the mechanisms underlying the effects of scandal, we can address the basic question of whether scandal resonates directly with voters. If allegations of misconduct solely influence elite behavior, then the impact on the vote choice observed in Table 5.3 should be unaccompanied by a corresponding impact on voters' subsidiary evaluations of their incumbent. Conversely, if scandal actually enters the consciousness of the voter, then CES respondents' conceptions of their House member should reflect this. Respondents were asked to assess the candidates in their districts in terms of both honesty and competence. We would take it as evidence that scandal directly influenced voters' perceptions if the occurrence of scandal lowered their evaluation of their incumbent's level of honesty. Moreover, we would take it as evidence that the impact of scandal was relatively refined rather than indiscriminate if scandal influenced their assessment of honesty but did not produce a corresponding effect on their assessment of competence.

To investigate this potential for differentiation, Table 5.4 presents ordinal logistic regression models of post-election respondent ratings of incumbent honesty and competence. Respondents were asked to evaluate how well the words "Honest" and "Competent" describe the sitting incumbent in their district. Ratings are measured on a 4-point scale, with higher values indicating more positive evaluations. Independent variables are defined as previously. Expounding upon the questions raised from the model of vote choice, in the context of the story presented thus far, what stands out immediately is that scandal matters for respondents' perception of incumbent honesty, but not for their perception of incumbent competence. Scandal achieves a high level of statistical significance when specified as a predictor of the post-election honesty rating, but fails to achieve statistical significance as a predictor of the post-election competence rating. The models presented in Table 5.4 are consistent with the idea that scandal not only resonated with voters, but in fact operated on their judgments in a discriminate fashion. It seems that respondents in scandal districts were consistently able to make the connection between scandal and honesty, but respondents did not view allegations of scandal as indictments of competence. Additionally, as in the vote model, strength of identification with the incumbent's party shows a strong, positive effect on evaluations of both honesty and competence. The effect of party is negatively signed in both models, but fails to achieve statistical significance in the model for honesty ratings (although this coefficient is on the cusp of significance at the $p < .05$ level).

The samples for the models in Table 5.4 consist of all respondents interviewed after Election Day for whom data are available on the covariates of interest. However, the CES panel component also allows us to control for baseline ratings of honesty and competence among those respondents interviewed in both the pre-election and post-election waves of the study. The pre- and post-election waves contained the honesty and competence questions

Table 5.4 Ordinal Logistic Regression Models of Incumbent Quality Ratings, All Respondents

	Post-Election Honesty Rating		Post-Election Competence Rating	
	Coefficient	Robust S.E.	Coefficient	Robust S.E.
Strength of Identification with Incumbent Party	0.389***	(0.046)	0.363***	(0.045)
Scandal	−0.793***	(0.219)	−0.307	(0.259)
Party of Incumbent	−0.343	(0.178)	−0.482**	(0.176)
1st Cut Point	−1.803	(0.235)	−2.039	(0.235)
2nd Cut Point	0.005	(0.211)	−0.303	(0.201)
3rd Cut Point	2.585	(0.266)	2.247	(0.244)
N	657		667	
Log-Pseudolikelihood	−720.138		−726.441	
Wald χ^2 (3 d.f.)	98.75***		77.70***	
Pseudo R^2	0.089		0.079	

Notes:
Cell entries are ordered logistic regression coefficients. Robust standard errors are in parentheses. Model is weighted to reflect oversampling of competitive congressional districts.
***p < 0.001, **p < 0.01, *p < 0.05

in the same wording, and it is appealing to control for the ratings provided prior to the election when evaluating the effects of scandal on post-election evaluations, as doing so offers powerful leverage on the possibility that developments occurring over the course of the campaign induced changes in voters' perceptions of incumbents' traits. Table 5.5 presents models of post-election honesty and competence ratings using only panel respondents, in which the pre-election evaluations are employed as controls. As expected, pre-election ratings are strongly, positively related (in both a substantive sense and a statistical sense) to post-election ratings. In terms of our main question about whether scandal actually resonated with voters, the story here remains the same. Even after controlling for pre-election honesty rating, the impact of scandal remains statistically significant. For the honesty model in Table 5.5, both the level of statistical significance and the magnitude of the coefficient are diminished only slightly from those in Table 5.4. And again we find that the presence

Table 5.5 Ordinal Logistic Regression Models of Incumbent Quality Ratings, Panel Respondents

	Post-Election Honesty Rating		Post-Election Competence Rating	
	Coefficient	Robust S.E.	Coefficient	Robust S.E.
Pre-Election Honesty Rating	1.797***	(0.227)		
Pre-Election Competence Rating			1.844***	(0.227)
Strength of Identification with Incumbent Party	0.249***	(0.059)	0.202**	(0.067)
Scandal	−0.767*	(0.390)	−0.492	(0.379)
Party of Incumbent	−0.272	(0.245)	−0.373	(0.237)
1st Cut Point	1.626	(0.576)	1.844	(0.227)
2nd Cut Point	4.278	(0.626)	4.081	(0.574)
3rd Cut Point	7.598	(0.743)	7.234	(0.685)
N	382		397	
Log-Pseudolikelihood	−340.022		−361.226	
Wald χ^2 (3 d.f.)	120.96***		112.52***	
Pseudo R^2	0.245		0.228	

Notes:
Cell entries are ordered logistic regression coefficients. Robust standard errors are in parentheses. Model is weighted to reflect oversampling of competitive congressional districts.
***p < 0.001, **p < 0.1, *p < 0.05

of scandal does not matter for evaluations of competence. Additionally, in each model presented in Table 5.5, we find that after controlling for the pre-election evaluation, the party of the incumbent seems not to matter.

Based on the model controlling for pre-election honesty rating as applied to Republican House incumbents, Figures 5.2a and 5.2b present cumulative probabilities of the number of panel respondents answering affirmatively to each of the four categories of the post-election honesty rating. Figure 5.2c depicts comparable results for Democratic incumbents. In these figures, lines represent the thresholds between categories, and the areas between lines indicate the predicted proportion of respondents in each category across the range of strength of partisanship. Each graph holds the level of pre-election honesty at its mean value. In the case of Republican scandal districts (Figure 5.2a), the proportion of respondents answering that "Honest" fits the incumbent "extremely well" becomes greater as identification with the incumbent's party grows stronger, the proportion answering "not too well" decreases, and the proportion answering "quite well" stays roughly the same. With pre-election rating held at its mean, a negligible proportion of respondents stated that honest fits the incumbent "not well at all." In the case of Republican non-scandal districts and Democratic non-scandal districts, the story is the same except for the fact that the proportion answering "quite well" decreases as identification with the incumbent's party grows stronger.

The interesting story appears when we compare across the three panels of the figure. It is clear that across the entire range of strength of partisanship, a greater mass of respondents in both Republican and Democratic non-scandal districts than in Republican scandal districts was willing to answer that honest described the incumbent "extremely well." Additionally, Democrats seemed to fare better than both categories of Republicans. And the story for the "not too well" category is just the opposite. Across the entire range of strength of partisanship, Republicans in scandal districts fared worse than Republicans in non-scandal districts, who in turn fared slightly worse than Democrats in non-scandal districts. It seems that even those who identified strongly with the other party were much more willing to give the incumbent a positive honesty rating when the incumbent was not tainted by scandal.

Thus, our results show that scandal influenced the 2006 vote choice, and that scandal altered voters' perception of their incumbent's level of honesty. Further, the fact that scandal mattered for honesty but not competence suggests that scandal operated on voters' perceptions with at least some level of precision. Following up on this point, the last matter to be considered is whether scandal produced spillover effects that hurt the electoral prospects of scandal-free Republicans in 2006. Spillover did apparently occur in some open seats, as voters elected Democrats to replace Tom DeLay, Mark Foley, and Bob Ney, Republicans forced by scandal to resign their posts. But what of those Republican incumbents who defended their seat? Did the scandals faced by their colleagues complicate their own re-election bid?

(a) Republican Scandal Districts

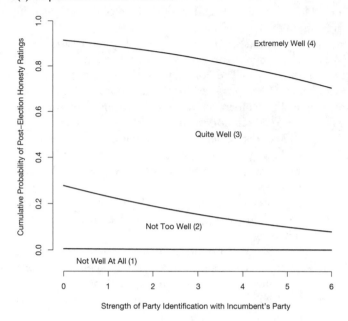

(b) Republican Non-Scandal Districts

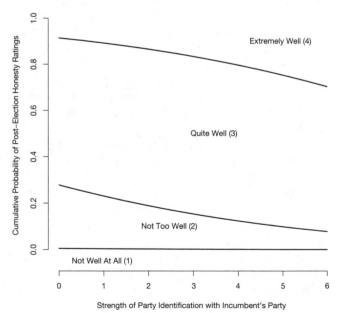

(c) Democratic Non-Scandal Districts

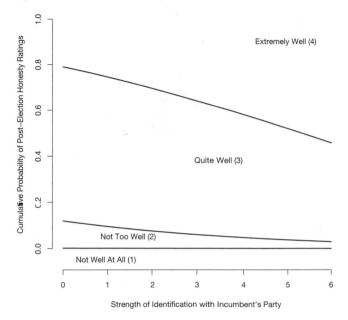

Figure 5.2 Cumulative Probabilities of Post-Election Honesty Ratings of House
Incumbents, Panel Respondents.

Note: All cumulative probability plots hold the level of the pre-election honesty rating at its mean value.

The question posed here defies easy answer. Results in Tables 5.2 and 5.3 reveal that *something* about being Republican was an electoral liability in 2006, but this hardly proves that scandal produced a spillover effect. The hypothesis under consideration is that voters thought less of all Republican incumbents because of the misdeeds of a few. To gain leverage on this hypothesis, we again make use of data on voters' perception of their incumbent's level of honesty. The analyses in Tables 5.4 and 5.5 establish that scandal induced a downgrading of the honesty rating of scandal-plagued incumbents. If spillover occurred, it follows that such a downgrading should be observable even among scandal-free Republican incumbents.

Panel respondents in the 2006 CES were posed the very same honesty question before and after the election. If scandal caused voters to think worse of even scandal-free incumbents, then post-election honesty ratings should lag behind the corresponding pre-election marks. With spillover operationalized in this manner, the data in Figures 5.3a and 5.3b for Republican incumbents and Figure 5.3c for Democrats reveal no such effects. Comparing Republicans implicated in scandals with scandal-free Republicans and scandal-free Democrats, we see that Republicans facing allegations of misconduct had

(a) Republican Scandal Districts

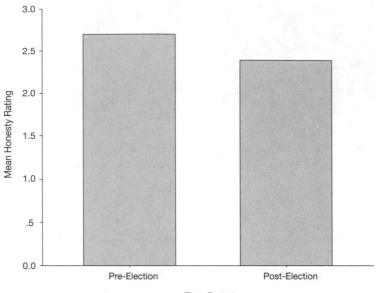

(b) Republican Non-Scandal Districts

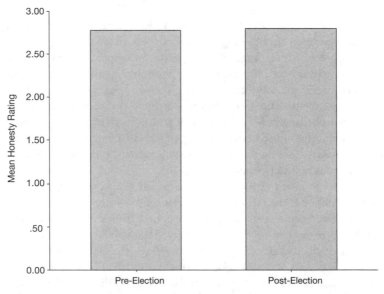

(c) Democratic Non-Scandal Districts

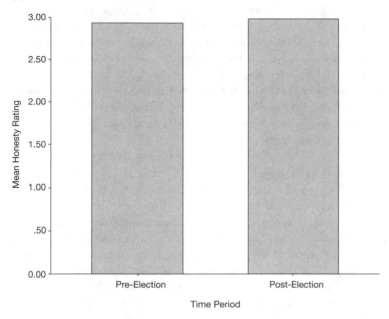

Figure 5.3 Mean Honesty Ratings of House Incumbents Before and After Election Day.

the lowest pre-election mean honesty rating. This is not surprising given that some information about scandal was available to most respondents by the time of their pre-election interview. However, despite starting with the lowest value, the mean honesty rating for scandal-plagued Republicans declined by a statistically-significant amount from the pre-election interview to the post-election interview.[18] This is evidence that events transpiring over the course of the campaign alerted voters to the allegations faced by these incumbents. But what is critical in these results is that no corresponding drop in mean honesty rating is observed for scandal-free Republican House members. For both scandal-free Democrats and Republicans, the mean honesty rating inched up negligibly, yielding no evidence whatsoever of a scandal spillover effect.[19]

Conclusions

In this chapter, we have sought to provide insight regarding how, and to what extent, scandal mattered in the 2006 House elections. Scandal unquestionably was among the many factors that contributed to the Republicans' loss of Congress in 2006. Numerous Republican House members found themselves embroiled in a scandal. Although some of these incumbents won re-election, scandal was a force in several of the races in which Republican incumbents were toppled or Republican-held open seats swung to the Democrats. Our best estimate is that scandal was the decisive force in as many as 13 of the seats lost by the Republicans in 2006. Our analyses have demonstrated that allegations of misconduct led some voters to downgrade their assessment of their incumbent's level of honesty, and, more importantly, to turn against their incumbent on Election Day. What we have not found, however, is concrete evidence that scandal produced spillover effects. For scandal-free Republican incumbents who fared poorly in the 2006 elections, culpability does not rest with their disgraced colleagues.

Four aspects of our findings warrant emphasis. First, scandal was a factor in the vote. In seats held by Republicans heading into the 2006 elections, our analysis shows that scandal brought a substantial drop in vote margins and in the probability of a vote for the incumbent party's candidate in both defended and open seats. But second, although sizeable, the mean effects of scandal were not crippling. Most tellingly, scandal-plagued Republican House incumbents in 2006 lost more electoral support for being Republican than for being accused of wrongdoing. Further, although scandal cost Republican candidates between 4 and 7 percentage points in the final vote tallies, the effect is less than that seen in past aggregate analyses (Peters and Welch 1980; Welch and Hibbing 1997). Third, the electoral effects of scandal did not operate wholly at the elite level. It is possible that an incumbent's involvement in scandal might have aided the opposing party in its efforts to recruit a high-quality, well-funded candidate, and nothing in our results suggests that this did not occur in 2006. However, data from the 2006 CES reveal that scandal corresponded with lower appraisals of an incumbent's level of honesty, and, as importantly, that scandal did not alter perceptions of competence. Together, these findings suggest that many voters were aware of and responsive to allegations questioning the integrity of some incumbents. Lastly, the rising tide did not swamp all ships. It is difficult to devise a definitive test regarding whether scandal hurt all Republicans in 2006. The possibility of marginal indirect effects certainly should not be ignored. For instance, were Republicans not placed on the defensive by scandal, the Republican party may have been able to do more to bolster scandal-free incumbents in vulnerable districts. But the steady stream of news about the likes of Jack Abramoff, Mark Foley, Bob Ney, and Don Sherwood produced no discernible effects on voters' perceptions of the honesty of scandal-free Republicans.

To a substantial degree, present results corroborate past findings regarding the electoral significance of scandal. As in previous research, we have seen that scandal did matter in 2006, but it hardly dominated the elections. Viewed more broadly, two key implications emerge from present findings. First, to the extent that scandal provided several Democrats with their margin of victory, these seats constitute targets of opportunity for Republicans in 2008 and beyond. Memories of implicated incumbents will fade, and Republican challengers will be able to highlight the fact that some of these Democratic incumbents are a poor fit for their district. The Democrats' majority in the House is nearly as thin as was the Republican majority prior to the election. A strong showing by Republicans in the next round of elections may return some of these seats to Republican control.

Second, if there is a lesson in present results regarding the collective wisdom of the electorate, we see that lesson as positive. Like Popkin (1994), we consider it reasonable for voters to draw on information about an incumbent's competence and integrity. Voters *should* desire a skilled and principled representative, and if strong evidence of malfeasance emerges, voters *should* take that information into account when ascertaining whether their incumbent warrants re-election. But voters also are wise to consider factors other than scandal. And in 2006, they did. As a determinant of the vote, scandal did not trump political considerations, but, importantly, scandal was not cast aside. Given the nature of scandal and of the broader political context in 2006, this outcome strikes us as appropriate.

Notes

1 Quoted in Caroline Daniel, Stephen Wyatt, and Holly Yeager, "Rove Off the Hook as Party Blames Iraq and Individual Ethics," *Financial Times*, 10 November 2006.

2 For examples of these accounts, see Caroline Daniel, Stephen Wyatt, and Holly Yeager, "Rove Off the Hook as Party Blames Iraq and Individual Ethics"; Dana Milbank, "The Thumpees Try Their Luck at the Blame Game," *Washington Post*, 9 November 2006; Lee Drutman, "Myths about the Election," *The Providence Journal*, 25 November 2006; Richard Wolffe, "The Architect's Faulty Specs," *Newsweek*, 20 November 2006; Jim Rutenberg and Adam Nagourney, "A Tough Road Ahead for the President's Closest Adviser," *New York Times*, 19 November 2006; Peter Baker, "Rove Remains Steadfast in the Face of Criticism," *Washington Post*, 12 November 2006. Although discussion of ethics concerns was widespread leading up to the 2006 elections, very little of this discussion centered on charges involving Democratic incumbents. Three exceptions are Patrick Kennedy (D-RI), Alan Mollohan (D-WV), and William Jefferson (D-LA), all of whom were re-elected in 2006.

3 Other analyses reach similar conclusions. For example, John Hood claimed that "the corruption issue played a significant role in at least a dozen GOP House losses." See John Hood, "GOP Car Wreck," *National Review*, 4 December 2006.

4 In this category, we include Arizona's 5th congressional district, California's 11th, Kansas' 2nd, New Hampshire's 2nd, New York's 19th and 20th, North Carolina's 11th, and Pennsylvania's 7th, 8th, and 10th.

5 These include Florida's 16th congressional district, Ohio's 18th, and Texas' 22nd.

6 Martha T. Moore, "Sex and Money Scandals Figure into Some House Races," *USA Today*, 8 November 2006.
7 This phrase was used by Democrats frequently during the 2006 election cycle as a means to disparage Republican congressional leadership. For a discussion, see Rich Lowry, "The Culture of Corruption Loses," *National Review Online*, 10 November 2006.
8 For a history of the Abramoff scandal, see Stone 2006.
9 Todd Mason and John Shiffman, "FBI is Said to be Probing Weldon Over His Influence," *Philadelphia Inquirer*, 14 October 2006.
10 Bill Gertz, "FBI Chief Orders Internal Probe: Inquiry Centers on Pre-Election Leak of Investigation of Lawmaker," *Washington Times*, 27 September 2007.
11 Scott Shepard, " 'Deeply Sorry' Hastert Digs In: Speaker Says He Didn't Know about Explicit E-Mails." *Atlanta Journal Constitution*, 6 October 2006.
12 For related laboratory approaches, see Rundquist, Strom, and Peters (1977) and Funk (1996).
13 The negative influence of scandal is elevated by more than 1 percentage point when we include those incumbents who did not face major party competition in 2004. The only incumbents implicated in scandal in 2006 who did not face a major party challenge in 2004 were Tom Feeney and Don Sherwood.
14 The models exclude districts from Louisiana, due to its unusual electoral system, and thus omit the third Democrat implicated in scandal in 2006, William Jefferson.
15 These nine Republicans were J.D. Hayworth (AZ 5th), Richard Pombo (CA 11th), Jim Ryun (KS 2nd), Charlie Bass (NH 2nd), Sue Kelly (NY 19th), John Sweeney (NY 20th), Charles Taylor (NC 11th), Mike Fitzpatrick (PA 8th), and Don Sherwood (PA 10th).
16 Districts in our sample coded as scandal districts were AZ 5th, CA 4th, CA 11th, FL 16th, IL 14th, KS 2nd, MO 7th, NC 11th, NH 2nd, NM 1st, NY 19th, NY 20th, OH 15th, OH 18th, PA 6th, PA 7th, PA 8th, PA 10th, RI 1st, TX 22nd, and WV 1st. All districts other than RI 1st and WV 1st were Republican seats in 2006.
17 RI 1st had six respondents, and WV 1st had four.
18 Because the two bars in Figures 5.3a, 5.3b, and 5.3c include the same respondents interviewed before and after the election, significance levels are calculated using paired *t*-tests.
19 Given that scandal-free Democrats have higher honesty ratings than do scandal-free Republicans, an alternate interpretation of the data in Figures 5.3a, 5.3b, and 5.3c is that there was indeed a scandal spillover effect, but one that had already operated by the time our pre-election data were gathered. This seems unlikely given that many of our pre-election interviews were conducted before the Foley, Ney, and Sherwood stories received media attention. Nonetheless, to explore this possibility, we split pre-election interviews at the median by date, and compared honesty ratings for scandal-free Republicans as measured before and after the cut-off date. The mean was *higher* (although insignificantly so) after the cut-off date, precisely the opposite of what would have been observed if campaign events activated a late-game scandal spillover.

References

Alford, John, Holly Teeters, Daniel S. Ward, and Rick K. Wilson. 1994. "Overdraft: The Political Cost of Congressional Malfeasance." *Journal of Politics* 56: 788–801.

Banducci, Susan A. and Jeffrey A. Karp. 1994. "The Electoral Consequences of Scandal and Reapportionment in the 1992 House Elections." *American Politics Quarterly* 22: 3–26.

Canache, Damarys, Jeffery J. Mondak, and Ernesto Cabrera. 2000. "Voters and the Personal Vote: A Countefactual Simulation." *Political Research Quarterly* 53: 663–76.

Dimock, Michael A. and Gary C. Jacobson. 1995. "Checks and Choices: The House Bank Scandal's Impact on Voters in 1992." *Journal of Politics* 57: 1143–59.

Funk, Carolyn L. 1996. "The Impact of Scandal on Candidate Evaluations: An Experimental Test of the Role of Candidate Traits." *Political Behavior* 18: 1–24.

Groseclose, Timothy and Keith Krehbiel. 1994. "Golden Parachutes, Rubber Checks, and Strategic Retirements from the 102d House." *American Journal of Political Science* 38: 75–99.

Jacobson, Gary C. and Michael A. Dimock. 1994. "Checking Out: The Effects of Bank Overdrafts on the 1992 House Elections." *American Journal of Political Science* 38: 601–24.

Kulisheck, Michael R. and Jeffery J. Mondak. 1996. "Candidate Quality and the Congressional Vote: A Causal Connection?" *Electoral Studies* 15: 237–53.

Maestas, Cherie, Sarah A. Fulton, L. Sandy Maisel, and Walter J. Stone. 2006. "When to Risk it? Institutions, Ambitions, and the Decision to Run for the U.S. House." *American Political Science Review*. 100: 195–208.

McCurley, Carl and Jeffery J. Mondak. 1995. "Inspected by #1184063113: The Influence of Incumbents' Competence and Integrity in U.S. House Elections." *American Journal of Political Science* 39: 864–85.

Mondak, Jeffery J. 1995. "Competence, Integrity, and the Electoral Success of Congressional Incumbents." *Journal of Politics* 57: 1043–69.

Mondak, Jeffery J. and Robert Huckfeldt. 2006. "The Accessibility and Utility of Candidate Character in Electoral Decision Making." *Electoral Studies* 25: 20–34.

Mondak, Jeffery J., Carl McCurley, and Steven R. L. Millman. 1999. "The Impact of Incumbents' Levels of Competence and Integrity in the 1994 and 1996 U.S. House Elections." In Herbert E. Weisberg and Janet M. Box-Steffensmeier, eds., *Reelection 1996: How Americans Voted*. New York: Chatham House.

Peters, John G. and Susan Welch. 1980. "The Effects of Charges of Corruption on Voting Behavior in Congressional Elections." *American Political Science Review* 74: 697–708.

Popkin, Samuel L. 1994. *The Reasoning Voter: Communication and Persuasion in Presidential Campaigns*, 2nd ed. Chicago: University of Chicago Press.

Rundquist, Barry S., Gerald S. Strom, and John G. Peters. 1977. "Corrupt Politicians and Their Electoral Support: Some Experimental Observations." *American Political Science Review* 71: 954–63.

Stone, Peter. H. 2006. *Heist: Superlobbyist Jack Abramoff, His Republican Allies, and the Buying of Washington*. New York: Farrar, Straus and Giroux.

Stone, Walter J. and L. Sandy Maisel. 2003. "The Not-So-Simple Calculus of Winning: Potential U.S. House Candidates' Nomination and General Election Chances." *Journal of Politics* 65: 951–77.

Stone, Walter J., L. Sandy Maisel, and Cherie D. Maestas. 2004. "Quality Counts: Extending the Strategic Political Model of Incumbent Deterrence." *American Journal of Political Science* 48: 479–95.

Welch, Susan and John R. Hibbing. 1997. "The Effects of Charges of Corruption on Voting Behavior in Congressional Elections, 1982–1990." *Journal of Politics* 59: 226–39.

Chapter 6

Perceptions and Realities of Issue Voting

Dona-Gene Mitchell

> This tendency of voters to attribute desired policy positions to candidates they like rather than to like candidates who have desirable policy positions is incredibly damning to those who stress the causal importance of policies.
> (Hibbing and Theiss-Morse (2002, 22))

In American politics, each election cycle provides citizens an opportunity to voice their views on the political direction of the country. Policy failures weigh heavily in voters' minds as they decide how to cast their ballots. As a result, incumbents often pay the price for unpopular policies associated with their party. This certainly appears to have been the case in the 2006 midterm elections where the Democrats captured 30 seats in the House and six in the Senate, more than enough to regain control of both chambers. To many, the Democratic sweep of Congress signaled widespread dissatisfaction among voters eager for policy change. Most observers concluded that issues, particularly President Bush's policies in Iraq, may have been the deciding force that pushed voters toward the Democrats. In short, issues appeared to have influenced voters' evaluations in the 2006 elections. Empirically assessing how issues influenced electoral decision making is my purpose in this chapter. Before reviewing the potential ways issues can influence voters, I begin by briefly discussing some of the central issues that came into play during the 2006 campaigns.

Congressional races, especially in midterm years, typically are determined by domestic and local issues, but in 2006 such concerns were largely over-shadowed by the war in Iraq and national security issues. In an ironic twist of events, many of the same Republicans who campaigned in 2002 and 2004 on their party's foreign policy strengths desperately were trying to distance themselves from an unpopular war and the president behind it. In the days and months preceding the elections, the Bush administration emphasized its unwavering commitment to continue "full speed ahead" in Iraq, while Democrats offered a change of course by arguing for phased troop withdrawal.[1] Even Saddam Hussein's execution on the eve of Election Day was not enough to relieve the public's disenchantment with the situation in Iraq.[2] Exit poll data revealed that a solid majority, nearly six in ten, disapproved of the war, and the likelihood of voting Democratic increased with the importance attached to the war.[3] Political scientist Thomas Patterson's assessment of the election was simply: "Iraq is the biggest single factor for the shift in opinion. This election is really a referendum on Iraq."[4]

Other foreign policy issues believed to have had a bearing on voters include terrorism and immigration policy. Since the terrorist attacks of September 11th, voters had been willing to entrust national security to Republicans. Although most Americans still considered terrorism a very important issue— nearly three-fourths according to exit poll data—less than half were willing to identify either party as more capable of protecting the nation from future terrorist attacks.[5] In the early months of 2006, immigration policy debate, centered on proposed legislation to build a 700-mile fence along the U.S.–Mexican border and legalize millions of undocumented workers, sparked widespread unrest that erupted in massive protest demonstrations across the country. By November, the issue of immigration reform had taken a back seat to the war in Iraq. Nevertheless, some analysts argued that immigration may have been a deciding factor in pockets of the country with large Latino populations.[6]

Although foreign policy dominated the 2006 campaigns, a host of domestic issues also received significant attention, including the unsteady state of the economy and President Bush's delayed reaction in the aftermath of Hurricane Katrina. The debate over stem cell research received extensive coverage in several local races and generated national controversy when conservative radio host Rush Limbaugh accused Michael J. Fox of using his acting skills to play up the symptoms of Parkinson's disease in several political advertisements where Fox asked viewers to vote Democratic.[7] On his show, Limbaugh went so far as to state, "He is exaggerating the effects of the disease. He's moving all around and shaking and it's clearly an act."[8]

The salience of issues in 2006 is undeniable. Less clear is *how* issues influenced electoral decision making. In this chapter, using data from the 2006 Congressional Elections Study (CES), I aim to assess how voters viewed and used issue information when evaluating their incumbent House member. Although issue information pervaded the campaigns, this does not mean that individuals considered issues important to their House vote. The 2006 survey provides a unique opportunity to explore the importance citizens attached to issues when deciding how to cast their ballots. The next logical step is to explore how well voters' perceptions correspond with reality. In other words, if voters perceive themselves as policy-minded, did they in fact use issue information to inform their assessments of the candidates? And if so, how did issue information contribute to candidate evaluations? I seek to address these questions below. First, I review how issues may influence citizens' evaluations of political candidates based on the lessons learned from prior political science research. I will then report and assess my findings.

Issue Information and Electoral Decision Making

Despite decades of research on how citizens navigate the political world, questions abound regarding how voters make use of issue information. General consensus in the literature is that issues probably matter in some way. There is less agreement, however, as to how citizens process and store information about a candidate's stances on the issues. Prior research points to several possible scenarios, which I explore in more detail below. Perhaps individuals factor issues directly into their evaluations by considering which candidate's positions on the issues are closest to their own. It is hard to ignore the cognitive demands such calculations require of voters, especially within the context of low-information House races where news coverage is less abundant and candidates rarely discuss their issue positions. Thus, it may be more realistic that voters encounter issue information, use it to update their impressions of the candidates and then discard the specifics in the name of cognitive efficiency. Using data from the 2006 CES, I examine whether voters had an adequate information base to engage in the type of classic issue voting described in the first scenario. Did voters form their views of the candidates on the basis of policy-specific information or were their assessments influenced by more extraneous considerations such as partisanship or ideology? I also explore whether voters were more likely to engage in on-line processing as portrayed in the second scenario. When individuals are presented with issue information, do they use it to update their summary judgments of the candidates regardless of whether they estimate policy distance measures of the sort associated with issue voting?

Issue Information and Proximity Preferences

The extent to which issue positions matter in American politics remains unclear. On the one hand, politicians behave as if their electoral fates rest on the policy stances they take. Likewise, campaign coverage often emphasizes the candidates' views on current hot button issues. But on the other hand, most citizens know little about politics generally, and even less about policy specifics (Delli Carpini and Keeter 1996). A substantial literature explores whether individuals are likely to factor issue positions directly into their candidate evaluations by estimating policy distance measures, a deliberate and time-consuming task. As a preview of the findings to be reviewed below, the lack of policy-specific knowledge among the electorate is a major handicap that most voters are unwilling to overcome. Rather than policy preferences driving candidate evaluations, candidate preferences are much more likely to determine policy preferences (Page and Jones 1979; Hibbing and Theiss-Morse 2002). For example, a voter is likely to feel favorably toward a candidate and then infer that the candidate shares her views on the issues—regardless of whether the candidate does, in fact, share the voter's position. Knowledge of the candidate's actual policy positions is irrelevant.

One way issues can inform citizen preferences is based on the spatial proximity between the voter's positions on the issues and the issue positions held by the candidates. As outlined by Downs (1957), voters who engage in what is often referred to as issue voting should support candidates whose issue positions are closest to their own (see also Hotelling 1929; and Davis, Hinich, and Ordeshook 1970). For instance, a voter who supports loosening the current restrictions on federal funding of embryonic stem cell research should feel more favorable toward a candidate who supports such research as long as it only involves currently existing stem cell lines than toward a candidate who opposes federally funding stem cell research of any kind. The candidate who supports only slight restrictions on stem cell research has a position much closer to the voter's view that stem cell research should have fewer restrictions as opposed to the candidate who opposes stem cell research regardless of the circumstances. To process issue information in this manner is cognitively demanding. Not only do voters need to possess knowledge of the issues and hold actual positions on the issues (and such actual positions may or may not exist—see Converse 1964), but they also must be aware of the candidates' positions on the issues.

The idea that citizens will favor candidates based on their issue positions enjoys normative appeal. The evidence, however, suggests that when citizens use issue information to inform their preferences, most probably do not do so by attending to which candidate's issue positions are closest to their own in the rigorous manner associated with classic depictions of issue voting. Rather than investing the time and cognitive effort to estimate the proximity of the candidates' issue positions, voters are much more likely to evaluate candidates on the basis of other considerations such as partisanship, personality, or character (e.g., Campbell *et al.* 1960; Converse and Markus 1979; Popkin 1991; McCurley and Mondak 1995). These kinds of considerations tend to be used more frequently because voters find such information to be highly cognitively accessible.

Additionally, candidates frequently find it in their best interest to use ambiguous campaign rhetoric when it comes to discussing policy positions (e.g. Page and Brody 1972; Alvarez and Franklin 1994; Hinich and Munger 1994). It becomes incredibly difficult for voters to calculate relative issue distances. Left with only half of the equation, citizens often will project their own issue positions onto their preferred candidates. Put more bluntly by Page and Jones (1979, 1078): "might not some of a candidate's supporters, in lieu of genuine opinions, give facile responses to policy questions corresponding to what they think their preferred candidate stands for?" In their analysis of two presidential elections, Page and Jones (1979) found that issue voting did occur but that candidate preferences influenced issue positions much more than issue positions influenced candidate preferences. In other words, voters appeared to attribute issue positions to their favored candidates rather than support candidates based on their policy stances. If anything, such an inferential process seemingly should be all the more likely in typical low-information congressional elections.

Issue Information and On-Line Evaluations

Perhaps the most common critique of classic issue voting is that citizens simply fail to live up to its expectations. In short, such models may be psychologically unrealistic. In a series of papers, Lodge and his colleagues (Lodge, McGraw, and Stroh 1989; Lodge, Stroh, and Wahlke 1990; McGraw, Lodge, and Stroh 1990; Lodge, Steenbergen, and Brau 1995) propose a specific alternate, on-line processing or impression-driven processing. The primary appeal of the on-line model is its cognitive efficiency. Lodge, McGraw, and Stroh caution, "When, as here, the citizen is conceived as a bounded rationalist, it is incumbent on us to construct models of candidate evaluation that do not require more capacity and processing skills than human beings are known to possess" (1989, 402). Building on research in psychology (see especially Hastie and Park 1986), Lodge and his colleagues contend that specific information can influence candidate evaluations even if voters later fail to recall that information. What happens, the authors suggest, is that voters attend to new information—whether about policy positions, candidate characteristics, etc.—long enough to update their summary evaluations of a candidate. Later, the summary evaluation is recalled—voters know to what extent they favor or oppose a given candidate—even though the specific substantive data that informed that summary judgment is not stored in memory.

Studying the dynamics of information processing within an actual campaign is incredibly difficult. As a result, most scholars have elected to take advantage of the strengths of the controlled experiment. The core studies reported by Lodge and his colleagues took place within the confines of the laboratory where participants were exposed to a single round of information exposure. Additionally experimental studies have incorporated dynamic elements into their carefully crafted mock campaigns. For instance, Lodge *et al.* (1995) investigate memory decay over a span of 31 days and Redlawsk (2001) develops a computer-based experiment to simulate the changing availability of information during a campaign. Despite the ability to monitor the release and effect of issue information, findings from past experiments leave at least some doubt as to how voter behavior in an intense 20-minute or half-hour "campaign" relates to the actions of voters in real-world elections, voters who enter elections with prior opinions about many candidates, and who tune in and tune out of a given contest multiple times over the course of two or three months. I see it as at least possible that information processing operates differently when voters receive an abundance of issue information in the span of 20 or 30 minutes about a hypothetical candidate as occurred in previous experimental studies versus when the voter receives pieces of issue information about a House candidate over the span of an actual weeks-long low-information campaign. Using data from the CES, I seek to investigate this possibility by providing voters issue information during an actual election campaign.

Distorted Perceptions: Voters and Issues

Although scholars generally agree that issues matter for electoral decision making, exactly *how* issues influence voters' decisions remains a matter of debate. A related and understudied question is how important are issues to voters when formulating a vote choice. Past studies have focused on how citizens process issue information without first assessing the extent to which voters value such information. Before evaluating how issues may have mattered in the 2006 House elections, let us take a closer look at whether voters considered issues important when deciding how to cast their votes. Post-election data from the 2006 survey provide unique insight as to the perceived importance of numerous factors in the decision to vote for the chosen U.S. House candidate. Respondents were asked to indicate how important or unimportant the candidate's positions on the issues and voting record were to their vote choice.[9] Data on the importance of these two factors are depicted in Figure 6.1. Respondents overwhelmingly perceive themselves as valuing the candidate's issue positions; 83.1 percent of respondents considered the candidate's issue positions important to their vote decision. Moreover, just over half of the respondents selected the "very important" category on our 5-point measure. Similarly, 60.1 percent of respondents claimed that the candidate's voting record was important when deciding how to vote. Most respondents perceive of themselves as policy-minded when forming their vote choice. According to an overwhelming majority of respondents, the candidate's issue stances and even the candidate's voting record were important determinants of their 2006 vote choice. Based on these perceptions, we do not know yet *how* voters processed issue information but we should at least expect voters to make use of issue information in some manner when evaluating the candidates. Political scientists may have concerns regarding the cognitive demands of classic issue voting, but voters themselves appear undaunted.

By most democratic standards, a policy-minded electorate is certainly desirable. After all, what better way to ensure representation and hold government accountable than if voters evaluate candidates on the basis of their issue stances? But additional probing of the data reveals reasons to suspect that these self-perceptions among voters may represent nothing more than unfulfilled expectations and wishful thinking. Although respondents perceive of themselves as valuing the candidates' issue positions and voting records, findings indicate that citizens may not use issue information to inform their views. If respondents value issue information as they claim, then it is not unreasonable to expect them to possess knowledge of the candidates' issue stances *and* to use that information to inform their views of the candidates. This assumption encompasses the basic logic of issue voting. At a minimum, issue voting requires some knowledge on the part of the voter. In short, before issues can influence decisions, voters must possess knowledge about the issues and the candidates' positions on those issues. It is possible with present data to at least gain a sense of whether voters' views of their incumbent's issue positions stem from factual information about their representative or if voters are more likely to project issue positions onto the candidate based on more readily accessible information such as partisanship and ideology.

Respondents were asked to place their district's House candidates' views on three issues: troop withdrawal from Iraq, fighting terrorism using the Patriot Act, and stem cell research.[10] In 2006, these three issues received extensive coverage by the media and the candidates. Information about these particular policies was widely available. If voters were indeed mindful of the issues as they claim, did they use this information to inform their views about their incumbent's issue positions? In the case that issue information specific to the House incumbent had an effect, it is reasonable to expect that the incumbent's actual voting record would influence perceptions of the incumbent's issue positions. Conversely, if respondents deduced their incumbent's policy preferences based on more extraneous cues, it may be that the incumbent's actual stand

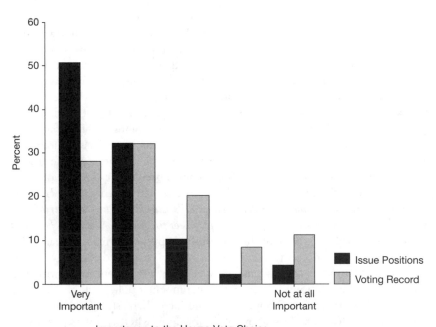

Figure 6.1 Perceived Importance of Issues to the House Vote.

on the issues had little or no effect on respondents' views and other factors may have been more influential, factors such as the incumbent's partisanship or ideology.

It is possible to test this account using present data. With the incumbent's perceived policy position modeled as a function of the incumbent's partisanship, ideology, and the relevant roll-call vote, this offers an opportunity to assess if voters' views of their incumbents' issue positions are indeed factually informed. The roll-call measure tells how the House member actually voted on the issue in Congress. Therefore, results from this model will reveal whether respondents formed their views of the incumbents' issue stances on the basis of genuine policy-specific information or if voters were more likely to infer the candidates' policy positions based on partisanship or ideology irrespective of the incumbents' actual legislative actions. The incumbent's partisanship is coded 1 for Republicans and 0 for Democrats. Ideology of the incumbent is measured using ADA scores[11] and the policy vote is coded 1 for a yes vote and 0 for a no vote.[12]

Coefficient estimates from three versions of the logit model, representing each of the three issues, are reported in Table 6.1. When it comes to withdrawing troops from Iraq or fighting terrorism at the expense of civil liberties, respondents rely heavily on the incumbent's partisanship to determine where they believe their member of Congress stands on these issues. The effect for partisanship indicates that, controlling for the impact of other information, when the incumbent is a Republican, respondents are more likely to believe their representative leans toward having U.S. troops remain in Iraq until it is secure rather than having the troops withdrawn as soon as possible. Respondents are also more likely to believe that when the incumbent is a Republican, their member of Congress leans toward fighting terrorism with measures such as the Patriot Act at the expense of protecting civil liberties. In the case of Iraq and stem cell research, ideology has a significant effect on the incumbent's perceived policy positions. Thus, controlling for the impact of other information, the more liberal the incumbent, the more likely respondents are to believe that their representative leans toward withdrawing the troops and supporting stem cell research. The notably absent effect in each of these models involves the incumbent's roll-call vote on the given policy. *How the respondent's House member actually voted on bills related to Iraq, the Patriot Act, and stem cell research did not affect perceptions of the incumbents' issue positions on these policies.* Perceptions of the incumbent's policy leanings appear to be projections based on considerations such as the party and ideology of the incumbent. Although respondents view themselves as concerned with the candidates' issue positions, in reality, the incumbent's policy actions were not used to inform their views about where the incumbent stood on the issues. This finding at least casts a shadow of doubt upon whether voters possess an information base that is adequate for classic issue voting. In order to estimate policy distance measures voters must know where they stand on the issues *and* the candidates' stances on the issue. I have shown that voters' views of the candidates' issue positions are not grounded in reality. Without this critical piece of the equation, voters in 2006 may have used issue information but it does not appear that they did so in the manner prescribed by classic issue voting.

If citizens did not factor issues directly into their votes via a process akin to classic issue voting, perhaps issues still influenced political judgments through on-line processing. That is, perhaps voters *did* attend to policy information, and *did* use such information to update appraisals of their incumbents, but then forgot the details of the policy information once those updates were formed. It should be clear that this is a difficult thesis to explore, especially outside of the laboratory. However, the results in Table 6.1 call this account into question. After all, the models do not test whether respondents *recalled* their House members' votes, but rather whether those policy votes mattered for perceptions of the incumbents irrespective of whether the votes themselves had been committed to memory by the respondents.

As a further test of this account within the context of an actual election while controlling the release of issue information, I included a set of district-specific items on the 2006 survey. I supplied respondents with information pertaining to their incumbent's voting record on two issues under the guise of asking them a pair of survey questions that recorded how much respondents agreed

Table 6.1 Unfounded Perceptions of Incumbent Policy Positions

Variable	Iraq: Troop Withdrawal		Patriot Act		Stem Cell Research	
	Coefficient	S.E.	Coefficient	S.E.	Coefficient	S.E.
Partisanship	2.09***	0.46	1.73***	0.43	0.70	0.57
Ideology	−0.01*	0.01	−0.002	0.01	−0.02**	0.008
Policy Vote	0.19	0.27	0.44	0.33	0.04	0.32
1st Cut Point	−1.49	0.62	−1.49	0.62	−2.16	0.66
2nd Cut Point	−0.20	0.60	−0.20	0.60	−0.93	0.64
3rd Cut Point	1.62	0.60	1.62	0.60	0.39	0.63
4th Cut Point	3.33	0.61	3.33	0.61	1.63	0.64
N	521		518		459	
Wald χ^2	145.64		105.40		78.55	
Pseudo R^2	0.16		0.10		0.09	

Notes:
Dependent Variable: Incumbent's Perceived Policy Position
* Indicates logit coefficient estimate significant at 0.10 level
** Indicates logit coefficient estimate significant at 0.05 level
*** Indicates logit coefficient estimate significant at 0.001 level
Robust standard errors are reported

or disagreed with their representative's recent votes on two issues.[13] The first question provided information about an issue where the incumbent had voted along party lines, while the second question revealed a vote the incumbent cast that was at odds with his partisan affiliation. For example, respondents from Tim Johnson's (R-IL) district were asked whether they agreed with his recent vote to pass a constitutional amendment to ban gay marriage and his vote to increase the federal minimum wage. These two types of questions were included to account for the possibility that partisan consistent and partisan inconsistent information may have differential influences on candidate evaluations. Early on the pre-election survey, respondents were asked to rate their favorability toward the candidates. Then, near the end of the survey, respondents were asked to indicate their approval of their incumbent's job performance.[14] Thus it is possible to see if new issue information about the House incumbent influenced evaluations within the short span of the survey that lasted an average of 33 minutes.

The dependent variable, *Incumbent Job Performance Approval*, is constructed with data from the 4-point approval measure of the incumbent's performance as a legislator (1 = strongly approve to 4 = strongly disapprove). Recall that this question was asked near the end of the pre-election survey. The first independent variable, *Initial Incumbent Favorability*, is measured using the first question on the pre-election survey about the House candidates, the 5-point favorability scale (1 = most unfavorable to 5 = most favorable).[15] This measure represents the baseline impressions of the incumbent before the new issue information was released. Even if, according to on-line processing, voters adjust their initial impressions of the incumbent based on the new issue information, initial impressions should still matter because they represent the accumulated prior evaluations of the candidate. Thus I expect to obtain a large positive coefficient for *Initial Incumbent Favorability*. I also control for the incumbent's partisanship and ideology by including two variables. The first variable, *Partisanship*, is measured using a modified 7-point scale (0 = the respondent strongly identifies with the party opposite of the incumbent's to 6 = the respondent strongly identifies with the party of the incumbent). The second variable, *Ideology*, is constructed in a similar manner (0 = the respondent's ideological leaning was opposite of the incumbent's to 6 = the respondent's ideological leaning was the same as the incumbent's).[16] To be cautious I include both variables but I do not expect either to have significant effects on candidate evaluations because the variable, *Initial Incumbent Favorability*, should capture the respondent's initial impression of the incumbent which presumably is formed in part on the basis of the representative's partisanship and ideology. Regressing the respondent's initial impression of the candidate on the incumbent's partisanship and ideology shows that this is indeed the case.

According to the logic of on-line processing, voters will use new issue information to update their candidate evaluations. If this is the case, informing respondents how their district's representative recently voted should lead respondents to adjust their impressions of the incumbent. Two critical variables are used to represent exposure to new issue information. The first issue variable, *Consistent Vote*, is coded 0 (respondent strongly disagrees with the incumbent's partisan consistent vote) to 4 (respondent strongly agrees with the incumbent's partisan consistent vote). The second issue variable, *Inconsistent Vote*, is constructed in exactly the same manner but pertains to the vote where the incumbent trespassed party lines. A significant effect for either or both of these issue variables would suggest that voters, at least in the short run, appear to incorporate issues via an on-line process. Whether issues provide any sort of enduring foundation to candidate evaluation would remain an open question that could be addressed with data from the post-election survey. The first step is to evaluate if issues mattered in the short period of 30 minutes, about the time it took most people to complete the survey.

Although the initial impression of the candidate should capture the effects of any prior information exposure voters may have encountered regarding the three popular issues of Iraq, the Patriot Act, and stem cell research,[17] it is possible that the survey may have primed respondents to consider these three policies. To account for this possibility, I also include three policy distance measures: *Iraq Policy Distance*, *Patriot Act Policy Distance*, and *Stem Cell Policy Distance*. Each is constructed by taking the absolute value of the difference between the respondent's self placement and the respondent's placement of the incumbent on the three policy issues. Note that any effects for these variables would suggest a circularity to candidate evaluation: voters use the incumbent's party and ideology (and *not* the incumbent's actual roll-call vote) to infer the incumbent's policy stance, and then use that policy stance to assess the incumbent.

The coefficient estimates from the logit model are reported in Table 6.2. The large coefficient for the respondent's initial impression of the incumbent measured at the beginning of the survey—the variable *Initial Incumbent Favorability*—was to be expected. Thus the respondent's feelings toward his or her representative at the beginning of the pre-election survey are a good indication of how the respondent will evaluate the incumbent at the end of the survey. It is also no surprise that the incumbent's partisanship and ideological leanings—the variables *Partisanship* and *Ideology*—are insignificant because these considerations should be captured in the measure of the incumbent's initial favorability rating. All of the policy distance measures are correctly signed, indicating that as the distance between the respondent's and incumbent's perceived positions on the issues grow, candidate evaluations suffer. However, only the variable that involves stem cell research, *Stem Cell Policy Distance*, is significant. The fact that the policy distance measures are largely inconsequential is to be expected. The effect of prior issue exposure that occurred before completing the survey should be captured by the respondent's initial impression of the incumbent measured at the beginning of the survey.

But what of new issue information released during the survey? Recall that the only new information voters received from the time they provided their initial impression of the candidate to the time they evaluated the incumbent's job performance pertained to the issue stances I revealed that their incumbent took on two recent House votes. Respondents claim that issues are important to them. We have already seen that the prospects for classic issue voting are slim. Respondents do not appear to have an adequate information base necessary to factor issues directly into their evaluations by estimating policy distances. Did voters, then, instantaneously incorporate issues into their evaluations, whether through on-line processing or any other mechanism? According to Table 6.2, they did not. Talk is cheap and respondents were more than willing to report that the candidates' issue positions were important to their vote choice. But even when information about how their incumbent stood on the issues was made available, respondents did not use it to update their summary evaluations.

Insignificant effects for both issue variables—*Consistent Vote* and *Inconsistent Vote*—suggest that new issue information received during the course of a short survey had no effect on candidate evaluations offered less than half an hour later. Because there were no short term effects of new issue information, the prospects of any sort of enduring effects are bleak. Evidence from the post-election survey supports this suspicion. Following the election, respondents were asked how their incumbent voted on the two policies included on the pre-election survey. Most of the post-election interviews were completed two weeks after

Table 6.2 Determinants of House Incumbent Job Performance Approval

Variable	Coefficient	Robust Standard Error
Initial Incumbent Favorability	0.99**	0.14
Partisanship	−0.13	0.08
Ideology	0.08	0.08
Consistent Vote	0.12	0.09
Inconsistent Vote	−0.07	0.09
Iraq Policy Distance	−0.23	0.15
Patriot Act Policy Distance	−0.11	0.12
Stem Cell Policy Distance	−0.32*	0.12
1st Cut Point	−1.19	0.63
2nd Cut Point	0.82	0.64
3rd Cut Point	4.38	0.71

Notes:
Dependent Variable: Incumbent's Job Performance Approval
* Indicates logit coefficient estimate significant at 0.01 level
** Indicates logit coefficient estimate significant at 0.001 level
Observations = 356
Wald χ^2 = 105.94
Pseudo R^2 = 0.23

Table 6.3 House Incumbent Voting Information Recall Rates

	Consistent Vote	Inconsistent Vote
Never Heard Position	57.4%	48.4%
Correctly Identified Position	27.9%	18.5%
Incorrectly Identified Position	14.7%	33.1%

Election Day or a month after most respondents completed the pre-election survey where information was released concerning how the incumbent voted on two pieces of legislation. As seen in Table 6.3, a sizable number of respondents claimed that they had not heard anything about how their incumbent voted; 57.4 percent for the consistent vote where the incumbent adhered to party lines and 48.4 percent for the inconsistent vote where the incumbent's vote was at odds with his partisan affiliation. Although respondents claim that issues are important, a sizable percentage of respondents appear to have largely ignored such information to the point that a month later they never even recall encountering it. For the consistent vote, only 27.9 percent of respondents accurately identified the incumbent's position on the issue and a mere 18.5 percent of respondents correctly recognized the incumbent's inconsistent vote. These findings suggest that voters do not use new issue information to inform their candidate evaluations in the short run and within a month nearly half of respondents forget ever encountering the information.[18]

Conclusions

Issues pervaded the political scene of the 2006 House races and appeared to play a critical role in the election outcome. Observers speculated that the Republicans' stances on the issues led to their downfall and that by offering a change in direction, Democratic candidates were able to capitalize on the situation and sweep the Congress. Concluding that issues matter in a given election is easy. Showing *how* issues matter is a much more difficult task and is the one I have attempted to tackle in this chapter. I have focused on assessing how citizens view and use issue information to inform their candidate evaluations. In short, my analyses reveal a disconnect between perceptions and reality. Voters claim to be policy-minded but do not appear to use issue information to inform their views even when the information is provided to them.

An overwhelming majority of respondents claimed that the candidate's issue positions and voting records were important factors they took into consideration when deciding how to cast their ballot. Evidence of a disconnect emerged when I examined two specific ways suggested by previous research—proximity preferences and on-line processing—that issues could influence electoral decision making. Citizens purport that the candidates' issue positions are important to them, but most voters lack the knowledge necessary to estimate which candidate's issue positions are closest to their own in the manner prescribed by classic issue voting. Most voters are missing an important piece of the equation. In lieu of knowledge about the candidates' actual policy stances, in 2006, voters used extraneous cues such as partisanship and ideology to deduce where the candidates stood on the issues. Voters did not fare well when it came to meeting the demands required to form proximity preferences.

Additionally, respondents exhibited no signs of using on-line updating to process new issue information. By virtue of the study's design, respondents were provided with clear information about the policy stances their incumbent had taken in the past year. Even when this information was made available during the survey, respondents did not use it to update their summary judgments of the candidates offered less than half an hour after receiving the new issue information. In previous research, on-line processing is typically depicted as commencing at the point new information is encountered. An overlooked possibility is that individuals may never attend to new issue information at all. It appears that many respondents may have simply ignored the issue information because after a month almost half of the respondents failed to recognize ever encountering the information in the first place. If citizens do not use issue information to update their impressions of the candidates under conditions where the information search costs are essentially reduced to zero, then it seems improbable that voters will take the time to research the candidates' positions on the issues, positions that at least in low-information House races may be difficult to uncover.

I have shown, first, that citizens lack an adequate information base necessary to form the type of proximity preferences associated with issue voting. Second, even when respondents are hit over the head with the policy stances of their incumbent House member, they still do not use that information to update their impressions of their representative. This finding at least casts doubt on whether individuals are likely to engage in on-line processing because it is less cognitively demanding. Another possibility suggested by my findings is that citizens may simply choose to ignore issue details altogether. What I have not shown is either that 1) issues were completely inconsequential or 2) that on-line processing does not occur at all. I have neither tested nor excluded the possibility that coarse impressionistic views of the issues may have influenced electoral decision making. For instance, one would be hard pressed to find a voter who had not at least considered the situation in Iraq before deciding which House candidate to support. But evaluating issues in a coarse impressionistic manner essentially equates to a form of on-line processing. Thus, even if the logic of on-line processing applies to the issue information citizens *do* make use of, it does not imply that voters made use of all of the issue information they encountered. If voters *are* policy-minded as they claim, it is possible that they may only attend to a relatively small number of issues.[19] Thus, it may still be the case that voters use on-line processing to update their summary evaluations but only when the information pertains to the few issues they consider important. Or, even less generously, it may be that dominant issues such as the Iraq War transform a congressional election into a simple referendum on the president. In this scenario, issues would matter, yet would add no precision to the vote choice beyond that already captured by the party label.

Testing two possible ways issue information may influence candidate evaluation within the context of an actual campaign reveals a less than flattering portrait of the electorate, one that does not live up to the expectations held by voters themselves. Although most voters claim to be policy-minded, the evidence overwhelmingly falls short. Proximity preference formation of the sort associated with issue voting seems out of the question given that voters were unaware of their incumbents' actual policy stances. As for on-line processing, respondents did not update their summary judgments of the candidates even when the issue information was readily available and more than half forgot ever encountering the information. Although the logic of on-line processing may apply to some issues, if voters do update their assessments of the candidates on the basis of policy considerations, the number of considerations is likely to be small.

Notes

1 E.g., John M. Broder, "Bush's Gamble: Turning the Spotlight on Iraq War as Republicans Try to Dim It," *The New York Times*, 26 October 2006; Michael A. Fletcher, "Cheney Vows 'Full Speed Ahead' on Iraq War," *The Washington Post*, 4 November 2006; Edward Luce, "Mid-terms Will Not Deflect Us in Iraq, Vows Cheney," *Financial Times*, 6 November 2006.

2 Toby Harnden, "End to Unfinished Business for Bush but Iraq Will Still Haunt Him," *The Daily Telegraph*, 6 November 2006.

3 Michael Grunwald, "Opposition to War Buoys Democrats," *The Washington Post*, 8 November 2006.

4 Quoted in Derwin Pereira, "Tables Turned in US Mid-term Polls; Democrats Likely to Take Congress as Voters Turn Sour on Iraq Policy," *The Straits Times*, 28 October 2006.

5 "Highlights from Exit Poll Economy to Scandal," *Chinadaily.com.cn*, 9 November 2006.

6 Teresa Watanabe and Nicole Gaouette, "Latinos Throw More Support to Democrats; Analysts say GOP Candidates' Stance against Immigration Helped Defeat them," *Los Angeles Times*, 10 November 2006.

7 Andrea Stone, "Limbaugh Says Actor Fox Exaggerating His Disease as Stem Cell Issues Churn," *USA Today*, 25 October 2006.

8 Quoted in Sheldon Alberts, "Fox Laughs at Accusation He's 'Acting': Limbaugh Attack of His TV Tremors Draws Liberal Ire," *National Post*, 26 October 2006.

9 The actual wording of the questions was as follows: "On a scale of 1 to 5 with 1 being very important and 5 being not at all important, how important was the candidates' positions on the issues to your vote choice?" and "On a scale of 1 to 5 with 1 being very important and 5 being not at all important, how important was the candidates' voting record to your vote choice?" I treat answers of "4" and "5" as indicating perceived importance.

10 The actual wording of the questions was as follows: "Some people believe it is important to get U.S. troops out of Iraq as soon as possible even if Iraq is not fully safe and secure, while others believe that U.S. troops should remain in Iraq as long as it takes to secure the country even if this is a long time," "Some people believe it is important to fight terrorism, even if individual rights are sometimes not fully protected. Other people believe it is important to protect individual rights, even if that limits the fight against terrorism," and "Some people oppose embryonic stem cell research because they believe it involves destroying innocent human life, while others support this type of research because it has the potential to save many lives."

11 Americans for Democratic Action (ADA) scores are often used in political science research to place members of Congress on a conventional left–right ideological scale. Based on how the member voted on a set of key issues, it is possible to obtain a score of 0 considered conservative to a score of 100 considered liberal. In the model involving stem cell research, 2005 ADA scores were used because the relevant policy vote on stem cell research was included in the 2006 ADA score calculations. For the other models, 2006 ADA scores were used.

12 Fortunately, in the preceding year, the 109th Congress voted on bills related to each of the three issues included on the survey. This made it possible to obtain the relevant roll-call votes for each incumbent from every district included in our sample.

13 The actual wording of the questions was "As you may know, the U.S. House member in your district voted this year _____." followed by "The House member in your district also voted this year _____." After each question, respondents were asked "To what extent do you agree or disagree with your representative's vote on this issue?"

14 The questions were worded as follows: "Using any number from 1 to 5, how would you rate the Republican/Democratic candidate for the House of Representatives in your district? One means you feel most unfavorable and five means you feel most favorable." and "What about the job your current representative in the U.S. House of Representatives is doing as a legislator in Washington D.C. Do you strongly approve, somewhat approve, somewhat disapprove or strongly disapprove?"

15 Respondents were asked to rate the Republican and Democratic candidates running in their district's House race. Only data pertaining to favorability of the incumbent were used. Thus, open seats are omitted from the analysis.

16 When constructing this variable, I assumed Republican incumbents were conservative and Democratic incumbents were liberal.

17 When the initial impression of the candidate is regressed on the policy distance measures, two of three issues (the Patriot Act and stem cell research) are significant predictors of *Initial Incumbent Favorability* even after controlling for the incumbent's partisanship and ideology.

18 It should be clear that the results in Table 6.2 do not definitively rule out the possibility that a) issues do matter to voters, perhaps through a mechanism such as on-line processing, but b) voters' perceptions of their incumbents had solidified to such an extent by the time the pre-election survey was conducted that no new information could alter voters' appraisals. However, there is reason to be skeptical of this alternate interpretation. First, results in Table 6.1 suggest that any solidification of incumbent evaluations occurred on the basis of partisanship and ideology, not issue information. Second, results elsewhere in this volume (Hendry *et al.*, Chapter Five) reveal volatility between the pre- and post-election surveys in respondents' evaluations of incumbent *character*; hence, some new information got through to voters over the course of the campaign, just not information about issues.

19 See work on issue publics, e.g., Converse (1964), Key (1966), RePass (1971), and Krosnick (1990).

References

Alvarez, R. Michael and Charles H. Franklin. 1994. "Uncertainty and Political Perceptions." *Journal of Politics* 56: 671–88.

Campbell, Angus, Philip E. Converse, Warren E. Miller, and Donald E. Stokes. 1960. *The American Voter*. New York: John Wiley & Sons.

Converse, Philip E. 1964. "The Nature of Belief Systems in Mass Publics." pp. 206–61 in *Ideology and Discontent*, edited by D.E. Apter. London: Free Press of Glencoe.

Converse, Philip E. and Gregory B. Markus. 1979. "Plus ca change . . .: The New CPS Election Study Panel." *American Political Science Review* 73: 32–49.

Davis, Otto A., Melvin J. Hinich, and Peter C. Ordeshook. 1970. "An Expository Development of a Mathematical Model of the Electoral Process." *American Political Science Review* 64: 426–48.

Delli Carpini, Michael X. and Scott Keeter. 1996. *What Americans Know about Politics and Why it Matters*. New Haven: Yale University Press.

Downs, Anthony. 1957. *An Economic Theory of Democracy*. New York: Harper and Row.

Hastie, Reid and Bernadette Park. 1986. "The Relationship between Memory and Judgment Depends on Whether the Task is Memory-Based or On-Line." *Psychological Review* 93: 258–68.

Hibbing, John R. and Elizabeth Theiss-Morse. 2002. *Stealth Democracy: Americans' Beliefs about How Government Should Work*. New York: Cambridge University Press.

Hinich, Melvin J. and Michael Munger. 1994. *Ideology and the Theory of Political Choice*. Ann Arbor: University of Michigan Press.

Hotelling, Harold. 1929. "Stability in Competition." *Economic Journal* 39: 41–57.

Key, V. O., Jr. 1966. *The Responsible Electorate*. Cambridge, Mass.: Harvard University Press.

Krosnick, Jon A. 1990. "Government Policy and Citizen Passion." *Political Behavior* 12: 59–92.

Lodge, Milton, Kathleen M. McGraw, and Patrick Stroh. 1989. "An Impression-Driven Model of Candidate Evaluation." *The American Political Science Review* 83: 399–419.

Lodge, Milton, Marco R. Steenbergen, and Shawn Brau. 1995. "The Responsive Voter: Campaign Information and the Dynamics of Candidate Evaluation." *American Political Science Review* 89: 309–26.

Lodge, Milton, Patrick Stroh, and John Wahlke. 1990. "Black-Box Models of Candidate Evaluation." *Political Behavior* 12: 5–18.

McCurley, Carl and Jeffery J. Mondak. 1995. "Inspected by #1184063113: The Influence of Incumbents' Competence and Integrity in U.S. House Elections." *American Journal of Political Science* 39: 864–85.

McGraw, Kathleen M., Milton Lodge, and Patrick Stroh. 1990. "On-Line Processing in Candidate Evaluation: The Effects of Issue Order, Issue Importance, and Sophistication." *Political Behavior* 12: 41–58.

Page, Benjamin I. and Richard A. Brody. 1972. "Policy Voting and the Electoral Process: The Vietnam War Issue." *American Political Science Review* 73: 1071–89.

Page, Benjamin I. and Calvin Jones. 1979. "Reciprocal Effects of Policy Preferences, Party Loyalties, and the Vote." *American Political Science Review* 73: 1071–89.

Popkin, Samuel L. 1991. *The Reasoning Voter*. Chicago: University of Chicago Press.

Redlawsk, David P. 2001. "You Must Remember This: A Test of the On-Line Model of Voting." *Journal of Politics* 63: 29–58.

RePass, David E. 1971. "Issue Salience and Party Choice." *American Political Science Review* 65: 389–400.

Chapter 7

The President, the War, and Voting Behavior in the 2006 House Elections

Gary C. Jacobson

In the 2006 midterm elections, Democrats won control of Congress for the first time in 12 years. They picked up 30 seats in the House to win a 233–202 majority, one seat larger than that held by the Republicans in the previous Congress. They also gained six Senate seats, all taken from Republican incumbents, to win a one-seat majority in the upper house. Remarkably, Democrats lost not a single seat in either chamber, the first election in U.S. history in which a party retained all of its congressional seats.

The Democrats' victory brought a major reconfiguration of national power, ending, in particular, the George W. Bush administration's easy dominance of a compliant Republican Congress (Jacobson and Kernell 2008). The 2006 midterm thus joins the list of pivotal midterm elections that, over the past half-century, have wrought highly consequential changes in national politics: 1958, 1966, 1974, and 1994.[1] Considering the list, it is arguable that midterm elections are at least as likely to produce historically-important shifts in the distribution of political power as are presidential election years (Busch 1999). In this light, the National Science Foundation's decision to stop funding midterm National Election Studies after 2002 was particularly short-sighted, interrupting the time series just when the forces shaping voting behavior appear to have diverged rather dramatically from the midterm norm.

Fortunately, two major academic studies—the 2006 Congressional Elections Study (CES), a telephone survey conducted under the leadership of Edward Carmines by the Center for Survey Research at Indiana University, and the Cooperative Congressional Election Study (CCES), an internet-based survey conducted by Polimetrix for a consortium of scholars at 39 universities led by Steve Ansolabehere and Lynn Vavreck—filled the vacuum. Unfortunately, however, neither study can be regarded as replicating the NES time series, raising questions of continuity; and each study has its peculiarities that justify caution in making comparisons to earlier studies (see Jacobson 2007a, Appendix). But as I shall argue in this chapter, analyzed together (along with the national Exit Poll and, for some comparisons, the vestigial data in the 2006 NES pilot study), these surveys support a highly consistent interpretation of the 2006 election: to a degree unique among modern midterm congressional elections, it featured an extraordinarily polarized electorate engaging in a national referendum on a president and his gravest policy decision.

The Referendum

Although other factors clearly contributed to the pro-Democratic national tide in 2006—notably, scandals that weakened some Republican members and cast a negative light on the whole congressional party—its primary source was the electorate's unhappiness with the Iraq War and the president responsible for it. Midterm elections are always to some extent referendums on the administration's performance (Jacobson 2004, 154–70), but the degree to which opinions on George W. Bush's job performance and his decision to invade Iraq shaped individual voting in 2006 was exceptionally large by any standard. To be sure, the unpopularity of Bush and the war were necessary but not sufficient to produce the Democrats' victory; as always, taking seats from the opposition required qualified, well-financed challengers capable of exploiting national issues locally and thus depended on the party's effective recruitment of candidates and strategic distribution of campaign resources (Jacobson 2007b). But the influx of candidates and resources on the Democratic side was also itself a reflection of the intense Democratic antipathy as well as the pro-Democratic political environment occasioned by the president and the war.

Well before the election, surveys provided ample reason for believing that opinions of George W. Bush would have an unusually large effect on voters in 2006, especially among those holding negative views of his performance. Figure 7.1 shows that, compared to electorates in previous midterms going back to 1982, voters in 2006 were more likely to say that their congressional vote would be about the president (54 percent, compared to between 34 and 46 percent in the earlier midterms); more importantly, over one third said that their vote for Congress would be a vote *against* Bush, a noticeably larger proportion than for any of his three predecessors at midterm, including Bill Clinton in 1994, the only other midterm in this series in which a president was, by this measure, a net drag on his congressional party. The reversal from 2002, when an unusually high proportion of voters said their vote would be an expression of support for President Bush, is especially striking.

Post-election surveys indicate that voters did what they said they would do; as Figure 7.2 shows, the proportion of the electorate whose House vote was consistent with their evaluations of Bush—voting Republican if they approved of his performance, voting Democrat if they disapproved—reached around 85 percent, more than 10 percentage points higher than in the earlier midterm elections for which data are available.[2] The problem for Republican House candidates was that Bush was also considerably less popular than any of his midterm predecessors in this group (Clinton, who arguably cost the Democrats control of Congress in 1994, comes closest; see Jacobson 1996); indeed, Bush's

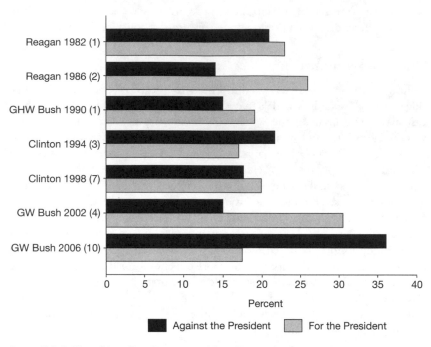

Figure 7.1 Is Your Vote For Congress a Vote For or Against the President?

Note: The number of surveys averaged is in parentheses.
Source: Pew Research Center for the People & the Press, "October 2006 Survey on Electoral Competition: Final Topline," October 17–22, 2006, at http://people-press.org/reports/questionnaires/293.pdf, accessed November 15, 2006.

38 percent approval rating in the Gallup Poll taken just before the election was the lowest for any president at midterm since Harry Truman in 1950. The uniformity of findings from the four separate 2006 surveys makes it most unlikely that these results are a product of chance variation or survey methodology rather than a particular feature of the election itself.

A major reason for the consonance between presidential approval and House (and Senate[3]) voting in 2006 is no doubt the unprecedented degree of partisan polarization the Bush presidency has provoked. The presidential approval ratings offered by ordinary Republicans and Democrats had, by 2006, become more widely divergent for Bush than they have been for any president since modern polling began more than 60 years ago (Jacobson 2008). With the exception of a single poll taken during the Truman administration, no previous president had ever received single-digit ratings from the opposition in any Gallup Poll; Bush's ratings among Democrats were in single digits in a majority of the 27 Gallup surveys taken between January and November 2006, averaging just 9.6 points. Meanwhile his average approval rating among Republicans was a robust 80 percent. Before Bush and going back to Truman, the partisan

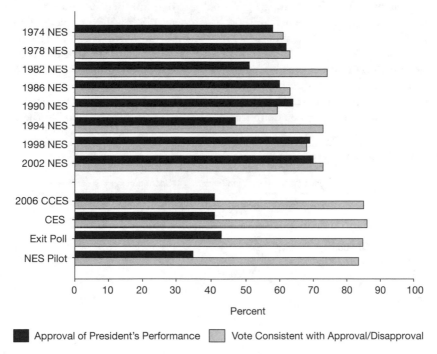

Figure 7.2 Consistency of Presidential Approval with the House Vote in Midterm Elections, 1974–2006.

difference in approval ratings had never exceeded 70 percentage points in any Gallup Poll. In the Gallup Polls taken between January and November 2006, the gap *averaged* more than 70 points and reached as high as 77 points.[4] Among independents, Bush's approval ratings averaged 29 percent during this period, 19 points higher than the Democratic mean, 52 points lower than the Republican mean.[5]

The uniqueness of the partisan divide on Bush's performance in 2006 is clear from Table 7.1 and Table 7.2. Table 7.1 presents data from the Gallup Polls taken just before midterm elections from 1950 through 2006. Bush received the lowest ratings among opposition party identifiers (10 percent approving) and independents (31 percent) of any president in the series, while his rating among his own partisans (82 percent) was above the average (78 percent) and precisely at the median. Thus the partisan gap for 2006, 72 points, was by a wide margin the largest yet recorded prior to a midterm. Data based on self-reported voters from the National Election Studies (1974–2002) and four 2006 surveys, reported in Table 7.2, reinforce this point. The drop in approval from 2002 to 2006 among independents and Democrats is especially striking in both tables.

In light of these data and the unusually strong link between presidential approval and the vote choice in 2006, it is no surprise to find unusually high levels of party-line voting and a substantial Democratic advantage among self-described independents. Table 7.3 displays the relevant data from midterms since 1974; comparisons between 2006 and elections during the recent period of Republican dominance (1994 onward) are the most informative, because prior to then, majority status and the incumbency advantage gave Democratic candidates a boost among Republicans and independents.[6] According to these

Table 7.1 Partisan Differences in Presidential Approval at the Midterm, 1950–2006

	President's Party	Independents	Opposition Party	Difference
1950	57	34	17	40
1954	90	71	51	39
1958	83	57	39	44
1962	80	61	38	42
1966	62	41	26	36
1970	82	53	41	41
1974	72	59	37	35
1978	54	40	27	27
1982	77	44	21	56
1986	88	61	42	46
1990	86	59	53	33
1994	72	41	14	58
1998	87	64	36	51
2002	93	62	47	46
2006	82	31	10	72

Source: Gallup Polls, August–October of the election year.

Table 7.2 Partisan Differences in Presidential Approval among Midterm Voters, 1974–2006

	President's Party	Independents	Opposition Party	Difference
1974 NES	76	59	44	32
1978 NES	79	64	31	48
1982 NES	89	61	24	65
1986 NES	90	64	38	52
1990 NES	88	71	46	42
1994 NES	83	43	16	67
1998 NES	94	66	39	55
2002 NES	96	71	38	58
2006 CCES	85	27	6	79
2006 CES	84	31	5	79
2006 Exit Poll	85	33	11	74
2006 NES Pilot	77	23	7	70

Table 7.3 Partisanship and Voting in Midterm House Elections, 1974–2006 (Percent Voting for the Republican)

	Republicans	Democrats	Independents
1974 NES	77	14	37
1978 NES	72	17	48
1982 NES	84	17	46
1986 NES	72	16	45
1990 NES	71	12	41
1994 NES	88	18	54
1998 NES	86	24	53
2002 NES	84	16	52
2006 CCES	87	11	42
2006 CES	82	6	33
2006 Exit Poll	93	7	42
2006 NES Pilot	86	5	41

data, Republican House candidates did not lose more of their own partisans than usual (although some data suggest Republican turnout may have been slightly depressed) but they did notably worse than recent midterms among Democrats and independents (Jacobson 2007b).

The Iraq War

Both the president's low overall approval ratings and the sharp partisan divisions on his performance are tightly linked to the public's reactions to the Iraq War. As popular support for the war has declined, so have the president's approval ratings (Figure 7.3).[7] While presidential approval and support for the war have declined in parallel, both going from above 70 percent to below 40 percent, the relationship between the two has remained strong and stable, with an average of about 83 percent of respondents offering consistent evaluations— for the war and approving of Bush's performance, or opposing the war and disapproving of Bush's performance. This level of consistency is far higher than it was for evaluations of Truman and the Korean War (averaging 60 percent) or Johnson and the Vietnam War (averaging 64 percent).

Like assessments of Bush, opinions on the Iraq War were strongly shaped by partisanship. In responses to 105 survey items (using a variety of question wordings) assessing the public's views of the Iraq War during 2006, support for the war averaged 75 percent among Republicans, 18 percent among Democrats, and 36 percent among independents (see Jacobson 2008 for further details). The partisan gap of 57 percentage points stands in sharp contrast to comparable data from previous engagements in Korea, Vietnam, the Persian Gulf, Kosovo, and Afghanistan. For none is the partisan gap anywhere nearly as wide as it has become for the Iraq War. Ironically, the gap is lowest for the most controversial of these engagements, Vietnam, averaging only 5 percentage points. Party differences over involvement in Korea and Kosovo averaged 11 to 12 points; they were about the same magnitude for Afghanistan until recently, when they began to grow (while remaining considerably smaller than for Iraq). Bush's father's Gulf War produced the widest initial partisan gap in this set. Still, the party difference averaged only 21 points and peaked at 29 points, months after the fighting had concluded. Clearly, partisan differences on the Iraq War are in a class by themselves, two to ten times as large as for any comparable engagement (Jacobson 2008, 134–8). Again, the distribution of opinions on the war among independents was considerably closer to that of Democrats than of Republicans.

The War, the President, and the House Vote

It is no great leap to infer from these data that assessments of the war contributed powerfully to the sharp partisan divisions expressed by voters in 2006 and to the desertion of Republican candidates by independent voters documented in Table 7.3. The CES, CCES, and Exit surveys permit a more detailed analysis of these linkages, with differences in the war-related questions they posed offering alternative avenues for assessing the effect of views on the Iraq War and Bush on House voters in 2006. In the CCES survey, war support was measured retrospectively, by whether the respondent thought the war was a

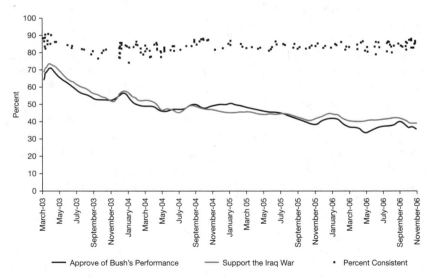

Figure 7.3 Support for the Iraq War and Approval of George W. Bush's Job Performance, 2003–2006.

mistake. The CES asks respondents to think prospectively, placing themselves on a 5-point scale in which 1 represents "leave Iraq as soon as possible" and 5 represents "remain in Iraq until it is secure" (basically, the Bush administration's position). The Exit Poll asked if voters approved or disapproved of the Iraq War. Obviously, these questions do not measure the same thing; a person could think the war a mistake or disapprove of it in general but still oppose withdrawal until security is established for fear of compounding the damage by leaving Iraq in bloody chaos. Nonetheless, the responses, combined with assessments of the president, are associated with the House vote in very similar ways.

The connections between party identification, support for the war, approval of Bush's job performance, and voting in the CCES are depicted in Table 7.4. Seventy-three percent of Republican respondents to the CCES supported the war and approved of Bush's performance, and of this group, 92 voted for the Republican House candidate. Among the small (9 percent) fraction of Republicans unhappy with both Bush and the war, more than half defected to the Democrat in these elections. Democrats were even more united, with 87 percent rejecting Bush and the war; among this group, only 7 percent voted for the Republican House candidate. In contrast, more than half of the tiny fraction (3 percent) of Democratic voters who supported the president and

Table 7.4 Presidential Approval, Assessments of the Iraq War, and the House Vote (CCES)

	Approve of Bush, War not a Mistake	Approve of Bush, War a Mistake	Disapprove of Bush, War not a Mistake	Disapprove of Bush, War a Mistake
Republicans (N = 7,747)				
Percent in category	73	3	4	9
Percent voting for Republican House candidate	92	83	75	44
Independents (N = 8,520)				
Percent in category	27	2	4	58
Percent voting for Republican House candidate	87	55	55	16
Democrats (N = 7,916)				
Percent in category	3	1	3	87
Percent voting for Republican House candidate	56	30	31	7
All Respondents (N = 24,183)				
Percent in category	34	2	3	52
Percent voting for Republican House candidate	89	64	56	12

the war voted for the Republican. The voting patterns of both sets of partisans with mixed views fell in between.

Notice that the gradients in the vote choice across these categories are steepest among independent voters; those independents who approved of Bush and the war voted Republican at rates 71 percentage points higher than those who rejected both. Thus it was greatly to the Republicans' disadvantage in 2006 that independents were more than twice common in the latter category than in the former. Notice also that only a small proportion of voters in this survey—around 5 percent overall—reported mixed views on the president and the war.

The results of a similar exercise using the CES survey are reported in Table 7.5. For this analysis, I classified positions 1 and 2 in the CES troop withdrawal question as advocating withdrawal, and positions 4 and 5 as favoring staying the course. Respondents who placed themselves at the center (3) are omitted; they comprise about 18 percent of the voters surveyed, compared to the 8 percent who could not be included in the CCES analysis because they lacked opinion on the war or the president. Again, we observe a highly polarized electorate and strong relationships between assessments of the president and views on troop withdrawal and the vote choice, with independents displaying the steepest gradient. Exit Poll results (Table 7.6) tell the same story, albeit with a slightly higher level of party loyalty. In all three surveys, the Republican

Table 7.5 Presidential Approval, Support for Staying in Iraq, and the House Vote (CES)

	Approve of Bush, keep troops in Iraq	Approve of Bush, withdraw troops	Disapprove of Bush, keep troops in Iraq	Disapprove of Bush, withdraw troops
Republicans (N = 272)				
Percent in category	64	7	4	6
Percent voting for Republican House candidate	92	86	30	41
Independents (N = 233)				
Percent in category	21	8	10	44
Percent voting for Republican House candidate	73	55	28	11
Democrats (N = 250)				
Percent in category	3	1	3	75
Percent voting for Republican House candidate	41	10	19	3
All Respondents (N = 755)				
Percent in category	30	5	6	41
Percent voting for Republican House candidate	86	67	27	9

Table 7.6 Presidential Approval, Approval of the Iraq War, and the House Vote (Exit Poll)

	Approve of Bush, Approve of War	Approve of Bush, Disapprove of War	Disapprove of Bush, Approve of War	Disapprove of Bush, Disapprove of War
Republicans (N = 1,941)				
Percent in category	77	6	3	11
Percent voting for Republican House candidate	96	87	81	71
Independents (N = 1,142)				
Percent in category	29	5	8	56
Percent voting for Republican House candidate	82	54	42	22
Democrats (N = 2,231)				
Percent in category	7	3	8	80
Percent voting for Republican House candidate	39	15	5	4
All Respondents (N = 5,533)				
Percent in category	39	5	6	48
Percent voting for Republican House candidate	90	59	32	15

disadvantage is clear, with a higher proportion of respondents falling into the right-hand column (disapproving of Bush and the war) than into the left-hand column (approving of Bush and the war).

The Iraq War and Approval of House Incumbents

Congressional elections are by no means purely national affairs, of course; in 2006, as always, respondents' evaluations of the local candidates were also strongly related to their vote choice (see below). However, a notable feature of 2006 was that evaluations of candidates—at least of House incumbents pursuing re-election—were linked to opinions on the Iraq War. In the CCES survey, 81 percent of voters who believed that the war was not a mistake approved of their Republican incumbent's performance, compared to 22 percent of voters who thought the war was a mistake. For Democratic incumbents, the pattern is reversed, with 75 percent of their districts' voters who opposed the war approving, compared with 33 percent of those supporting it. The CES survey asked respondents to rate the House candidates on a 5-point favorability scale (1 = most unfavorable, 5 = most favorable); combining positions

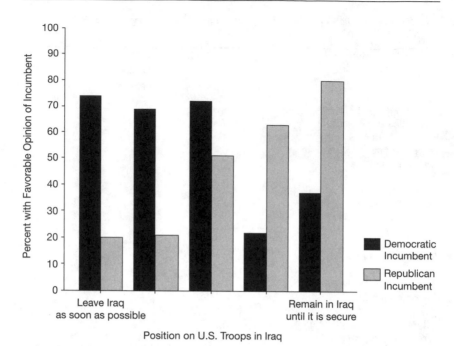

Figure 7.4 Opinions on Iraq and Favorability Toward House Incumbents.
Source: CES

4 and 5 as "favorable," we again observe a strong relationship between opinions on the Iraq War (here, the troop withdrawal question) and opinions on the House incumbents (Figure 7.4).

Evaluations of incumbents are deeply colored by partisanship, to be sure, but even with the voter's party, ideology, and assessments of Bush taken into account, opinions on the war still had a significant effect on opinions of House incumbents. Table 7.7 displays the results from the CCES, Table 7.8 the corresponding results from the CES.[8] Both tell a similar story. CCES respondents who thought the war a mistake rated Republican incumbents significantly lower, Democratic incumbents, significantly higher. Evaluations of Bush's performance affected incumbent approval in the same way and by a similar magnitude.

The CES survey asked respondents to place the congressional parties and House candidates (and Bush) on the troop withdrawal scale in addition to specifying their own positions. Their responses can thus be used to measure a voter's perceived proximity to the congressional parties and candidates on this issue. Because respondents were better able to specify the party than candidate positions (so fewer cases are lost), and relative proximity to parties was more strongly related to the House vote than relative proximity to the candidates, I use party proximity to test the effects of war-related opinions on favorability evaluations of House incumbents. The substantive results are similar regardless of which proximity measure is used. Opinions on troop withdrawals (as well as approval of Bush's performance) had a substantial effect on favorability ratings of incumbents of both parties, again controlling for presidential approval, party identification, and ideology. The latter two variables were unrelated to opinions of Democratic incumbents among Democrats, once the national political items—assessments of Bush and preferences on troop withdrawal—are taken in to account, a consequence of the collinearity among these sets of variables.

Table 7.7 Sources of Approval of House Incumbents' Job Performance (CCES)

	Republican Incumbents		Democratic Incumbents	
	Coefficient	S.E.	Coefficient	S.E.
Party Identification (1, 0, −1)	0.13***	0.01	−0.16***	0.02
Ideology (2, 1, 0, −1, −2)	0.14***	0.01	−0.14***	0.01
Approve of Bush's Performance (1, 0)	0.46***	0.02	−0.24***	0.03
Iraq War Not a Mistake (1, 0, −1)	0.22***	0.01	−0.16***	0.02
Constant	−0.12***	0.01	0.34***	0.02
Adjusted R²	0.44		0.27	
Number of Cases	12,401		8,673	

Notes:
The dependent variable is 1 if the respondent approves of the incumbent's performance, −1 if disapproves, 0 if neither; the independent variables are scored to be positive in the Republican direction.
*** p < 0.001

Table 7.8 Sources of Favorable Opinions of House Incumbents (CES)

	Republican Incumbents		Democratic Incumbents	
	Coefficient	S.E.	Coefficient	S.E.
Party Identification (1, 0, −1)	0.12*	0.06	0.01	0.08
Ideology (2, 1, 0, −1, −2)	0.13***	0.04	−0.00	0.05
Approve of Bush's Performance (1, 0)	0.58***	0.11	−0.64***	0.16
Party Closer on Iraq Withdrawal (1, 0, −1)	0.14**	0.05	−0.17*	0.08
Constant	−0.59***	0.13	0.55***	0.16
Adjusted R²	0.42		0.24	
Number of Cases	352		195	

Notes:
The dependent variable is 1 if the respondent chose 4 or 5 on the candidate favorability scale, 0 if on 3, and −1 if on 1 or 2); the independent variables are scored to be positive in the Republican direction.
*** p < 0.001, ** p < 0.01, * p < 0.05.

Multivariate Models of the Vote Choice in 2006

Although voters' party affiliation, ideological leanings, and attitudes toward the war, the president, and the candidates were tightly linked in 2006, each of these still had a large and separable impact on their reported House vote choice. The logit equations estimating the House vote reported in Table 7.9 include all of these variables, plus the incumbency status of the candidates. The salient results:

1   The effects on the vote of opinions on the Iraq War and the president remain substantial even under these controls. With the other variables set at their mean values, the probability of a Republican vote varies by .33 depending on whether the respondent thought the war was a mistake (CCES), by .28 depending on perceived proximity to the parties on Iraq (CES), and by .21 depending on whether the respondent approves of the Iraq War (Exit Poll).[9]

2   The respective probability differences arising from presidential approval or disapproval are .30, .17, and .36 in these three surveys.

3   The estimated effects on the vote of moving from the least and to the most pro-Republican values of the presidential approval and Iraq variables combined are quite similar across the equations: .57 for the CCES equation, .44 for the CES equation, and .53 for the Exit Poll equation.

4   Although the estimated effects of party identification and ideology vary across the three equations, in combination their effect on the probability of a Republican House vote are virtually identical: differences of .79, .80, and .80, respectively, between the least and most pro-Republican combinations of values.

5   The estimated benefits of House incumbency were notably larger for Democrats than for Republicans in 2006. Other things equal, incumbency status increased the probability of a vote for Democratic incumbents by about the same amount in all three equations (between .17 and .20); the coefficient on Republican incumbency was smaller in all three equations, insignificant in two, and had the wrong sign in one (CRS).

6   Opinions on the incumbent also had a major effect on the vote decision, as we would expect.[10] The Exit Poll did not ask an incumbent approval question, but it did ask if the respondent approved of Congress's performance. The estimated effect of congressional approval was considerably smaller than that of incumbent approval or favorability, but it did increase the probability of a Republican vote significantly.

7   These equations do an impressive job of predicting the House vote (88 to 91 percent correct), but remember that predictions are almost as accurate when just one of the independent variables is employed: presidential approval alone predicts 85 to 86 percent of votes correctly; opinion on the Iraq War by itself predicts 82 to 84 percent of votes correctly among voters with opinions on the war (who comprise a large majority).

Table 7.9 Logit Model of House Voting in 2006

	Coefficient	S.E.	Effect[a]	
A. CCES (N = 21,477)				
Democratic Incumbent (1, 0)	−0.75***	0.08	0.18	} 0.28
Republican Incumbent (1, 0)	0.43***	0.08	0.11	
Party Identification (1, 0, −1)	0.71***	0.04	0.34	} 0.79
Ideology (2, 1, 0, −1, −2)	0.73***	0.04	0.62	
Approve of Bush's Performance (1, 0)	*1.23***	*0.08*	*0.30*	} 0.57
Iraq War Not a Mistake (1, 0, −1)	*0.68***	*0.04*	*0.33*	
Incumbent Approval (1, 0, −1)	1.54***	0.03	0.65	
Constant	−0.50***	0.08		
Likelihood ratio chi square	19,253			
Percent correctly predicted (null = 54.1)	88.2			
Pseudo R²	0.65			
B. CES (N = 728)				
Democratic Incumbent (1, 0)	−0.89*	0.40	0.17	} 0.15
Republican Incumbent (1, 0)	−0.06	0.37	–	
Party Identification (1, 0, −1)	1.26***	0.22	0.48	} 0.80
Ideology (2, 1, 0, −1, −2)	0.75***	0.16	0.52	
Approve of Bush's Performance (1, 0)	*0.81**	*0.35*	*0.17*	} 0.44
Closer to Republicans on Troop				
Withdrawal (1, 0, −1)	*0.70***	*0.18*	*0.28*	
Favorable View of Incumbent (1, 0, −1)	2.03***	0.24	0.71	
Constant	−3.22***	0.61		
Likelihood ratio chi square	653			
Percent correctly predicted (null = 58.7)	91.1			
Pseudo R²	0.66			
C. National Exit Poll (N = 5,134)				
Democratic Incumbent (1, 0)	−0.84***	0.18	0.20	} 0.28
Republican Incumbent (1, 0)	0.31	0.17	0.08	
Party Identification (1, 0, −1)	1.85***	0.07	0.73	} 0.80
Ideology (1, 0, −1)	0.42***	0.07	0.20	
Approve of Bush's Performance (1, 0)	*1.51***	*0.14*	*0.36*	} 0.53
Approve of Iraq War (1, 0, −1)	*0.42***	*0.07*	*0.21*	
Congress Approval (1, 0, −1)	0.19***	0.06	0.16	
Constant	−0.50***	0.08		
Likelihood ratio chi square	4,267			
Percent correctly predicted (null = 51.3)	89.8			
Pseudo R²	0.60			

Notes:
a Estimated change in probability with the other variables set at their means.
Dependent variable takes the value of 1 if respondent voted for Republican, 0 if for Democrat; values of the independent variable are scored to by positive in the Republican direction.
*** p < 0.001, * p < 0.05.

Comparisons to Earlier Midterms

The degree of consistency in the findings produced by these models is impressive, especially considering the differences in the survey methodology used to create the three data sets (see the Appendix). The same degree of consistency was also apparent in the other analyses reported in this chapter. But how do these results compare to earlier midterm elections that were subjects of NES surveys? To answer this question, I had to simplify the equations, for none of the earlier studies has the equivalent of the Iraq War question and some omitted the incumbent approval question. I therefore estimated logit equations for the entire set of studies with the House vote as the dependent variable with only party identification, ideology, incumbency status, and presidential approval as independent variables. The 2006 NES pilot study included these variables so it can be included in the comparison set. Table 7.10 summarizes the results by listing the estimated effects of three sets of variables (party identification and ideology combined, the two incumbency dummies, and presidential approval) on the vote choice.

Table 7.10 Estimated Effects of Incumbency, Party ID and Ideology, and Presidential Approval on the Vote Choice in Midterm U.S. House Elections, 1974–2006

Year and Study	Party Identification and Ideology	Incumbency	Presidential Approval	Number of Cases
1974 NES	0.56	0.42	0.15	691
1978 NES	0.47	0.70	0.09	902
1982 NES	0.58	0.58	0.24	685
1986 NES	0.42	0.64	0.13	962
1990 NES	0.55	0.70	0.09	769
1994 NES	0.56	0.53	0.18	903
1998 NES	0.58	0.61	0.26	545
2002 NES	0.49	0.57	0.31	733
Average, 1974–2002 NES	0.53	0.59	0.18	
2006 CCES	0.76	0.33	0.53	21,506
2006 CES	0.73	0.27	0.47	728
2006 Exit Poll	0.82	0.28	0.51	5,134
2006 NES Pilot	0.84	0.26	0.32	359

Note:
Entries are the estimated changes in the probability of a Democratic vote as the value on the variables of interest vary from their lowest to highest scores, with the other variables set at their means. Results are based on logit equations estimating the House vote as a function of incumbency, party identification, and presidential approval scored as indicated in Table 7.9; ideology is measured by the 3-point scale used in Table 7.9c.

Not only are the results from all four 2006 surveys highly consistent with one another, they are without exception starkly different from those typically derived from the NES surveys of the previous eight midterm elections. The combined effects of party identification and ideology were much larger in 2006 than in any of the previous midterms examined, as were the effects of presidential approval.[11] The effects of incumbency status, on the other hand, were much lower in 2006 than in the earlier midterms. By this evidence, 2006 was indeed exceptional, much more of a national referendum on the president and parties, much less dominated by the local factor of incumbency, than previous midterms going back to at least 1974.

These results underline what a bad idea it was for the NSF to kill the NES midterm studies and how fortunate it was that multiple independent studies of 2006 were undertaken as replacements. Had only any one of these studies been available for comparing voting behavior in 2006 to that of earlier midterms, we would inevitably be debating whether the observed differences are the result of changes in voting behavior or changes in the survey methodology. But with four separate studies, each using a different approach, telling us the same basic story, we can be much more confident that the striking differences that appear in the 2006 data reflect reality and that 2006 was indeed unique among modern midterm elections.

Appendix: Data Sources

This chapter draws on four national survey studies of the 2006 midterm election, each employing a different methodology. All require the use of weights to approximate the sampled population, and all of the analyses reported in this chapter employed the weights.

1   Cooperative Congressional Election Study (CCES)
    The CCES was a survey of 38,443 Americans conducted during October and November of 2006 (Ansolabehere 2006). The survey had a pre/post design and was a cooperative venture of 39 universities and more than 100 political scientists. CCES was completed on-line and fielded by the survey research firm Polimetrix, Inc., located in Palo Alto, CA. Steve Ansolabehere (MIT) was the Principal Investigator of the project and Lynn Vavreck (UCLA) served as the Study Director. A design committee consisting of Steve Ansolabehere, Lynn Vavreck, Doug Rivers (Stanford), Don Kinder (Michigan), Bob Erikson (Columbia), Wendy Rahn (Minnesota), Liz Gerber (Michigan), Jeremy Pope (Brigham Young), and John Sides (George Washington) collaborated to write the first 40 questions of the survey, called the Common Content. All 38,443 respondents completed this part of the survey. Each CCES team then drafted its own unique content that followed the Common Content. Each team received 1,000 unique respondents who completed both the Common Content and the Team Module.

The Common Content sample for CCES is a nationally representative sample. Interviewed respondents were selected from the Polimetrix PollingPoint Panel using sample matching. A random sub sample of size 36,501 was drawn from the 2004 American Community Study (ACS), conducted by the U.S. Bureau of the Census, which is a probability sample of size 1,194,354 with a response rate of 93.1 percent (participation in the ACS is mandatory). For each respondent in the selected ACS sub sample, the closest matching active PollingPoint panelist was selected using the following measure of distance: d(x,y). Following matching, the sample marginals were raked to the ACS marginals for age, race, gender, and education. Raking was performed using iterative proportional fitting. The final weights were trimmed to lie between .33 and 3.[12]

2   Center for Survey Research 2006 Congressional Elections Study (CES)

The CES study is an RDD telephone survey of respondents in a random sample of 100 House districts plus an oversample of 72 districts identified as competitive or potentially competitive in 2006; 17 of the latter were in the original random sample of districts. It was designed by Edward Carmines (Indiana), Robert Huckfeldt (UC Davis), Jeff Mondak (Illinois), Walter Stone (UC Davis), John Hibbing, Dona-Gene Mitchell and Mike Wagner (Nebraska), and Herb Weisberg (Ohio State) and conducted by Indiana University's Center for Survey Research. Its pre/post format produced three overlapping studies: a pre-election cross-section, a post-election panel made up of the pre-election respondents, and a post-election cross-section supplemented with new respondents in the post election period. A total of 776 of the 1023 pre-election respondents completed post-election interviews; 401 respondents were interviewed for the post-election supplement. To produce the equivalent of a national sample, the respondents are weighted to adjust for the over-sample of competitive districts. For more details, see Huckfeldt (2007).

3   The National Exit Poll

The National Exit Poll was conducted by Edison Media Research/ Mitofsky International for a consortium of news organizations (ABC News, Associated Press, CBS News, CNN, Fox News, and NBC News). It surveyed 13,866 respondents, including 1,478 absentee/early voters contacted prior to the election by telephone. The regular election day respondents were chosen from a random sample of precincts in all 50 states. Precincts were selected with a probability proportionate to the number of voters in each precinct, except that in some states, precincts that have large minority populations were sampled at a higher rate than other precincts. Weights adjust for this over-sampling. Within each precinct, voters were sampled systematically throughout the voting day at a rate that gave all voters in a precinct the same chance of being interviewed. The telephone component used RDD; interviewing for the state absentee surveys began on October 27, 2006 and concluded on November 5, 2006. Before the telephone survey results were combined with the exit poll data they were weighted to reflect the probabilities of selection and to reflect demographic characteristics in that state. Respondents are also weighted based upon the size and distribution of the final tabulated vote within geographic regions of the state or of the nation. For more details, see Edison Media Research/ Mitofsky International (n.d.).

4   The 2006 NES Pilot Study

The 2006 NES Pilot Study was designed to test new questions and conduct methodological research to inform the design of future NES studies. As such, it was not part of the NES time series that has been conducted since 1948, and it included only those time series questions necessary to evaluate the new content. The work was supported by the National Science Foundation under grants SES-0535332 and SES-0535334; the principal investigators were Arthur Lupia (Michigan) and Jon Krosnick (Stanford). Data collection took place between November 13, 2006 and January 5, 2007. The original sample consisted of 1,211 individuals who completed a valid interview in the 2004 NES time series study; a total of 675 reinterviews were completed. The relevant questions for this study included a House vote question, presidential approval, and party identification; ideology was taken from the respondent's answers to the 2004 survey.

Notes

1 Democrats gained 49 House seats and 15 Senate seats in 1958, establishing the party's congressional dominance for the next 36 years; they lost 47 House seats and four Senate seats in 1966, ending Lyndon Johnson's "Great Society" ambitions. In 1974, Democrats picked up 49 House seats and four Senate seats, fueling a surge in congressional reform of party and budget processes. And in 1994, Republicans gained 52 House seats and eight Senate seats to win majorities in both chambers for the first time in more than four decades.

2 The data for 1974–2002 are from the National Election Studies cumulative data file; data for 2006 are from the small NES pilot study (which was not a midterm election study but included questions on presidential approval and the House vote), the Cooperative Congressional Election Study (CCES; see the Appendix for information on this study), and the National Exit Poll.

3 Presidential approval was also highly consonant with the vote for Senator in 2006; the consistency rates are 85 percent, 89 percent, and 84 percent, respectively, for the NES Pilot survey, CCES, and the Exit Poll.

4 The peak of polarization on evaluations of Bush was reached around the time of the 2004 election, 83 points in a couple of surveys (Jacobson 2008, 10–13).

5 Author's analysis based on Gallup Poll data acquired from the Roper Center for Public Opinion Research at www.ropercenter.uconn.edu.

6 The independent category includes partisan leaners in the analyses in this chapter to allow comparisons with the Exit Poll results; exit polls do not ask independents if they lean toward one of the parties.

7 The approval and war support trends are the Lowess-smoothed percentages of responses to the job approval question (N = 560) and responses to four of the many variants of the war support question (war was not a mistake, the U.S. did the right thing in attacking Iraq, the war has been worth the cost, favor the war; N = 503); the consistency measures come from the 149 surveys with which I have been able to do secondary analyses to produce the relevant cross-tabulations. Sources: 16 national media and academic surveys organizations, most results reported at www.pollingreport.com, some supplied by the Roper Center and the Pew Research Center for the People and the Press. See Jacobson (2008, 128 fn. 22).

8 The results are substantively the same if the relationships are estimated by ordered logit instead of OLS regression; I display the latter for ease of interpretation; includes only voters in contested districts.

9 Estimated using *CLARIFY* (Tomz, Wittenberg, and King 2001).

10 For the CES equation, the favorability variable is reconstituted to match the approval variable in the CCES equation as closely as feasible. It takes the value of 1 if the respondent had a favorable opinion of a Republican incumbent or an unfavorable opinion of a Democratic incumbent, a value of -1 if the respondent had a favorable opinion of the Democrat incumbent or an unfavorable opinion of the Republican incumbent, and 0 if neither candidate was an incumbent or the respondent had a neutral opinion of the incumbent.

11 The relationship between presidential approval and the combination of party identification and ideology was also stronger in 2006, with the R^2 averaging .47, compared to an average of .26 for the previous midterms.

12 For more information on sample matching see Rivers (2006).

References

The American National Election Studies. THE 1948–2004 ANES CUMULATIVE DATA FILE [dataset]. Stanford University and the University of Michigan [producers and distributors], 2005. At www.electionstudies.org, accessed July 7, 2007.

The American National Election Studies. 2007. THE 2006 ANES PILOT STUDY FULL RELEASE [dataset]. Stanford University and the University of Michigan [producers and distributors]. At www.electionstudies.org, accessed September 11, 2007.

Ansolabehere, Stephen. 2006. Cooperative Congressional Election Study—Common Content. Palo Alto, CA: Polimetrix.

Busch, Andrew. 1999. *Horses in Midstream: U.S. Midterm Elections and their Consequences, 1894–1998.* Pittsburgh: University of Pittsburgh Press.

Edison Media Research/Mitofsky International. n.d. Documentation for the 2006 General Election Exit Polls. At http://roperweb.ropercenter.uconn.edu/cgi-bin/hsrun.exe/Roperweb/Catalog40/StateId/RtIUwml1UeM00Tb7tR6gXCkO1WGTI-46zu/HAHTpage/file?fi = 55547, p. 84. Accessed June 6, 2007.

Huckfeldt, Robert. 2007. Weights for the 2006 Congress Study. Manuscript, June 7.

Jacobson, Gary C. 1996. "The 1994 House Elections in Perspective," *Political Science Quarterly* 111: 207–9.

Jacobson, Gary C. 2004. *The Politics of Congressional Elections.* 6th ed. New York: Longman.

Jacobson, Gary C. 2007a. "The President, the War, and Voting Behavior in the 2006 House Elections: Evidence from Four National Surveys." Presented at the Conference on Congressional Elections, University of Illinois Urbana–Champaign, October 18–19, 2007.

Jacobson, Gary C. 2007b. "Referendum: The 2006 Midterm Congressional Elections." *Political Science Quarterly* 122: 1–24.

Jacobson, Gary C. 2008. *A Divider, Not a Uniter: George W. Bush and the American People: The 2006 Election and Beyond.* New York: Pearson Longman.

Jacobson, Gary C. and Samuel Kernell. 2008. *The Logic of American Politics Under Divided Government: The Legacy of the 2006 Elections; A Supplement to the Logic of American Politics.* Washington, D.C.: Congressional Quarterly Press.

Rivers, Douglas. 2006. Sample Matching: Representative Sampling from Internet Panels. Palo Alto, CA: Polimetrix White Paper Series, available at www.polimetrix.com/learn.

Tomz, Michael, Jason Wittenberg, and Gary King. 2001. CLARIFY: Software for Interpreting and Presenting Statistical Results. At http://gking.harvard.edu/clarify/docs/clarify.html, accessed September 5, 2007.

Chapter 8

Americans' Perceptions of the Nature of Governing

John R. Hibbing, Elizabeth Theiss-Morse, and Eric Whitaker

Actual and perceived governmental processes, quite apart from actual and perceived substantive policy outputs, are of pressing concern. Processes shape the ability of government to respond to important societal challenges, they color people's evaluations of government, they influence the reform agenda surrounding governmental processes, they increase the likelihood of certain policies failing or securing passage, they encourage people to enter or to avoid the political process, and they even mold the extent to which people comply with collective outputs—an essential feature of developed polities. Given the importance of preferences for and perceptions of political processes, it is essential that we identify their sources and markers. Fortunately, the 2006 Congressional Elections Study (CES) organized by the University of Indiana contains an unusually useful battery of "process" items and these items will serve as the centerpiece for the data analysis contained in this chapter.

Literature Review and Background

How do Americans want their government to work? How do they want politically-relevant figures to behave? Are they satisfied with the way their government is functioning? Why do they think governing is often fractious? What are the consequences of dissatisfaction with processes? Though we know less than we should about the answers to these questions, recent interest in the processes involved with authoritative decision making has been stimulated by the research of social psychologist Tom Tyler on procedural justice. Tyler's work initially focused on the judicial branch where he discovered that even defendants who were found guilty were more likely to accept the verdict if they approved of the manner in which the trial was handled (Tyler 1994; Tyler and Mitchell 1994). Tyler subsequently analyzed data relevant to other decision-making situations, especially situations such as those typically found in the U.S. Congress or other legislative sessions. He found that people were more likely to approve of Congress if they believed Congress listened to all sides of an issue before deciding and if they believed Congress paid attention to ordinary people (Tyler 1994).

Political scientists are generally more concerned with substantive policy positions than with abstract procedural matters. To a certain extent, this is understandable. It is vital that students of politics identify the causes and consequences of public attitudes toward school prayer, tax cuts, and military action abroad. But adequate attention should also be given to process. Surveys of public opinion, both academic and popular, lavish items on key policies of the day but rarely tap people's deeper feelings regarding the manner in which government makes decisions and goes about its business. To be sure, survey respondents are often afforded the opportunity to pass judgment on their government. Do they trust it, have confidence in it, approve of it, or think it is doing a good job? But rarely are ordinary people asked to state their preferred and perceived procedures of government even though these preferences and perceptions have much to do with the mood of the masses and the chances for a successfully functioning polity. Giving people a forum for griping about government is not the same as either asking their perceptions of the reason government is not working well or pushing them to specify the type of procedures they would prefer. It is almost as though reflecting on the nature of government is an endeavor believed to be reserved for elite political theorists.

Valuable work by political scientists has been done on the likely consequences of procedural judgments. The classic exchange between Miller (1974) and Citrin (1974) on whether deep dissatisfaction with the political system was likely to lead to revolution or just an anti-incumbent election or two is an early example. Hetherington's recent research (2005) shows that process perceptions (such as that government is bungling and incompetent) affect policy preferences (such as that greater authority for healthcare should *not* be given to the government). And obviously the people's process perceptions have much to do with the popularity of all kinds of reform proposals in the last 20 years, including legislative term limits, recall elections, initiatives, referenda, and assorted, creative attempts to enact a more direct form of governing. That Americans (and, it turns out, citizens of virtually all developed democracies) are dissatisfied with the operation of their government and that this dissatisfaction has important consequences do not seem to be in dispute (for further discussion, see Chanley, Rudolph, and Rahn 2001).

Less agreement exists regarding what, if anything, should be done to make people more satisfied with governmental operations. Many observers advocate giving the people the more populist-oriented government they claim to want, broadening the use of New England town meetings (Bryan 2003), "mini-populi" (Dahl 1970), and citizen issue juries (Headlam 1933), establishing deliberation days (Ackerman and Fishkin 2004), and using the internet to create electronic democracies (Etzioni 1972; Becker and Slaton 2000). But Hibbing and Theiss-Morse (2002) argue that these reforms would only make people more upset with government, that people's apparent desire for more direct democracy is really just dissatisfaction with current decision-makers and that when faced with the tangible reality of spending significantly more time and energy on politics, the desire for rich personal involvement quickly vanishes. On the basis of their survey and focus group results they argue that both Russell Hardin and John Mueller had it right in the following quotes:

> It is hard to avoid the suspicion that deliberative democracy is the democracy of elite intellectuals . . . It is virtually impossible to avoid the suspicion that deliberation will work, if at all, only in parlor room discourse or in the small salons of academic conferences. Far too much of real politics is about winning and losing . . . Deliberative democracy clearly has the problem that Oscar Wilde saw in socialism. It would require too many evenings.
>
> (Hardin 1999, 112)

> Democratic theorists and idealists may be intensely interested in government . . . but it verges on the arrogant, even the self-righteous, to suggest that other people are somehow derelict unless they share the same curious passion.
>
> (Mueller 1999, 184–5)

These very different perceptions of the processes people want as well as of the processes likely to make them more satisfied (not always the same thing) make it essential that we probe more deeply to identify the specific nature of people's process attitudes. Only then will we be in a position to evaluate the need for change and the best manner to effect change. Research specifying the consequences of process dissatisfaction is not matched by research on dissatisfaction's exact nature, largely because ordinary people are rarely encouraged to move beyond voicing dissatisfaction with the government they have to specifying the government they want.

Moreover, once attitudes about governing are measured, care needs to be taken to identify the factors that shape these attitudes as well as people's differing perceptions of both the nature of government and the best way to go about governing. The few existing efforts to specify the correlates of attitudes toward governing have been notable for the variables that seem unrelated to procedural attitudes (see, for example, Hibbing and Theiss-Morse 1995; 2002). Are people's expectations for and perceptions of government shaped by their life situations as indicated by the traditional battery of demographic variables (age, sex, income, education, race, etc.)? Are they shaped by mere political expediency (whether their partisan and ideological compatriots are or are not in a position of dominance when the survey questions happen to be posed)? Or are they shaped by deeper factors, including personality traits that lead to preferences for the conduct of group life and the making of group-relevant decisions?

Posing the question in this fashion also makes it possible to clarify an issue of broader interest and this is the extent to which political attitudes and behaviors spring from ephemeral environmental events including parental socialization as opposed to deeper, bedrock, perhaps biological, factors. For more than 20 years, evidence has suggested a genetic link for political ideology (see Martin *et al.* 1986; Eaves *et al.* 1999; Alford *et al.* 2005) and recent evidence indicates a genetic link for voter turnout (Fowler *et al.* 2006), indirectly for vote choice (Hatemi *et al.* 2007), and for the intensity of party identification (Eaves and Hatemi 2007).

Personality traits have long been of intense interest to psychologists partially because they are known to be strongly heritable. For many people, personality is not something that changes with every environmental fluctuation. Using the so-called Big 5 personality traits, one thorough meta-analysis puts the heritability correlation of openness at .57, conscientiousness at .49, extraversion at .54, agreeableness at .42, and neuroticism at .48 (Bouchard and McGue 2003, 23). Personality traits have been shown to be heritable in animals where strict environmental controls are possible (Gosling and John 1999) and selective breeding of animals has been shown to produce vastly different personality morphs even when offspring never observe the behavior of parents (see especially Trut 1999). In humans, these highly heritable personality traits have been shown to influence a variety of political behaviors (see Mondak and Halperin 2008; Mondak 2008).

The connection of genetic and/or personality traits to preferences for the nature of governing, however, has never been tested even though the issue has surfaced in different incarnations. To take one example, numerous studies have reported that approval of Congress, somewhat surprisingly, tends to be lower among those with a substantial amount of information regarding the institution specifically or politics generally. This led to the notion that familiarity breeds contempt (or at least disapproval) when it comes to the first branch of government. Elsewhere, Mondak *et al.* (2007) suggest that it is not information per se that leads directly to disapproval but rather that information serves as an indicator of the type of evaluator the subject happens to be. Mondak reports "extremely strong and consistent personality effects on knowledge levels" and properly speculates that "political knowledge functions in part as a positional marker of sorts" (personal communication). Everyone seems in agreement that simply throwing information at people is unlikely to improve their perceptions of Congress and of governing generally. Either information makes people more exacting in their expectations and evaluation criteria or, if Mondak is correct, knowledge is best seen as an endogenous marker for deeper personality traits. Either way, force-feeding information to the populace, as many advocates of civic education propose, is likely to have little effect at all.

Data and Research Design

All told, numerous intriguing questions surround public attitudes toward the governing process and the correlates of those attitudes, particularly if these potential correlates include personality items. In many respects, active, salient legislative bodies such as the U.S. Congress serve as the best referent for process items. In the U.S. case, Congress is the first branch—the branch where representative democracy is seen in action. In contrast, the judicial branch is not particularly democratic and deliberations there go on behind curtains, and even the executive branch, though certainly democratic, is hierarchically structured, with reasonably closed internal deliberations. But Congress is an open, collegial institution with procedures and disagreements visible for all to see, and with members who represent demarcated constituencies (Hibbing and Theiss-Morse 1995). As a result, items concerning Congress are frequently the best opportunity to obtain people's opinions on the governmental processes they perceive and the governmental processes they prefer. Still, surveys rarely take advantage of this fact, choosing instead to focus on respondents' policy and candidate preferences—important topics to be sure but not the only important topics.

Fortunately, the 2006 CES organized by Indiana University and funded by several organizations and congressional scholars is an exception to typical surveys in that it contains several process-related items and, very unusually for political science surveys, even a small battery of personality items. No doubt an important part of the explanation for the presence of so many procedural items is the key financial and organizational role played by former U.S. Representative Lee Hamilton. His long-standing concern with the public image of Congress specifically and representative government generally is reflected in the broad range of process items included. Given our objectives, we intend to take advantage of this valuable new data set to further understanding of the nature and correlates of the American public's preferences for governing processes.

This survey took place in two parts: a pre-election wave with 1,197 respondents and a post-election wave with 1,167 usable respondents. Seven hundred and sixty-six of the individuals in the pre-election wave agreed to be re-interviewed after the 2006 election and this group was then supplemented with 401 new participants to enlarge the post-election wave. The survey was conducted over the telephone and the sample was drawn nationwide using random digit dialing with oversampling of respondents living in electorally competitive congressional districts (see Chapter 1).

Most of the procedural items referenced above were contained in the pre-election wave but a goodly portion of the variables we wish to test for relationships with the procedural responses, including the personality items, are found in the post-election wave, so our analyses will be limited to the 766 respondents in both the pre- and post-waves. Though this restriction leaves an ample number of cases, it does enhance the bias toward politically active and intelligent respondents that is present in virtually all surveys. The kind of people who are willing to subject themselves to two separate, reasonably lengthy interviews regarding their political beliefs and behaviors can not be expected to be completely representative of the larger population of interest and they are not.

In terms of political participation and knowledge, the 766 people in the two-wave sample would appear to be head and shoulders above the respondents in just one of the waves who in turn are head and shoulders above typical American adults. Eighty-three percent of the respondents in the panel claimed to have voted in 2006 compared to 76.8 percent in the post-election survey (the difference is statistically significant—$p < .01$). Nationwide, the actual turnout in 2006 (as calculated by Michael MacDonald, http://elections.gmu.edu/voter_turnout.htm) was 41.3 percent. The 2006 post-election respondents were not asked to report their voting behavior in 2004 but those in the pre-election survey were. Though 89.8 percent of respondents who participated in both waves reported voting in 2004, just 82.5 percent of those in the pre-election survey only reported voting ($p < .01$). These self-reports compare to an actual national average of 61 percent.

Because it is well known that in order to be socially acceptable survey respondents often claim to have voted when they did not, a portion of the sizable differences between actual turnout and reported turnout is no doubt attributable to over-reporting, but it is also likely that turnout is simply higher among those people willing to answer a large number of political items posed by a stranger over the telephone. In other words, part of the difference may be attributable to the nature of obtaining a sample rather than the tendency of respondents to dissemble. Support for this line of thinking comes from the fact that, as evident in Table 8.1, subjects completing only one wave were much less likely to report voting than those completing both waves and it is unlikely the pressure to be socially acceptable applies more strongly to those doing two waves.

Table 8.1 Assessing the Representativeness in the 2006 Congressional Elections Study Sample

	Panel	Pre	Post	χ^2	t-test
Vote in 2006 House Election	83.1	–	76.8	6.70***	–
Vote in 2004 Presidential Election	89.8	82.5	–	12.9***	–
Mean Political Knowledge	4.1	3.0	3.7	–	14.75*** 4.19***
% High Knowledge (≥ 4 correct)	77.0	33.4	67.0	219.7*** 14.5***	–

Notes:
* $p \leq 0.10$, ** $p \leq 0.05$, *** $p \leq 0.01$
N = 766 (panel), N = 431 (pre-election), and N = 397 (post-election)

A similar pattern from panel respondents to post-election-only respondents applies to the knowledge items. The CES employed what has become the standard five-item knowledge battery for surveys these days (Which branch decides constitutionality? Who nominates federal judges? How is a presidential veto overridden? And which party controls each house of Congress?). Though there is no known comparison figure for the average knowledge level of the entire American adult population, it should be noted that the knowledge levels displayed by the survey respondents are extremely high overall and, once again, even higher for those completing both waves than for those completing either just the pre-election survey or just the post-election survey (p < .01). On average, respondents in the panel portion of the survey get more than four of the five questions correct, a truly impressive performance. Voters in the post-election survey only, on average, get 3.7 of the questions correct and voters in the pre-election survey only get just 3.0 correct. Both of these are significantly different from the panel respondents and it makes sense that respondents in the pre-only do worse than respondents in the post-only since respondents in the pre-only refused (or were unavailable) to take the post-survey. Some respondents in the post-only may have been willing to complete a second political survey if they had been asked and this may explain why their average knowledge level is higher than those not interested in doing a second political survey. The same pattern, not surprisingly, is apparent when knowledge is dichotomized by separating those who correctly answered at least four of the items from those who correctly answered three or less. Seventy-seven percent of the panel respondents could be classified as "high knowledge" while 67 percent of the post-only respondents and just 33.4 percent of the pre-only respondents merited this classification. All these differences easily attain statistical significance.

Thus, as further results are considered, it should be kept in mind that the panel survey respondents we will be analyzing are well above the norm in political participation and knowledge. Partly for this reason, whenever possible, such as in describing the univariate results in the next section, we will use all those to whom the pertinent item was posed (in this case, all pre-election respondents) rather than only those responding in both waves.

How Should Political Decisions be Made?

The CES reveals that, except for one item, when it comes to preferences for the manner in which government should and does operate, Americans are hardly of one mind. The exception pertains to whether members of Congress should "take action without engaging in such lengthy discussions about the issues or discuss issues more thoroughly before taking action." As can be seen in Figure 8.1, debate is strongly supported given this wording. Just 19.4 percent of valid respondents opt for the "take action" procedure while 80.6

percent prefer that issues be discussed more thoroughly. These results are in stark contrast to the results from a 1998 survey in which 86 percent of the respondents felt that "elected officials should stop talking and take action" (Hibbing and Theiss-Morse 2002, 136). Whether these different results are due to alterations in the question wording ("talking" and "discussing issues more thoroughly" may have different implications) or to changes in the nature of the times is an open question.

But on the other central procedural items the public is remarkably divided. When asked "would you prefer that members of Congress stand up for their principles come what may or compromise with their opponents in order to get

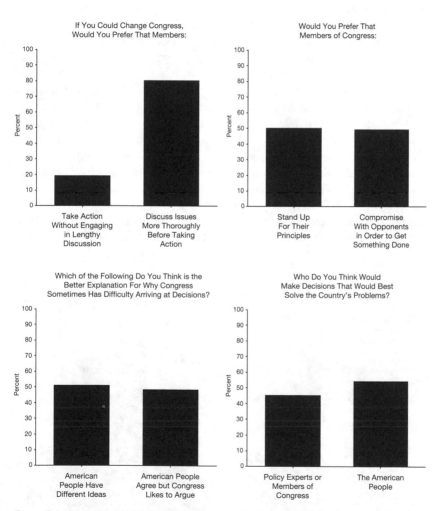

Figure 8.1 Assessing Variability in the Process Preferences of the American People.

something done," 50.3 percent say "stand up for principles" and 49.7 percent say "compromise with opponents." When asked "which of the following do you think is the better explanation for why Congress sometimes has difficulty arriving at decisions," 51.2 percent respond that it is because the "American people have different ideas" and 48.8 percent say it is because the "American people agree but Congress likes to argue." Finally, when asked "who do you think would make decisions that would best solve the country's problems," 54.6 percent say the "American people" and 45.4 percent say either "members of Congress" or governmental "policy experts."

Certainly, each of the four central procedural items we have chosen is quite different. The first and second ask how key decision-makers (in this case, members of Congress) should approach their responsibilities. Should they quit engaging in such lengthy discussions or should they discuss more before taking action? Should they stand up for their principles come what may or should they be willing to compromise in order to get something done? The third asks the reason for the difficulties Congress is perceived to have in arriving at decisions. Is it because the American people themselves are conflicted about the best course of action and, therefore, any proper representative institution would reflect these deep divisions or are differences of opinion rare among real Americans and Congress unnecessarily constructs arguments where there need not be any? And the final item asks who would best solve the country's problems. Is it the American people or is it governmental officials, either members of Congress or "policy experts working for the government?"

But all relate to the nature of representative government and together they address its central procedural issues: who best to make decisions, how decision-makers, whoever they are, should approach their duties, and what is

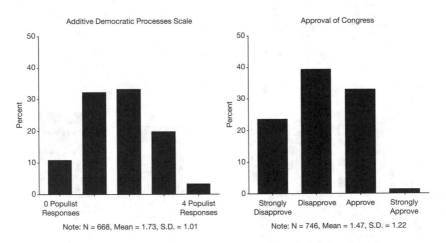

Figure 8.2 Democratic Process Preferences and Approval of Congress.

the context in which decisions tend to be made (consensual or not). The substantial division present in the survey marginals for three of the four items indicates that there is not a single governmental form that will appeal to all or even to a clear majority of Americans. This in itself is revealing. Often the impression is given that governing and institutional design would be easier if politicians would only listen to the people, but these even splits suggest listening to the people will not yield a clear signal. Many people think there is mass agreement about the way government should work in America, but this is far from the truth.

Despite the diversity of these four items and the fact that we make no claim they fit neatly into an overarching vision of governmental processes, we present in Figure 8.2, for comparison purposes, the distribution of respondents on an additive index of these four items with the more "populist" response (take action, do not compromise, the people are in agreement but Congress likes to argue, and decisions would be better if made by the people) coded with the highest value. Finally, Figure 8.2, again for comparison purposes, presents the distribution of respondents on the standard congressional approval item (strongly approve, somewhat approve, somewhat disapprove, or strongly disapprove). As of October 2006, approval of the manner in which the U.S. Congress was handling its job was quite low. Just 1.5 percent of respondents strongly approved, 33.1 percent somewhat approved, 39.4 percent somewhat disapproved, and 23.6 strongly disapproved (the remaining respondents volunteered an answer of "neither approved nor disapproved") of the job Congress was doing—a reasonably negative assessment that is widely believed to have helped set the stage for a rejection of Republican control of the national legislature in the 2006 midterm elections.

Accounting for Variation in Preferences for Governmental Processes

While the deep divisions in preference for process pose challenges for those designing government, they are welcome from the point of view of statistical analysis since such analysis demands variance. Just what type of person tends to value action over debate? Just what type of person tends to believe that sticking to principles is better than compromising in order to get something done? What type of person believes the American public is in general agreement on controversial political issues? And what kind of person believes that ordinary people would make better political decisions than either members of Congress or bureaucrats? We now turn our attention to these matters.

As outlined above, three of the four items of central interest are forced-choice and therefore dichotomous. The fourth permits respondents three options: decisions would be better if made by the American people, members of Congress, or policy experts working for the government. The latter two options are collapsed so that the item becomes whether people want the American people or government officials to make political decisions. As before, the position associated with what might be described as the more populist approach to governmental processes is assigned the higher value. Thus, preferring action to debate, principles to compromise, and the American people to government officials, along with seeing the American people as in agreement and Congress as unnecessarily fractious are all given the value of 1 and the alternatives 0. Given the dichotomous nature of these variables, we employ logistic regression to estimate effects for the four individual process items and the results are presented in Table 8.2. The two variables in Figure 8.2—the additive combination of the process items as well as the four-point congressional approval item—are estimated with OLS and the results are presented in Table 8.3.

The explanatory variables included in the models can best be seen as falling into three distinct categories. First are some standard demographic items: sex (female = 1; male = 0); race (nonwhite = 1; white = 0); age (in years); and education (post-graduate degree = 1.0; college graduate = .75; some college and/or associate degree = .50; vocational-technical training = .25; and high school degree or less = 0). Income is not included because several dozen respondents refused to answer that item and the results are largely unchanged with income included (income is never statistically significant regardless of the dependent variable), so we decided to keep the larger number of cases and omit income. Next come several political items including dummy variables for identification with the Democratic party, identification with the Republican party, a conservative ideology, a liberal ideology, and the five-point measure of political knowledge (higher values equate with more knowledge). Finally, we include the five components of the Big 5 personality inventory. Because these items are rarely used in political science work, a few descriptive comments are in order.

Assessing personality has a long and somewhat contentious history in social psychology. Though it would be a mistake to imply that a universal consensus has been reached, repeated factor analyses have identified five, largely distinct, personality traits. These are extroversion, agreeableness, conscientiousness, neuroticism, and openness, the so-called Big 5. The preferable way of measuring these traits is to pose scores of individual items to respondents. Given the need to hold the CES to a manageable length while still including the traditional political items, a stripped down version of the personality inventory, with just ten items, was included. Though this ten-item version of the Big 5 inventory has demonstrated certain admirable qualities, it remains unavoidably imperfect. Respondents are asked to report whether on a scale running from 0 to 10 they are sympathetic or unsympathetic, unkind or kind (agreeableness); hard-working or lazy, sloppy or neat (conscientiousness); relaxed or tense, nervous or calm (neuroticism); outgoing or shy, introverted or extraverted (extraversion); and philosophical or unreflective, not an intellectual or an intellectual (openness). The two items for each personality trait are correlated with each other though not always as strongly as might be desired; nonetheless, the opportunity to include even a somewhat rough-and-ready personality battery is exciting. All of the personality items were coded such that higher values for each personality dimension are indicative of traits that are, on their face, more socially-desirable.

Previous work attempting to account for variations in the American public's procedural preferences and perceptions has not been particularly successful (e.g., Hibbing and Theiss-Morse 2002, 146). Demographic items are typically not statistically significant, though there is some indication that in their procedural preferences conservatives tend to be more "populist" and Democrats less so. The question now becomes whether results are enhanced with more recent data, with more extensive procedural items, and with personality traits included.

The ill-developed state of the literature in this area makes it difficult to specify particular hypotheses. In terms of demographic variables, conventional wisdom might suggest that populist-style process preferences would be the province of uneducated, politically uninformed, young males but the limited extant empirical work finds little support for these expectations. Moreover, while a conservative political philosophy seems somewhat more consistent with populist notions (get government out of the hands of officials and into the hands of local government and real people), the political realities prior to the election of 2006 were such that the elected officials in charge were Republicans and conservatives, thus creating obvious cross-pressures. And because personality traits have so rarely been used in political science research, expectations regarding them pose special challenges except that perhaps those who are more intellectually open could be expected to be more supportive of debate, compromise, a divided public, and decisions being made by government officials rather than by the people. Expectations concerning the remaining personality variables are decidedly less clear.

The main results of this chapter are presented in Table 8.2 for the four dichotomous procedural variables and in Table 8.3 for the other two dependent variables. Beginning with people's views of the value of political debate, the results are somewhat more encouraging than previous work indicated. Certain variables from each of the three categories—demographic, political, and personality—show statistical significance and some sense of substantive significance can be obtained by noting the reported change in the dependent variable (Y) generated by a standardized change in each individual independent variable with the other independent variables held constant at their mean (the change reported is that resulting from a one standard deviation increase in the case of non-dichotomous variables and a change from 0 to 1 in the case of dichotomous variables). Among the demographic variables, it appears as though males and young people are the most likely to advocate taking action without extended discussion. Among the political variables, Republicans are more likely than Independents or Democrats to support Congress taking action rather than engaging in extended debate. Notably, neither education

Table 8.2 Predicting the Process Preferences of the American People (Logistic Regression)

Variable	Take Action			Stand Up for Principles			Congress Indecisive Because of Members			Best Solutions from American People		
	Coeff.	S.E.	Δ in Y	Coeff.	S.E.	Δ in Y	Coeff.	S.E.	Δ in Y	Coeff.	S.E.	Δ in Y
Sex (Female = 1)	-0.547**	0.229	-0.019	0.336*	0.175	0.084	-0.378**	0.175	-0.094	-0.098	0.169	-0.025
Race (Non-white = 1)	-0.644	0.569	-0.017	0.351	0.370	0.087	0.676*	0.385	0.166	0.542	0.363	0.131
Age	-0.023**	0.007	-0.044	0.000	0.000	0.0003	0.000	0.000	0.001	-0.000	0.000	-0.0002
Education	0.015	0.333	0.0002	-0.483*	0.260	-0.043	-0.730***	0.259	-0.065	-0.296	0.249	-0.027
Democrat	-0.379	0.302	-0.012	0.065	0.210	0.016	0.312	0.212	0.078	0.059	0.203	0.015
Republican	0.584**	0.256	0.022	-0.044	0.209	-0.011	0.034	0.207	0.009	-0.371*	0.200	-0.092
Liberal	0.239	0.333	0.008	-0.186	0.251	-0.047	-0.259	0.252	-0.064	-0.397*	0.239	-0.099
Conservative	0.022	0.251	0.001	0.993***	0.206	0.241	0.018	0.200	0.005	0.050	0.194	0.012
Political Knowledge	0.858	0.573	0.008	-0.451	0.412	0.026	0.357	0.403	0.021	-0.121	0.391	-0.007
Extroversion	0.683	0.482	0.006	0.180	0.369	0.010	0.850**	0.373	0.048	0.590*	0.357	0.033
Agreeableness	-0.381	0.644	-0.002	0.760	0.508	0.034	0.062	0.508	0.003	-0.159	0.493	-0.007
Conscientiousness	0.534	0.598	0.036	-0.358	0.463	-0.017	0.819*	0.462	0.039	0.628	0.443	0.030
Emotional Stability	-1.02*	0.555	-0.006	-0.401	0.424	-0.020	0.048	0.424	0.002	-0.042	0.408	-0.002
Openness	-1.14*	0.683	-0.006	-0.789	0.521	-0.034	-0.979*	0.522	-0.042	0.086	0.503	0.004
Constant	0.016	0.850		0.500	0.612		-0.471	0.603		-0.193	0.584	
-2 Log Likelihood	612.33			909.66			908.80			974.92		
% Correctly Predicted	81.0			62.0			59.6			57.8		
Nagelkerke R²	0.112			0.099			0.072			0.035		
N	674			695			684			718		

Notes:
*** $p \leq 0.01$, ** $p \leq 0.05$, * $p \leq 0.10$.
All variables were coded on a 0 to 1 scale. The impact score (Δ in Y) was calculated using a one standard deviation increase while holding all other values at their mean. The variable was recoded to range from 0 to 1.

Table 8.3 Predicting Process Preferences and Congressional Support (OLS Regression)

Variable	Cumulative Process Preferences		Approval of Congress	
	Coeff.	S.E.	Coeff.	S.E.
Sex (Female = 1)	−0.118	0.087	0.287**	0.095
Race (Non-white = 1)	0.309*	0.183	−0.447**	0.193
Age	0.000	0.000	−0.000	0.000
Education	−0.292**	0.130	−0.174	0.139
Democrat	0.034	0.104	−0.105	0.113
Republican	−0.001	0.104	0.501***	0.112
Liberal	−0.179	0.125	−0.113	0.132
Conservative	0.208**	0.101	0.181*	0.108
Political Knowledge	−0.053	0.203	−0.516**	0.220
Extroversion	0.433**	0.183	0.255	0.199
Agreeableness	−0.034	0.253	0.014	0.276
Conscientiousness	0.377	0.230	0.166	0.248
Emotional Stability	−0.307	0.230	0.382*	0.227
Openness	−0.504**	0.255	−0.955***	0.279
Constant	1.91***	0.302	2.14***	0.330
F	3.03***		9.52***	
Adj. R^2	0.043		0.146	
N	631		700	

Notes:
*** $p \leq 0.01$, ** $p \leq 0.05$, * $p \leq 0.10$.
All independent variables were recoded on a 0 to 1 scale. Cumulative process preferences are calculated as an additive index of the four dependent variables included in Table 8.2.

nor political knowledge is related to support for political discussion once the other variables in the model are controlled. Turning to personality traits, none of the Big 5 achieves significance at the .05 level but two do at the .1 level. The more intellectually "open" an individual and the more emotionally stable (the less neurotic) the individual, the more the individual values extended discussion as opposed to taking immediate action. Extraversion, agreeableness, and conscientiousness are unrelated to the perceived value of debate in this formulation.

The pattern of support for standing up for principles as opposed to compromising is slightly different. Whereas females are more supportive of debate, there is some indication they are less supportive of compromise, as indicated by the positive sign of the coefficient for female (p < .1). This desire to both talk problems through but also to stand firm on principles is an interesting combination. Education is the only other demographic variable to show a connection to the compromise/principles item, with more educated people, as expected, being more supportive of compromise (significant only at the .1 level). Political knowledge is not significantly related to the perceived desirability of compromise but political conservatives are strongly in favor of standing up for principle. Part of this relationship may be due to the diminished need of the majority party to compromise (especially when that party also controls the White House) but the size of this coefficient and the results of previous empirical work suggest that, compared to liberals, conservatives in general may have a stronger philosophical desire to stand on principle. This finding is also consistent with recent work in psychology indicating political conservatives have a stronger affinity for order, structure, and predictability than do liberals (see Jost 2006; Amodio *et al.* 2007). None of the Big 5 is significantly related to perceptions of the value of compromise.

Are the American people so divided on policy issues that Congress cannot avoid disagreement or does Congress manufacture disagreement despite a relatively monolithic public? Less educated, minority males are more likely to believe the American people are united whereas well educated white females are more likely to realize that political disagreement among the people is rampant. None of the political variables—party identification, political ideology, and political knowledge—is related to perceptions of the source of disagreement but three of the five personality measures are. According to the 2006 CES, individuals who are conscientious, extroverted, and less intellectually open are more likely to believe that the American people are united.

Finally, what explains the substantial variation in people's tendencies to believe either the American people or governmental officials are best equipped to solve difficult political problems? The short answer is virtually none of the variables included in our model. No independent variable in the model reaches significance at the .05 level though a few surface at the more permissive .1 level. All in all, preferences as to the proper locus for political decisions are strangely difficult to explain.

Turning to Table 8.3, a cumulative preference for populist procedures is predicted by a relatively low level of education, minority status, a conservative ideology, extroversion, and a lack of intellectual openness. Approval of Congress, on the other hand, is predicted by Republican party identification (not surprising since Republicans were the majority party in Congress when the question was posed), a relative lack of political knowledge (consistent with previous research), being female, being white, and being less intellectually open.

Conclusion

This chapter is admittedly more exploratory than theoretically grounded. Still, it is driven by the sincere beliefs that 1) public preferences for governmental processes are important and poorly conceptualized by scholars and perhaps by the people themselves; 2) an understanding of the reasons for variations across people in these important process perceptions and preferences is virtually nonexistent; and 3) deep-seated human characteristics traceable to personality traits and perhaps to biology have for too long been ignored in empirical political science research of this sort.

The results indicate massive levels of disagreement on even the most fundamental procedural matters. Though respondents on the CES were strongly supportive of the need for extended discussions in Congress, they were evenly divided on whether compromise is needed to get things done or is an abrogation of principled stands. They were also evenly divided on whether the unfortunate level of disagreement in the American polity is due to an argumentative Congress or to authentic differences of opinion among ordinary citizens. And, though respondents tended to believe the American people would make better political decisions, a very large minority believed either members of Congress or governmental policy experts would make better decisions. The locus of decisions, the level of agreement among the people, and the role of debate and compromise are as basic to democratic processes as could be, yet Americans are divided virtually down the middle on most of these fundamental procedural issues.

The results further indicate that explaining the substantial variation in people's procedural preferences is a tall order. Standard demographic and political variables achieve only spotty success in accounting for variance in the four main procedural items serving as dependent variables in this analysis. Some might claim that people hold no honest philosophical position on democratic processes but instead choose whichever process will temporarily assist their partisan or ideological leanings. Others might claim that liberals and Democrats are intrinsically more open to the intricacies and uncertainties of debate, compromise, and indirect representation. Neither of these orientations receives unequivocal support from these data. On occasion Republicans could be observed advocating power for elected officials because at the federal level elected officials at the time of the survey were primarily Republicans and also could be observed coming down firmly on the side of principles (an easy position to take if winning is likely) rather than compromise.

Political knowledge and education are of special interest to many people. The results here indicate increased political acumen is sometimes consistent with more sophisticated process attitudes but that many other times this is not the case. Neither the educated nor the politically knowledgeable, for example, is more likely to advocate extended political discussions rather than immediate action just as they are not more likely to say that members of Congress or governmental policy experts are likely to make better decisions than the American public. Political knowledge is, however, inversely related to approval of Congress even when personality traits and demographic variables are controlled (Table 8.3).

Personality traits offer intriguing possibilities for future research on political variables, whether attitudinal or behavioral. The initial results here are mixed, with the trait of openness, as expected, appearing to be the most connected to procedural attitudes but with other personality traits occasionally giving hints of relevance. All told, it may be that the best role for personality variables is in interaction with other concepts (see Mondak 2008).

In sum, we must conclude that much remains to be learned about the source of procedural attitudes. Either they are idiosyncratic or they emanate from sources not best captured by standard demographic concepts, by political partisanship and ideology, and by relatively crude measures of personality. But if we do not more vigorously pursue the nature and sources of people's preferences for the manner in which governmental decisions should be made, we will be doomed to misdiagnosing those desires as well as their wellsprings.

References

Ackerman, Bruce and James S. Fishkin. 2004. *Deliberation Day*. Chicago: University of Chicago Press.

Alford, John R., Carolyn L. Funk, and John R. Hibbing. 2005. "Are Political Orientations Genetically Transmitted?" *American Political Science Review* 99: 153–68.

Amodio, David M., John T. Jost, Sarah L. Master, and Cindy M. Yee. 2007. "Neurocognitive Correlates of Liberalism and Conservatism." *Nature Neuroscience* (9 September): 1–2.

Becker, Theodore Lewis and Christa Daryl Slaton. 2000. *The Future of Teledemocracy*. Westport, Conn.: Praeger.

Bouchard, T.J., Jr. and Matt McGue. 2003. "Genetic and Environmental Influences on Human Psychological Differences." *Journal of Neurobiology* 54: 4–45.

Bryan, Frank M. 2003. *Real Democracy: The New England Town Meeting*. Chicago: University of Chicago Press.

Chanley, Virginia A., Thomas J. Rudolph, and Wendy M. Rahn. 2001. "Public Trust in Government in the Reagan Years and Beyond." In John R. Hibbing and Elizabeth Theiss-Morse, eds., *What is it about Government that Americans Dislike?* Cambridge: Cambridge University Press.

Citrin, Jack. 1974. "Comment: The Political Relevance of Trust in Government." *American Political Science Review* 68: 973–88.

Dahl, Robert A. 1970. *After the Revolution: Authority in a Good Society*. New Haven, Conn.: Yale University Press.

Eaves, Lindon, J., Andrew C. Heath, Nicholas G. Martin, Hermine H. Maes, Michael C. Neale, Kenneth M. Kendler, Katherine Kirk, and Linda Corey. 1999. "Comparing the Biological and Cultural Inheritance of Personality and Social Attitudes in the Virginia 30,000 Study of Twins and their Relatives." *Twin Research* 2: 62–80.

Eaves, Lindon J. and Peter K. Hatemi. 2007. "We Get Opinions from Our Parents, but Not How We Think We Do: Genetic and Social Components of the Familial Transmission of Political Attitudes." Unpublished Manuscript, Virginia Commonwealth University.

Etzioni, Amitai. 1972. "Minerva: An Electronic Town Hall." *Policy Sciences* 3: 457–74.

Fowler, James H., Laura A. Baker, and Christopher T. Dawes. 2006. "The Genetic Basis of Political Cooperation." Paper presented at the Hendricks Conference on Biology and Politics, Lincoln, Nebr., October 2006.

Gosling, Samuel D. and Oliver P. John. 1999. "Personality Dimensions in Nonhuman Animals: A Cross-species Review." *Current Directions in Psychological Science* 8: 69–75.

Hardin, Russell. 1999. "Deliberation: Method, Not Theory." In Stephen Macedo, ed., *Deliberative Politics: Essays on Democracy and Disagreement.* Oxford: Oxford University Press.

Hatemi, Peter K., Sara E. Medland, Katherine I. Morley, Andrew C. Heath, and Nicholas G. Martin. 2007. "The Genetics of Voting: An Australian Twin Study." *Behavior Genetics* 37: 435–48.

Headlam, James Wycliffe. 1933. *Election by Lot at Athens* (Second Edition). Cambridge: Cambridge University Press.

Hetherington, Marc J. 2005. *Why Trust Matters: Declining Political Trust and the Demise of American Liberalism.* Princeton, NJ: Princeton University Press.

Hibbing, John R. and Elizabeth Theiss-Morse. 1995. *Congress as Public Enemy.* Cambridge: Cambridge University Press.

Hibbing, John R. and Elizabeth Theiss-Morse. 2002. *Stealth Democracy.* Cambridge: Cambridge University Press.

Jost, John T. 2006. "The End of the End of Ideology." *American Psychologist* 61: 651–70.

Martin, Nicholas G., Lindon J. Eaves, Andrew C. Heath, Rosemary Jardine, Lynn M. Feingold, and Hans J. Eysenck. 1986. "Transmission of Social Attitudes." *Proceedings of the National Academy of Sciences* 15: 4364–8.

Miller, Arthur H. 1974. "Political Issues and Trust in Government, 1964–70." *American Political Science Review* 68: 951–72.

Mondak, Jeffery J. 2008. "Politics and the Psychology of Individual Differences." Unpublished Manuscript.

Mondak, Jeffery J., Edward G. Carmines, Robert Huckfeldt, Dona-Gene Mitchell, and Scot Schraufnagel. 2007. "Does Familiarity Breed Contempt? The Impact of Information on Mass Attitudes toward Congress." *American Journal of Political Science* 51: 34–48.

Mondak, Jeffery J. and Karen Halperin. 2008. "A Framework for the Study of Personality and Political Behavior." *British Journal of Political Science* 38: 335–62.

Mueller, John. 1999. *Capitalism, Democracy and Ralph's Pretty Good Grocery.* Princeton, NJ: Princeton University Press.

Trut, Lyudmila N. 1999. "Domestication: The Farm Fox Experiment." *American Scientist* 87: 160–9.

Tyler, Tom R. 1994. "Psychological Models of the Justice Motive: Antecedents of Distributive and Procedural Justice." *Journal of Personality and Social Psychology* 67: 850–63.

Tyler, Tom R. and Glenn Mitchell. 1994. "Legitimacy and the Empowerment of Discretionary Legal Authority: The United States Supreme Court and Abortion Rights." *Duke Law Journal* 43: 703–814.

Index